LAW AND LEGAL ISSUES IN THE UNITED STATES:
ANALYSES AND DEVELOPMENTS

CRIMINAL JUSTICE

GOVERNMENT POLICIES AND PROGRAMS

LAW AND LEGAL ISSUES IN THE UNITED STATES: ANALYSES AND EVELOPMENTS

Additional books and e-books in this series can be found on Nova's website under the Series tab.

LAW AND LEGAL ISSUES IN THE UNITED STATES: ANALYSES AND DEVELOPMENTS

CRIMINAL JUSTICE

GOVERNMENT POLICIES AND PROGRAMS

QUINCY FRANKS

snova
New York

Additional color graphics may be available in the e-book version of this book.

Library of Congress Cataloging-in-Publication Data

ISBN: 978-1-53614-196-2

Published by Nova Science Publishers, Inc. † New York

CONTENTS

PREFACE

The United States has gradually shifted its formal drug policy from a punishment-focused model toward a more comprehensive approach–one that focuses on prevention, treatment and enforcement. The federal government has demonstrated growing support for the drug court model primarily through financial support of drug court programs, federal drug courts, research and various drug court initiatives. This book includes an overview on federal support for drug courts; an overview of recent trends in the enforcement of the Bank Secrecy Act (BSA), the principal U.S. anti-money laundering law regulating financial institutions; an overview on the mandatory minimum sentencing of federal drug offenses; a discussion on the legislative provisions that govern the US Department of State's production of the annual TIP (Trafficking in Persons) Report, reviews country ranking trends in the TIP Report, and identifies recent congressional oversight of and legislative activity to modify the TIP report; an finally, an analysis of the use of special prosecutors and independent counsels under now-expired provisions of the Ethics in Government Act of 1978, as well as the use of special counsels that are currently authorized by DOJ regulations.

In: Criminal Justice
Editor: Quincy Franks
ISBN: 978-1-53614-196-2

Chapter 1

MURDEROUS SCHEMES ARE NOT VIOLENT CRIMES?*

Charles Doyle

The U.S. Court of Appeals for the Fourth Circuit (Fourth Circuit) recently held in *U.S. v. McCollum* that conspiracy to murder is not a violent crime for federal sentencing purposes. The comments of a concurring judge seem to capture the frustration of the panel with the result: "The dissent ends with the ... lament, 'Heaven help us.' Frankly, I would be satisfied if Congress or the Supreme Court would help us. The law in this area, which Judge Duncan faithfully follows, leads to some seemingly odd results with which I do not think any of us are particularly happy."

The case marks the latest judicial effort to identify what constitutes a crime of violence for purposes of federal law. The task has been complicated by the multiplicity of state statutes that often serve as predicates for federal sentencing enhancements. Congress has made

* This is an edited, reformatted and augmented version of a Congressional Research Service report, LSB10120, dated April 17, 2018.

adjustments. For example, it established a general definition to permit uniform application through the federal criminal code, 18 U.S.C. § 16. Yet the difficulties persist.

The Armed Career Criminal Act (ACCA) is primarily responsible for the more than a dozen instances when the Supreme Court has addressed the "violent crime" question. The ACCA calls for a 15-year mandatory minimum term of imprisonment for those convicted of unlawful firearm possession that have three or more prior federal or state serious drug felony or violent felony convictions. A felony is an ACCA "violent felony" if it qualifies under any of the three categories of offenses. One category includes crimes that involve the actual, attempted, or threatened use of physical force against another individual. A second consists of specific crimes, such as burglary, arson, and extortion. A third, the so-called residual clause, encompasses offenses that "otherwise involve[] conduct that presents a serious potential risk of physical injury to another."

Beginning with *Taylor v. United States*, the Supreme Court developed a "categorical" approach to determine whether a particular federal or state crime conviction constitutes a violent felony conviction for ACCA purposes. However, after trying four times, from *James v. United States* through *Sykes v. United States*, to apply the approach to residual clause cases, the Court gave up. In *Johnson v. United States,* it declared the ACCA's residual clause unconstitutionally vague. *Johnson* raised questions of the continued validity of the remaining categories of the ACCA violent felony definition, as well as the validity of the general definition in Section 16 and the sentencing enhancing definition in the Sentencing Guidelines. The Supreme Court has, or soon will, address these issues.

The Court has two "crime of violence" cases pending. One, *Sessions v. Dimaya*, addresses the Section 16 issue and the other, *Stokeling v. United States*, the "use of physical force" category of the ACCA definition. The Court has already held, in *Beckles v. United States*, that the Sentencing Guideline's crime of violence definition is not *unconstitutionally* vague, even though it was modeled after the definition found unconstitutional in *Johnson*. The Court in *Beckles* explained that the constitutional void-for-vagueness doctrine did not apply to the Guidelines because they are not binding on a sentencing court, although failure to accurately account for the Guidelines' recommendations constitutes reversible error. All of which left the Fourth Circuit with the task of applying the *Taylor* categorical approach in *McCollum*.

McCollum pleaded guilty to possession of a firearm by a convicted felon. In the calculation of McCollum's sentence, the U.S. District Court for Western District of North Carolina added in a "crime of violence" enhancement based on the McCollum's prior conviction for conspiracy to murder in aid of racketeering. The Fourth Circuit held that was a mistake. The court determined that the enhancement was not appropriate because the conspiracy-to-murder statute imposed no overt act requirement.

The Fourth Circuit's analysis relied on the "categorical" approach, which the Supreme Court first established in *Taylor v. United States* and which the Supreme Court and lower courts have used since in "crime of violence" cases. The approach involves comparing the elements of an offense at issue, here conspiracy to murder, with the elements of a "crime of violence" as defined in the statute or Guidelines. The crime at issue is not a crime of violence unless it matches or is narrower than the crime envisioned in the statute or Guidelines, that is, unless it falls within the same category as the statute or Guideline description of a crime of violence.

The Sentencing Guidelines define a crime of violence as an "offense under federal or state law" that "(1) has an element the use, attempted use, or threatened use of physical force against the person of another, or (2) is murder ... or [3] is an offense of ... conspiring ... to commit such offenses." (USSG 4B1.2). The Fourth Circuit concluded that the *Taylor* line of cases compels use of the generic, contemporary meaning of "conspiracy" and noted that thirty-six states, the District of Columbia, three U.S. territories, and the general federal conspiracy statute all define "conspiracy" to include an overt act element. The conspiracy to commit murder in aid of racketeering statute, however, does not have an overt act requirement. The Fourth Circuit consequently held that "[b]ecause [the conspiracy statute] does not require an overt act, it criminalizes a broader range of conduct than that covered by generic conspiracy. McCollum's [conspiracy] conviction therefore cannot support his enhanced sentence because it is not categorically a crime of violence."

Unless the Supreme Court or Congress clarifies what constitutes a violent crime, results like those in *McCollum* are likely to continue to occur.

In: Criminal Justice
Editor: Quincy Franks
ISBN: 978-1-53614-196-2

Chapter 2

FEDERAL SUPPORT FOR DRUG COURTS: IN BRIEF*

Lisa N. Sacco

ABSTRACT

The United States has gradually shifted its formal drug policy from a punishment-focused model toward a more comprehensive approach—one that focuses on prevention, treatment, and enforcement. The proliferation of drug courts in American criminal justice fits this more comprehensive model. These specialized court programs are designed to divert certain defendants and offenders away from traditional criminal justice sanctions such as incarceration while reducing overall costs and helping these defendants and offenders with substance abuse issues.

Drug courts present an alternative to the traditional court process for some criminal defendants and offenders—namely those who are considered nonviolent and are known to abuse drugs and/or alcohol. While there are additional specialized goals for certain types of drug courts, the overall goals of adult and juvenile drug courts are to reduce

* This is an edited, reformatted, and augmented version of a Congressional Research Service report, R44467, dated March 20, 2018.

recidivism and substance abuse among nonviolent offenders. Drug court programs may exist at various points in the justice system, but they are most often employed postarrest as an alternative to traditional criminal justice processing.

The federal government has demonstrated growing support for the drug court model primarily through financial support of drug court programs, federal drug courts, research, and various drug court initiatives. For example, each year, the Bureau of Justice Assistance (BJA) and Substance Abuse and Mental Health Administration (SAMHSA) distribute grants to states and localities to support the creation and enhancement of drug courts. In FY2017, over $100 million in federal funding was appropriated for drug courts.

As the opioid epidemic continues, policymakers may debate whether drug courts could be an effective tool in efforts to address opioid abuse. Policy options include, but are not limited to, increasing federal funding for drug courts and reauthorizing (with or without amendments) the Drug Court Discretionary Grant Program (Drug Courts Program). Further, Congress may wish to maintain the exclusion of violent offenders from the Drug Courts Program, or, conversely, broaden the pool of eligible offenders that may participate in BJA-funded drug court programs to include some violent offenders.

INTRODUCTION

The United States has gradually shifted its formal drug policy from a punishment-focused model[1] toward a more comprehensive approach—it is now one that focuses on prevention, treatment, and enforcement. The Obama Administration stated that it coordinated "an unprecedented government-wide public health and public safety approach to reduce drug use and its consequences."[2] In its FY2018 budget request, the Trump Administration requested funds for both public health and public safety efforts to combat the opioid epidemic.[3]

---

[1] For further discussion, see CRS Report R43749, *Drug Enforcement in the United States: History, Policy, and Trends*.

[2] Executive Office of the President under President Barack Obama, Office of National Drug Control Policy, *About ONDCP*, https://obamawhitehouse.archives.gov/ondcp/about.

[3] *President Trump's First Budget Commits Significant Resources to Fight the Opioid Epidemic*, May 23, 2017, https://www.whitehouse.gov/the-press-office/2017/05/23/president-trumps-first-budget-commits-significant-resourcesfight-opioid.

The proliferation of drug courts in American criminal justice fits this new comprehensive model. Broadly, these specialized court programs are designed to divert some individuals away from traditional criminal justice sanctions such as incarceration. Many drug courts offer a treatment and social service alternative for those who otherwise may have faced traditional criminal sanctions for their offenses. In some drug courts, individuals that have been arrested are diverted from local courts into special judge-involved programs; these courts are often viewed as "second chance" courts. Other drug court programs offer reentry assistance after an offender has served his or her sentence. According to some research, these courts help save on overall criminal justice costs, provide treatment for defendants/offenders with substance abuse issues, and help offenders avoid rearrest.[4]

This chapter will explain (1) the concept of a "drug court," (2) how the term and programs have expanded to include wider meanings and serve additional subgroups, (3) how the federal government supports drug courts, and (4) research on the impact of drug courts on offenders and court systems. In addition, it briefly discusses how drug courts might provide an avenue for addressing the opioid epidemic and other emerging drug issues that Congress may consider.

WHAT ARE DRUG COURTS?

The term "drug courts" refers to specialized court programs that present an alternative to the traditional court process for certain criminal defendants[5] and offenders. Traditionally, these individuals are first-time, nonviolent offenders who are known to abuse drugs and/or alcohol. While there are additional specialized goals for different types of drug courts (e.g., veterans drug courts, tribal drug courts, and family drug courts), the

---

[4] See research discussion further along in this chapter. Also, see National Institute of Justice, *Drug Courts*, January 2017, https://nij.gov/topics/courts/drug-courts.

[5] Defendants are individuals who have been charged with committing an offense for which they have not yet been convicted.

overall goals of adult and juvenile drug courts are to reduce recidivism and substance abuse.

Drug court programs may exist at various points in the justice system, but they are often employed postarrest as an alternative to traditional criminal justice processing. Figure 1 illustrates a deferred prosecution, pretrial drug court model where defendants are diverted into drug court *prior* to pleading to a criminal charge. In many drug court programs, participants have the option to participate in the program.

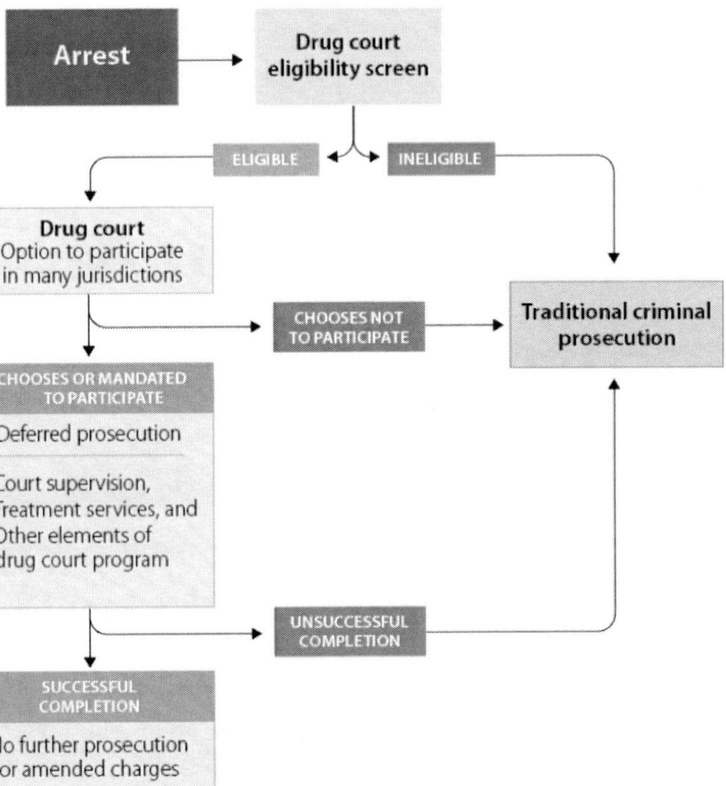

Source: CRS illustration of pretrial, deferred-prosecution drug court model.

Notes: The defendant does not have to enter a plea to charges under this drug court model. For an example of a pretrial model involving a deferred prosecution drug court program, see the Felony Pre-Trial Intervention Program operated by the Florida Department of Corrections, http://www.sao17.state.fl.us/felony-pti.html.

Figure 1. Deferred-Prosecution Drug Court Model.

Figure 2 illustrates a postadjudication model where defendants must plead guilty to charges (as part of a plea deal) in order to participate in the drug court program. Upon completion of this type of program, their sentences may be amended or waived, and in some jurisdictions, their offenses may be expunged.

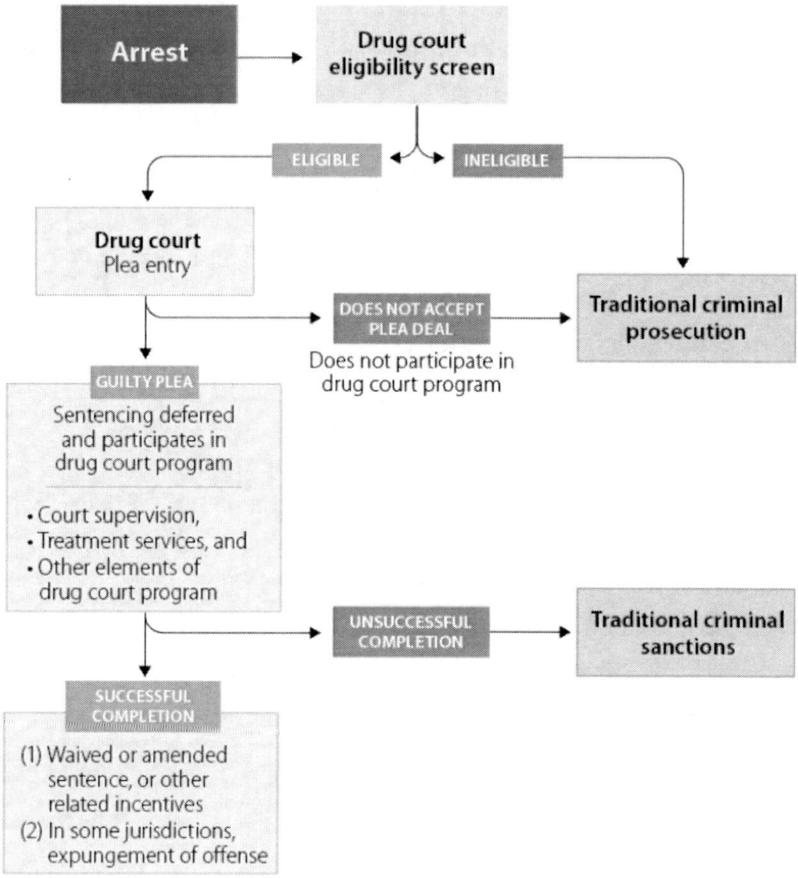

Source: CRS illustration of postadjudication drug court model.

Notes: For an example of a postadjudication model involving a guilty plea of the offender, see the Denver Drug Court of Denver, CO, http://www.denverda.org/prosecution_units/Drug_Court/Drug_Court.htm.

Figure 2. Postadjudication Drug Court Model.

These diagrams illustrate two common models of drug courts, but other models (or variations on the above) have been developed around the country. For example, some drug court referrals may come as a condition of probation. Many drug courts, including some federal drug court programs, are actually reentry programs that assist a drug-addicted prisoner with reentering the community while receiving treatment for substance abuse.

While drug courts vary in composition and target population, they generally have a comprehensive model involving

- offender screening and assessment of risks and needs,
- judicial interaction,
- monitoring (e.g., drug and alcohol testing) and supervision,
- graduated sanctions and incentives, and
- treatment and rehabilitation services.[6]

Drug courts are usually managed by a team of individuals from (1) criminal justice,[7] (2) social work, and (3) treatment service.[8]

Drug courts typically utilize a multiphase treatment approach including a stabilization phase, an intensive treatment phase, and a transition phase. The stabilization phase may include a period of detoxification, initial treatment assessment, and education, as well as additional screening for other needs. The intensive treatment phase typically involves counseling and other therapy. Finally, the transition phase could emphasize a variety of reintegration components including social integration, employment, education, and housing.[9]

---

[6] U.S. Department of Justice, National Institute of Justice, *Drug Courts*, January 2017, http://www.nij.gov/topics/.

[7] Including judges, prosecutors, defense attorneys, and community corrections officers.

[8] U.S Department of Justice, Office of Justice Programs, *Drug Courts*, June 2015, https://www.ncjrs.gov/pdffiles1/nij/ 238527.pdf.

[9] U.S Department of Justice, Office of Justice Programs, Bureau of Justice Assistance, *Defining Drug Courts: The Key Components*, Drug Courts Resource Series, NCJ 205621, October 2004, https://www.ncjrs.gov/pdffiles1/bja/ 205621.pdf.

Expansion of Drug Courts

A group of criminal justice professionals established the first drug court in Florida in 1989; they are credited with sparking a national movement of problem-solving courts that address specific needs and concerns of certain types of offenders.[10] There are around 3,000 drug courts (of various types) operating in the United States.[11] Drug courts have diversified to serve specialized groups including veterans, juveniles, and college students. Many drug courts are hybrid courts and address issues beyond drug abuse including mental health and alcohol-impaired driving. In some ways, the term "drug courts" appears to be a catch-all phrase for specialized programs for addicted defendants and offenders at various points in the criminal justice process.

Federal Drug Courts

While the Judicial Conference of the United States has long opposed the creation of specialized federal courts,[12] there has been growing support within the federal court system and the Department of Justice (DOJ) for reentry programs that incorporate some features of drug courts.[13] While some federal district courts have created special programs for drug-involved offenders—these programs are sometimes referred to as "drug

[10] Florida Courts, *Drug Courts*, 2015, http://www.flcourts.org/resources-and-services/court-improvement/problemsolving-courts/drug-courts/.

[11] The National Institute of Justice states there were 3,142 drug courts operating in the United States as of June 2015. See National Institute of Justice, *Drug Courts*, March 2015, http://www.nij.gov/topics/courts/drug-courts/.

[12] See, for example, Administrative Office of the U.S. Courts (A.O. Courts), *Report of the Proceedings of the Judicial Conference of the United States*, September 1986, p. 60, and September 1990, p. 82, http://www.uscourts.gov/aboutfederal-courts/reports-proceedings-judicial-conference-us. See also CRS correspondence with A.O. Courts on April 1, 2016.

[13] Steven E. Vance, "Federal Reentry Court Programs: A Summary of Recent Evaluations," *Federal Probation*, vol. 75, no. 2 (September 2011); and Department of Justice, *Deputy Attorney General James M. Cole Speaks on Alternatives to Incarceration Program: the Use of "Drug Courts" in the Federal and State Systems*, Justice News, May 21, 2012, https://www.justice.gov/opa/speech/deputy-attorney-general-james-m-cole-speaks-alternatives-incarceration-programuse-drug.

courts"—they are largely reentry programs that manage an inmate's reintegration to the community. A few federal drug court programs, however, manage offenders with "front end" diversion options. There have been questions about the effectiveness of drug court programs at the federal level due to the nature of federal crimes and the individuals who are arrested for allegedly committing them.

Federal district courts fund these specialized programs from decentralized allotments[14] given to the districts for general treatment and supervision of offenders.[15] As federal districts have budget autonomy, they may elect to establish these specialized court programs.[16]

Of note, in 2017 the President's Commission on Combating Drug Addiction and the Opioid Crisis recommended that DOJ establish a federal drug court in every federal judicial district.[17]

Federal Drug Courts and the 21st Century Cures Act

Enacted in 2016, Section 14003 of the 21st Century Cures Act (the Cures Act; P.L. 114-255) required DOJ to establish a pilot program to determine the effectiveness of federal drug and mental health courts. Within one year of enactment, DOJ, with assistance from the Administrative Office of the United States Courts and the United States Probation Offices, must establish a pilot program in at least one U.S. judicial district[18] that will divert certain offenders with mental illness or intellectual disabilities from federal prosecution, probation, or prison and

---

14 Governance, including the budget, of the federal judicial system is decentralized. After Congress and the Administration enact appropriations for the Judiciary, funding is then distributed to federal court units. For more information, see Administrative Office of the United States Courts, *Understanding the United States Judiciary's National Budget Process*.

15 Currently, there are no specific funding data for these programs.

16 Conversation between CRS and the Administrative Office of the U.S. Courts on April 1, 2016.

17 The President's Commission on Combating Drug Addiction and the Opioid Crisis, *Final Report*, November 1, 2017, p. 11, https://www.whitehouse.gov/sites/whitehouse.gov/files/images/Final_Report_Draft_11-1-2017.pdf.

18 Before making a designation, the Attorney General must (1) obtain the approval of the U.S. Attorney and chief judge for the judicial district being designated, and (2) determine that the judicial district being designated has adequate behavioral health systems for treatment.

place the offenders in these specialized courts. As of January 2018, this pilot program is still in the planning stages.[19]

Veterans Treatment Courts

Postdeployment, many veterans face unique challenges in readjusting to civilian life, and these challenges may contribute to involvement with the criminal justice system. According to the Bureau of Justice Statistics' (BJS's) National Inmate Survey from 2011 to 2012, approximately 8% (181,500) of the total incarcerated population in the United States[20] are veterans.[21] For approximately 14% (25,300) of these incarcerated veterans, the most serious offense that led to their incarceration was a drug offense, and for approximately 4% (7,100), their most serious offense was driving while intoxicated or impaired.[22] Older BJS survey data indicate that 43% of veteran state prisoners and 46% of veteran federal prisoners met the criteria for drug dependence or abuse in 2004, as opposed to 55% of nonveteran state prisoners and 45% of nonveteran federal prisoners.[23] While veterans in state prison reported lower levels of past drug use than nonveterans, a larger percentage of veterans (30%) than nonveterans (24%) reported a "recent history of mental health services."[24]

In 2008, the first veterans court was created in Buffalo, NY, in response to the combined mental health and substance abuse treatment

---

[19] CRS correspondence with the Administrative Office of the U.S. Courts in January 2018. There is no publicly available information on this project from DOJ.

[20] Excluding military-operated facilities.

[21] Jennifer Bronson, Ann Carson, and Margaret E. Noonan, et al., *Veterans in Prison and Jail, 2011-12*, U.S. Department of Justice, Bureau of Justice Statistics (BJS), NCJ 249144, December 2015, http://www.bjs.gov/content/ pub/pdf/vpj1112.pdf. These are the most recent data available from BJS.

[22] Based on CRS calculation of 2011-2012 Bureau of Justice Statistics data.

[23] Margaret E. Noonan and Christopher J. Mumola, *Veterans in State and Federal Prison, 2004*, Bureau of Justice Statistics, NCJ 217199, May 2007, pp. 5-6, http://www.bjs.gov/ content/pub/pdf/vsfp04.pdf.

[24] Mental health services include an overnight stay in a hospital, use of a prescribed medication, or treatment by a mental health professional.

needs of justice system-involved veterans.[25] These court programs are a hybrid model of drug treatment and mental health treatment courts.[26] As of June 2015, there were approximately 306 veterans treatment courts and 6 federal veterans courts.[27]

FEDERAL SUPPORT FOR DRUG COURTS

The federal government has demonstrated growing support for the drug court model primarily through financial support of drug court programs, research, and various drug court initiatives.

Drug Court Discretionary Grant Program

The Department of Justice (DOJ) supports research on drug courts,[28] training and technical assistance for drug courts, and grants for their development and enhancement. The primary federal grant program that supports them is the Drug Court Discretionary Grant Program (Drug Courts Program).[29] DOJ's Office of Justice Programs (OJP), Bureau of

---

[25] Office of National Drug Control Policy, *Veterans Treatment Courts*, Fact Sheet, December 2010, https://www.whitehouse.gov/sites/default/files/ondcp/Fact_Sheets/veterans_treatment_courts_fact_sheet_12-13-10.pdf.

[26] For more information about mental health courts, see Council of State Governments Justice Center, *Mental Health Courts: A Primer for Policymakers and Practitioners*, A report prepared for the Bureau of Justice Assistance, 2008, http://ojp.gov/newsroom/testimony/2009/mentalhealthcourts.pdf.

[27] The National Institute of Justice, *Drug Courts*, January 2017, http://www.nij.gov/topics/courts/drug-courts/pages/ welcome.aspx. For an example of a federal veterans court, see the program created in the Eighth Judicial District of Montana: U.S. Department of Justice, *Veterans Court Now Available for Vets Charged with Federal Crimes in Montana*, March 26, 2015, https://www.justice.gov/usao-mt/pr/veterans-court-now-available-vets-charged-federalcrimes-montana.

[28] See the U.S. Department of Justice, National Institute of Justice, *Drug Courts*, March 2015, http://www.nij.gov/ topics/courts/drug-courts/ for DOJ-sponsored research on drug courts.

[29] 34 U.S.C. §§10611-10619. The Drug Court Discretionary Grant program was first authorized under Title V of the Violent Crime Control and Law Enforcement Act of 1994 (P.L. 103-322). It has been reauthorized twice: first, under the 21st Century Department of Justice Appropriations Authorization Act (P.L. 107-273), and second, under the Violence Against Women and Department of Justice Reauthorization Act of 2005 (P.L. 109-162). It was

Justice Assistance (BJA) jointly administers this competitive grant program along with the Substance Abuse and Mental Health Administration (SAMHSA) within the Department of Health and Human Services (HHS). Grants are distributed to state, local, and tribal governments as well as state and local courts themselves to establish and enhance drug courts for nonviolent offenders with substance abuse issues.[30] See Table 1 for a five-year history of DOJ appropriations for the Drug Courts Program.

Table 1. Enacted Funding under DOJ for the Drug Court Discretionary Grant Program and Veterans Treatment Courts, FY2013-FY2017 (Dollars in millions)

	FY2013	FY2014	FY2015	FY2016	FY2017
Drug Court Discretionary Grant Program	\$38.1[a]	\$40.5	\$41.0	\$42.0	\$43.0[b]
Veterans Treatment Courts	\$3.7[a]	\$4.0	\$5.0	\$6.0	\$7.0[b]

Source: FY2013 postsequestration amounts were provided by the Department of Justice. FY2014 enacted amounts were taken from the joint explanatory statement to accompany P.L. 113-76. FY2015 enacted amounts were taken from the joint explanatory statement to accompany P.L. 113-235. FY2016 enacted amounts were taken from the joint explanatory statement to accompany P.L. 114-113. FY2017 enacted amounts were taken from the joint explanatory statement to accompany P.L. 115-31.

[a] The FY2013 amounts include rescissions of FY2013 budget authority and the amount sequestered per the Budget Control Act of 2011 (P.L. 112-25).

[b] For FY2017, funding for this program was provided under the Opioid Initiative, which included other drug control-related activities.

Drug courts funded through this program may not use federal funding and matched funding to serve violent offenders. Offenders may be characterized as "violent" according to current or past convictions as well

---

amended by the Comprehensive Addiction and Recovery Act of 2016 (CARA; P.L. 114-198).

[30] SAMHSA jointly administers only part of the Drug Court Discretionary Grant Program with BJA. For more information on this program and how grant funds are used, see the program description and grant solicitations available at https://www.bja.gov/ProgramDetails.aspx?Program_ID=58.

as current charges.[31] Of note, an exception to the violent offender restriction is made for veterans treatment courts that are funded through the Drug Courts Program.

Grants for Veterans Treatment Courts

Since FY2013, BJA has funded the Veterans Treatment Court Program[32] through the Drug Courts Program using funds specifically appropriated for this purpose (see amounts in Table 1). As mentioned, these amounts are not subject to the violent offender exclusion according to BJA.[33] The purpose of the Veterans Treatment Court Program is "to serve veterans struggling with addiction, serious mental illness, and/or co-occurring disorders."[34] Grants are awarded to state, local, and tribal governments to fund the establishment and development of veterans treatment courts. While veterans treatment court grants have been part of OJP's Drug Courts Program for several years, the Comprehensive Addiction and Recovery Act of 2016 (CARA; P.L. 114-198), authorized DOJ to award grants to state, local, and tribal governments to establish or expand programs for qualified veterans,[35] including veterans treatment

---

[31] Under 34 U.S.C. §10613, the term "violent offender" means a person who "(1) is charged with or convicted of an offense that is punishable by a term of imprisonment exceeding one year, during the course of which offense or conduct—(A) the person carried, possessed, or used a firearm or dangerous weapon; (B) there occurred the death of or serious bodily injury to any person; or (C) there occurred the use of force against the person of another, without regard to whether any of the circumstances described in subparagraph (A) or (B) is an element of the offense or conduct of which or for which the person is charged or convicted; or (2) has 1 or more prior convictions for a felony crime of violence involving the use or attempted use of force against a person with the intent to cause death or serious bodily harm."

For the purposes of juvenile drug courts, the term "violent offender" means a juvenile who has been convicted of, or adjudicated delinquent for, a felony-level offense that "(1) has as an element, the use, attempted use, or threatened use of physical force against the person or property of another, or the possession or use of a firearm; or (2) by its nature, involves a substantial risk that physical force against the person or property of another may be used in the course of committing the offense."

[32] OJP identifies this program as a hybrid of drug and mental health court programs.

[33] See p. 5 of the FY2017 competitive grant announcement for the Adult Drug Court Discretionary Grant Program, https://www.bja.gov/funding/DrugCourts17.pdf.

[34] U.S. Department of Justice, Office of Justice Programs, *FY2017 Performance Budget*, p. 51, https://www.justice.gov/jmd/file/822366/download.

[35] CARA defines a qualified veteran as a preliminarily qualified offender who served on active duty in any branch of the Armed Forces, including the National Guard or Reserves, and was

courts, peer-to-peer services, and treatment, rehabilitation, legal, or transitional services for incarcerated veterans.

Based on a review of program activity at the Department of Veterans Affairs (VA), the VA does not offer funding for veterans treatment courts; however, the VA operates a Veterans Justice Outreach (VJO) program,[36] which provides outreach and linkage to VA services for justice system-involved veterans, including those involved with veterans courts or drug courts.

Other Grant Support

Other DOJ grants, including the Edward Byrne Memorial Justice Assistance Grants (JAG)[37] and Juvenile Accountability Block Grants (JABG),[38] may be used to fund drug courts. One of the broader purpose areas of the JAG program is to improve prosecution and courts programs as well as drug treatment programs. The JABG program includes a purpose area to establish juvenile drug courts. Of note, the last time JABG received an appropriation was in FY2013, and it has been unauthorized since it expired in FY2009.

The Office of National Drug Control Policy (ONDCP), under its Other Federal Drug Control Programs account, offers drug court training and technical assistance grants, as well as support for other initiatives.[39]

---

discharged or released from such service under conditions other than dishonorable, unless the reason for the dishonorable discharge was attributable to a substance abuse disorder.

[36] For more information about the VJO program, see http://www.va.gov/homeless/vjo.asp and https://www.ptsd.va.gov/professional/provider-type/community/veterans-PTSD-Justice-System.asp.

[37] For more information on the JAG program, see CRS Report RS22416, *Edward Byrne Memorial Justice Assistance Grant (JAG) Program: In Brief*, by Nathan James (available upon request to CRS).

[38] For more information on the JABG program, see CRS Report RL33947, *Juvenile Justice: Legislative History and Current Legislative Issues*, by Kristin Finklea.

[39] For more information, see Executive Office of the President, ONDCP, Grants & Programs, https://www.whitehouse.gov/ondcp/grants-programs.

Table 2. SAMHSA Funding for Drug Court Grants, FY2013-FY2017 (Dollars in millions)

FY2013	FY2014	FY2015	FY2016	FY2017
$39.40	$52.75	$50.00	$60.00	$58.00

Source: Enacted funding data for FY2014-FY2016 taken from the FY2015 and FY2016 operating plans for SAMHSA and enacted funding data for FY2013 and FY2017 provided by SAMHSA. Of note, funding for drug courts is taken from the appropriations line item, "criminal justice activities."

Notes: According to SAMHSA, funding goes toward the following agencies/programs to support drug courts: (1) DOJ, Office of Juvenile Justice and Delinquency Prevention (OJJDP); (2) Partnership with Robert Wood Johnson for four years; (3) DOJ, BJA, Drug Court Discretionary Grant Program; (4) SAMHSA, Children Affected by Methamphetamine/ Family Treatment Drug Court Program; and (5) SAMHSA, Grants to Develop and Expand Behavioral Health Treatment Court Collaborative.

As mentioned, SAMHSA jointly administers the Drug Courts Program with BJA. In addition, SAMHSA administers other grants that support drug courts.[40] Grants go toward the creation, expansion, and enhancement of adult and family drug courts and treatment drug courts.[41] For FY2016, SAMHSA funded 122 drug court continuations, 60 new drug court grants,[42] and four contracts. In FY2017, SAMHSA planned to fund 103 drug court continuations, 71 new drug court grants, and two contracts.[43]

IMPACT OF DRUG COURTS

Jurisdictions have sought to utilize drug courts to treat individuals' drug addictions, lower recidivism rates for drug-involved offenders, and lower costs associated with processing these defendants and offenders.

---

[40] SAMHSA supports drug courts under the broader category of criminal justice activities.

[41] For more information about treatment drug courts, see the SAMHSA FY2016 and FY2017 grant announcements and awards for drug court programs, https://www.samhsa.gov/grants.

[42] The 60 new drug court grants include new BJA jointly funded drug court grants.

[43] Department of Health and Human Services, Substance Abuse and Mental Health Services Administration, *Fiscal Year 2018 Justification of Estimates for Appropriations Committees*, https://www.samhsa.gov/sites/default/files/samhsa-fy-2018-congressional-justification.pdf. p. 196.

Since the inception of drug courts, a great deal of research has been done to evaluate their effectiveness and their impact on offenders, the criminal justice system, and the community. Much of the research yields positive outcomes.[44]

Over the last decade, the National Institute of Justice, through its CrimeSolutions.gov evaluation program, has evaluated 21 drug court programs and found that 19 of them had either "effective" or "promising" ratings while two had ratings of "no effects." Most reported positive results for recidivism outcomes. For cost evaluations, only some programs had these data and these evaluations showed mixed results. Some programs showed significant cost savings while others had insignificant findings for cost impacts.[45]

Several studies have demonstrated that drug courts may lower recidivism rates and/or lower costs for processing defendants and offenders compared to traditional criminal justice processing.[46] For example, one group of researchers examined the impact of a drug court over 10 years and concluded that treatment and other costs associated with the drug court (investment costs)[47] per offender were $1,392 less than investment costs of traditional criminal justice processing. In addition, savings due to reduced recidivism (outcome costs) for drug court participants were more than $79 million over the 10-year period.[48] A collaboration of researchers conducted a five-year longitudinal study of 23 drug courts from several regions of the

---

[44] U.S. Department of Justice, National Institute of Justice, *Do Drug Courts Work? Findings from Drug Court Research*, http://www.nij.gov/topics/courts/drug courts/Pages/work.aspx; Douglas B. Marlowe, *Painting the Current Picture: A National Report on Drug Courts and Other Problem-Solving Court Programs in the United States*, June 2011, http://www.ndci.org/sites/default/files/nadcp/PCP%20Report%20FINAL.PDF.

[45] See profiles for 21 drug court programs at https://www.crimesolutions.gov/Topic Details.aspx?ID=238.

[46] Several evaluations of drug court programs on CrimeSolutions.gov show reductions in postarrest recidivism, while cost-effectiveness evaluations show some positive and some insignificant outcomes. Also, see results from the Multisite Adult Drug Court Evaluation funded by NIJ and conducted by the Urban Policy Institute, Justice Policy Center, RTI International, and the Center for Court Innovation, see http://www.nij.gov/topics/courts/drug-courts/Pages/ madce.aspx.

[47] These include costs associated with arrest, booking, court, jail, and probation.

[48] Michael W. Finigan, Shannon M. Carey, and Anton Cox, *The Impact of a Mature Drug Court over 10 Years of Operation: Recidivism and Costs*, NPC Research, Final Report, April 2007.

United States and reported that drug court participants were significantly less likely than nonparticipants to relapse into drug use and participants committed fewer criminal acts than nonparticipants after completing the drug court program.[49]

Still, some are skeptical of the impact of drug courts. The Drug Policy Alliance[50] has claimed that drug courts help only offenders who are expected to do well and do not truly reduce costs. This organization also has criticized drug courts for punishing addiction because drug courts dismiss those who are not able to abstain from substance use.[51]

SELECTED ISSUES FOR CONGRESS

The Opioid Epidemic

Congress has long been concerned over illicit drug use and abuse in the United States. Recently, Congress has given attention to opioid abuse, and especially overdose deaths involving prescription and illicit opioids.[52] In 2015, there were 52,404 drug overdose deaths in the United States, including 33,091 (63.1%) that involved an opioid.[53] Also, in 2016 SAMHSA estimated that 329,000 Americans age 12 and older were current users[54] of heroin and approximately 3.8 million Americans were

[49] For a summary of and various publications discussing the Multisite Adult Drug Court Evaluation funded by NIJ and conducted by the Urban Policy Institute, Justice Policy Center, RTI International, and the Center for Court Innovation, see http://www.nij.gov/topics/courts/drug-courts/Pages/madce.aspx.

[50] The Drug Policy Alliance is a national advocacy group that advocates for drug law reform.

[51] Drug Policy Alliance, *Drug Courts are Not the Answer: Toward a Health-Centered Approach to Drug Use*, March 2011.

[52] For example, in July 2016 Congress passed and the President signed the Comprehensive Addiction and Recovery Act of 2016 (CARA; P.L. 114-198).

[53] Rose A. Rudd, Puja Seth, and Felicita David, et al., *Increases in Drug and Opioid Overdose Deaths—United States, 2010–2015*, Centers for Disease Control and Prevention, Morbidity and Mortality Weekly Report (MMWR), December 30, 2016, https://www.cdc.gov/mmwr/volumes/65/wr/mm655051e1.htm.

[54] "Current use" is defined as use in the past month.

current "misusers"[55] of prescription pain relievers.[56] Policymakers may debate whether drug courts are an effective tool in the package of federal efforts to address the opioid epidemic. Policy options include, but are not limited to, increasing federal funding for drug courts, expanding federal drug court programs, and amending the Drug Courts Program to possibly include a broader group of offenders, among other potential changes.

Inclusion of Violent Offenders

As discussed, grant recipients of the federal Drug Courts Program, with the exception of veterans treatment courts, must exclude violent offenders;[57] however, some argue that drug courts should include violent offenders. One group of researchers compared the outcomes for violent and nonviolent offenders and concluded that courts should consider the current charge rather than the offender's history of violence, and the type and seriousness of the offender's substance abuse problem when selecting individuals for drug court programs.[58] They found that while it appeared that individuals with a history of violence (defined as at least one violent charge before entering drug court) were more likely to fail the program

---

[55] SAMHSA defines misuse of prescription drugs as "use in any way not directed by a doctor including use without a prescription of one's own medication; use in greater amounts, more often, or longer than told to take a drug; or use in any other way not directed by a doctor." Prescription drugs do not include over-the-counter drugs.

[56] Subtypes of pain relievers include hydrocodone, oxycodone, tramadol, codeine, morphine, fentanyl, buprenorphine, oxymorphone, Demerol®, hydromorphone, and methadone. See HHS, SAMHSA, *Results from the 2016 National Survey on Drug Use and Health: Detailed Tables*, September 2016, Tables 1.1A and 1.1B, https://www.samhsa.gov/ data/population-data-nsduh/ and Methodological Summary and Definitions, Table C-1.

[57] Under 34 U.S.C. §10613, a "violent offender" means a person who "(1) is charged with or convicted of an offense that is punishable by a term of imprisonment exceeding one year, during the course of which offense or conduct—(A) the person carried, possessed, or used a firearm or dangerous weapon; (B) there occurred the death of or serious bodily injury to any person; or (C) there occurred the use of force against the person of another, without regard to whether any of the circumstances described in subparagraph (A) or (B) is an element of the offense or conduct of which or for which the person is charged or convicted; or (2) has 1 or more prior convictions for a felony crime of violence involving the use or attempted use of force against a person with the intent to cause death or serious bodily harm."

[58] Christine A. Saum, Frank R. Scarpitti, and Cynthia A. Robbins, "Violent Offenders in Drug Court," *Journal of Drug Issues*, vol. 31, no. 107 (2001), p. 124.

than those who never had been charged with a violent crime, the relationship between history of violence and drug court success disappeared when controlling for total criminal history.[59] More serious offenders are less likely than low-level or first-time offenders to abstain from crime, and some argue that drug courts may be the best option for these individuals.

Substance abuse and crime have long been linked,[60] and diversion and treatment may assist some individuals in avoiding criminal behavior. Congress may wish to maintain the exclusion of violent offenders from the Drug Courts Program, or it may consider broadening the pool of eligible offenders that may participate in BJA-funded drug court programs to include certain violent offenders.

ACKNOWLEDGMENTS

Amber Wilhelm contributed to the graphics used in this chapter.

---

[59] Ibid, p. 123. The offender's charges were coded into seven categories, and these categories were divided into four major offenses (violent, property, public order, drug) and three minor offenses (traffic, court—violation of probation, capiases, etc.; and other—juvenile offenses, conspiracy charges, and other miscellaneous offenses). The total number of lifetime charges for each participant indicates the extent of an offender's previous criminal involvement.

[60] See Bureau of Justice Statistics, *Drug and Crime Facts*, http://www.bjs.gov/content/dcf/duc.cfm.

In: Criminal Justice
Editor: Quincy Franks
ISBN: 978-1-53614-196-2

Chapter 3

TRENDS IN BANK SECRECY ACT/ANTI-MONEY LAUNDERING ENFORCEMENT*

Jay B. Sykes

ABSTRACT

This chapter provides an overview of recent trends in the enforcement of the Bank Secrecy Act (BSA), the principal U.S. anti-money laundering law regulating financial institutions.

The chapter begins by providing general background information on BSA penalties and enforcement. The chapter concludes by discussing three recent trends that commentators have observed in BSA enforcement: (1) an increase in the frequency with which BSA enforcement actions involve an assessment of money penalties, and an increase in the size of those penalties, (2) an increased emphasis by regulators on the acceptance of responsibility by institutions entering into

---

* This is an edited, reformatted, and augmented version of a Congressional Research Service report, R45076, dated January 12, 2018.

settlement agreements for BSA violations, and (3) an increased risk of individual liability for BSA violations.

BACKGROUND

The BSA is "the primary U.S. anti-money laundering (AML) law" regulating financial institutions.[1] Among other things, the Act and related regulations impose certain reporting and recordkeeping requirements[2] and require certain institutions to establish AML programs that meet specified minimum standards.[3] The BSA and related regulations provide for civil and criminal penalties for violations of their provisions, as well as the forfeiture of assets involved in a violation.[4] The level of BSA penalties varies based on the type of entity charged with a violation, the type of violation, and the defendant's level of intent.[5]

The Financial Crimes Enforcement Network (FinCEN), a bureau within the Department of the Treasury primarily charged with administering the BSA, has enforcement authority to bring administrative actions for failure to meet BSA requirements.[6] The Office of the Comptroller of the Currency (OCC),[7] the Federal Deposit Insurance Corporation,[8] the Federal Reserve,[9] the Securities and Exchange Commission,[10] the Financial Industry Regulatory Authority,[11] and the National Credit Union Administration[12] also have authority to enforce the BSA's requirements against the institutions they regulate. Moreover, the

---

[1] *BSA and Related Regulations*, OFFICE OF THE COMPTROLLER OF THE CURRENCY, https://www.occ.treas.gov/topics/compliance-bsa/bsa/bsa-regulations/index-bsa-regulations.html.

[2] *See* 31 U.S.C. §§ 5313-5316; 31 C.F.R. §§ 1010.300-1010.370, 1010.400-1010.440.

[3] *See* 31 U.S.C. § 5318(h); 31 C.F.R. §§ 1010.200-1010.230.

[4] 31 U.S.C. §§ 5321-5322; 31 C.F.R. §§ 1010.820-1010.840 (listing penalties).

[5] *See supra* note 4.

[6] *See* 31 U.S.C. § 310; 31 C.F.R. § 1010.810(a).

[7] *See* 12 U.S.C. § 1818(i)(2); 12 C.F.R. §§ 21.11, 21.21, 163.180.

[8] *See* 12 U.S.C. § 1818(i)(2); 12 C.F.R. § 326.8.

[9] *See* 12 U.S.C. § 1818(i)(2); 12 C.F.R. § 208.63.

[10] *See* 15 U.S.C. § 78u; 17 C.F.R. § 240.17a-8.

[11] *See* 31 C.F.R. § 1023.220.

[12] *See* 12 U.S.C. § 1786; 12 C.F.R. § 748.2.

Department of Justice (DOJ) regularly brings criminal charges for BSA violations.[13]

BSA Enforcement Trends

Increases in Penalty Frequency and Size

Commentators have noted an increase in the frequency with which BSA enforcement actions have involved an assessment by federal regulators of monetary penalties, and an increase in the size of those penalties.[14] According to a June 2016 study conducted by National Economic Research Associates, Inc. (NERA), nearly 90% of BSA/AML enforcement actions from 2012 through 2015 involved an assessment of money penalties, compared to less than half of such enforcement actions from 2002 through 2011.[15] NERA also observed that BSA/AML penalties "have grown substantially in both absolute terms and as a proportion of firm capital."[16] Specifically, NERA found that more than 80% of the total money penalties imposed for BSA/AML violations since 2002 have been

---

[13] *See*, e.g., *Banamex USA Agrees to Forfeit $97 Million in Connection with Bank Secrecy Act Violations*, U.S. DEP'T OF JUSTICE (May 22, 2017), https://www.justice.gov/opa/pr/banamex-usa-agrees-forfeit-97-million-connection-banksecrecy-act-violations; *Western Union Admits Anti-Money Laundering and Consumer Fraud Violations, Forfeits $586 Million in Settlement with Department of Justice and Federal Trade Commission*, U.S. DEP'T OF JUSTICE (Jan. 19, 2017), https://www.justice.gov/opa/pr/western-union-admits-anti money laundering and consumer fraud violationsforfeits-586-million; *Commerzbank AG Admits to Sanctions and Bank Secrecy Act Violations, Agrees to Forfeit $563 Million and Pay $79 Million Fine*, U.S. DEP'T OF JUSTICE (Mar. 12, 2015), https://www.justice.gov/opa/pr/commerzbank-ag-admits-sanctions-and-bank-secrecy-violations-agrees-forfeit-563-million-and. *See also* 5 U.S.C. §§ 510, 515-519; 28 C.F.R. § 0.55.

[14] Sharon Brown-Hruska, *Developments in Bank Secrecy Act and Anti-Money Laundering Enforcement and Litigation*, N ERA ECONOMIC CONSULTING (June 2016) at 12, http://www.nera.com/content/dam/nera/publications/2016/ PUB_Developments_BSA AM L_L it-06.16.pdf. *See also 2015 Year-End Review of BSA/AML and Sanctions Developments and Their Importance to Financial Institutions*, SULLIVAN & CROMWELL L L P at 2 (M ar. 3, 2016), https://www.sullcrom.com/siteFiles/Publications/SC_Publication_2015 Y ear_End_Review_of BSA A M L_3_3_16.pdf (noting that "[i]n 2015, we continued to see record-setting fines ... against financial institutions for violations of BSA/A M L ... laws.").

[15] Brown-Hruska, *supra* note 14 at 12.

[16] *Id.*

levied after 2012.[17] Moreover, according to that same report, since October 2009, nearly one-third of BSA/AML penalties have exceeded 10% of a defendant institution's capital.[18] By contrast, no penalty imposed before 2007 exceeded 9% of a defendant institution's capital.[19]

Two recent BSA/AML enforcement actions stand out for their size. In 2012, HSBC Holdings plc and HSBC Bank USA N.A. (together, HSBC) were assessed a $665 million civil money penalty, forfeited roughly $1.2 billion, and entered into a deferred prosecution agreement (DPA) based on, among other things, their failure to maintain an effective AML program and conduct appropriate due diligence on foreign correspondent account holders.[20] The HSBC enforcement action was pursued concurrently by the DOJ, the OCC, the Federal Reserve, and the Department of the Treasury.[21] Pursuant to the DPA, HSBC admitted responsibility for violating the BSA and associated regulations from 2006 to 2010.[22] Specifically, HSBC admitted that during the relevant time period, it "ignored the money laundering risks associated with doing business with certain Mexican customers and failed to implement a BSA/AML program that was adequate to monitor suspicious transactions from Mexico."[23] According to the DPA, as a result of HSBC's failures, at least $881 million in drug trafficking

---

[17] *Id.*

[18] *Id.* at 7.

[19] *Id.*

[20] United States v. HSBC Bank USA, N.A., No. 1:12-cr-00763, 2013 WL 3306161 (E.D.N.Y. July 1, 2013); Statement of Facts, United States v. HSBC Bank USA, N.A., No. 1:12-cr-00763 (E.D.N.Y., filed on Dec. 11, 2012) [hereinafter "Statement of Facts"], https://www.justice.gov/sites/default/files/opa/legacy/2012/12/11/dpa-attachment-a.pdf; *HSBC Holdings Plc. and HSBC Bank N.A. Admit to Anti-Money Laundering and Sanctions Violations, Forfeit $1.256 Billion in Deferred Prosecution Agreement*, U.S. DEP'T OF JUSTICE (Dec. 11, 2012), https://www.justice.gov/opa/pr/hsbcholdings-plc-and-hsbc-bank-usa-na-admit-anti-money-laundering-and-sanctions-violations. A "correspondent account" is an account established by a foreign bank or financial institution "to receive deposits from, or to make payments or other disbursements on behalf of" the foreign bank or financial institution, "or to handle other financial transactions related to" the foreign bank or financial institution. 31 C.F.R. § 1010.605(c)(1). BSA regulations require certain institutions to establish due diligence programs for foreign correspondent accounts that meet specified minimum standards. *Id.* § 1010.610.

[21] *See HSBC Holdings Plc. and HSBC Bank N.A. Admit to Anti-Money Laundering and Sanctions Violations, Forfeit $1.256 Billion in Deferred Prosecution Agreement*, *supra* note 20.

[22] Statement of Facts at 3.

[23] *Id.*

proceeds were laundered through HSBC Bank USA without being detected.[24]

In a series of other BSA enforcement actions, a number of federal regulators assessed large penalties against JPMorgan Chase Bank, N.A. (JPMorgan) in January 2014 for its role in the Bernard L. Madoff Ponzi scheme. JPMorgan entered into a DPA with the U.S. Attorney's Office for the Southern District of New York concerning Madoff-related BSA violations.[25] Pursuant to the DPA, JPMorgan admitted that it violated the BSA by failing to maintain an effective AML compliance program and failing to file suspicious activity reports (SARs) concerning transactions related to the Madoff scheme.[26] JPMorgan further agreed to forfeit $1.7 billion to compensate victims of the Madoff fraud—the largest-ever penalty for a BSA violation.[27] Separately, the OCC and FinCEN assessed civil money penalties of $350 million and $461 million, respectively, against JPMorgan for its Madoff-related BSA violations.[28]

---

[24] *Id.* As part of the DPA, HSBC also agreed to oversight by a corporate monitor to ensure the effectiveness of its AML reforms. HSBC announced last month that the DOJ agreed to release HSBC from the monitorship after finding that it had made sufficient improvements. *HSBC Holdings plc Expiration of 2012 Deferred Prosecution Agreement*, HSBC (Dec. 11, 2017), http://www.hsbc.com/news-and-insight/media-resources/media-releases/2017/hsbc-holdings-plcexpiration-of-2012-deferred-prosecution-agreement.

[25] *Manhattan U.S. Attorney and FBI Assistant Director-in-Charge Announce Filing of Criminal Charges Against and Deferred Prosecution Agreement With JPMorgan Chase Bank, N.A., In Connection With Bernard L. Madoff's Multi-Billion Dollar Ponzi Scheme*, U.S. DEP'T OF JUSTICE (Jan. 7, 2014), https://www.justice.gov/usao-sdny/pr/manhattanus-attorney-and-fbi-assistant-director-charge-announce-filing-criminal.

[26] *Id.*

[27] *Id.*

[28] Consent Order for the Assessment of a Civil Money Penalty, In the Matter of JPMorgan Chase Bank, N.A., JPMorgan Bank and Trust Company, N.A., Chase Bank USA, N.A., AA-EC-13-109, OFFICE OF THE COMPTROLLER OF THE CURRENCY (Jan. 7, 2014), https://www.occ.treas.gov/topics/laws-regulations/enforcement-actions/bankenforcement-actions/ea-2014-001.pdf; *JPMorgan Admits Violation of the Bank Secrecy Act for Failed Madoff Oversight; Fined $461 Million by FinCEN*, FINANCIAL CRIMES ENFORCEMENT NETWORK (Jan. 7, 2014), https://www.fincen.gov/news/news-releases/jpmorgan-admits-violation-bank-secrecy-act-failed-madoff-oversightfined-461. Note that FinCEN deemed its penalty satisfied by JPMorgan's payment to the U.S. Attorney's Office for the Southern District of New York. *Id.*

Emphasis on Acceptance of Responsibility

A second recent trend in BSA/AML enforcement is an increased emphasis by regulators on the acceptance of responsibility by institutions charged with BSA violations.[29] In 2013, FinCEN Director Jennifer Shasky Calvery indicated that FinCEN had changed its approach of generally allowing financial institutions charged with BSA violations to enter into settlements "without admitting or denying" the facts alleged in a penalty assessment.[30] Shasky Calvery noted that in FinCEN's most recent enforcement actions, defendant institutions had been required to stipulate to a statement of facts, reflecting the agency's new position that "[a]cceptance of responsibility and acknowledgment of the facts is a critical component of corporate responsibility."[31] Two years later, FinCEN's Director of Enforcement confirmed the agency's changed approach when she indicated that FinCEN operates under a "presumption" that "a settlement of an enforcement action will include an admission to the facts, as well as the violation of law."[32] Along these lines, NERA's 2016 study found that four of the six largest BSA/AML violations charged between 2010 and 2015 "required the [defendant] financial institution to admit the accuracy of government claims and accept responsibility for the actions of its officers, agents, and employees who violated BSA/AML regulations."[33]

---

[29] *See* Brown-Hruska, *supra* note 14 at 2-3; *Remarks of Stephanie Brooker, Associate Director of Enforcement, Financial Crimes Enforcement Network (FinCEN)*, 2015 Bank Secrecy Act Conference (June 18, 2015), https://www.fincen.gov/news/speeches/remarks-stephanie-brooker-associate-director-enforcement-financial-crimes-0 [hereinafter "Remarks of Stephanie Brooker"]; *Remarks of Jennifer Shasky Calvery, Director, Financial Crimes Enforcement Network*, American Bankers Association/American Bar Association Money Laundering Enforcement Conference (Nov. 19, 2013) [hereinafter "Remarks of Jennifer Shasky Calvery"], https://www.fincen.gov/sites/default/files/shared/20131119_ABA_ABA.pdf.

[30] Remarks of Jennifer Shasky Calvery at 4.

[31] *Id.*

[32] Remarks of Stephanie Brooker.

[33] Brown-Hruska, *supra* note 14 at 4.

Increased Risk of Individual Liability

Finally, commentators have noted an increased risk of individual liability for BSA violations.[34] In December 2014, FinCEN assessed a $1 million civil money penalty against Thomas Haider, the former Chief Compliance Officer of MoneyGram International for willful violations of the BSA's program requirements and failure to timely file SARs concerning fraudulent telemarketing operations and other schemes.[35] FinCEN's enforcement action led to litigation over the application of the BSA to individuals. In January 2016, a federal district court held in *U.S. Department of Treasury v. Haider* that individuals can be liable for violations of the BSA's AML program requirements.[36] In that case, Haider argued that individuals cannot be liable for violations of the BSA's program requirements because the relevant BSA provision provides that "financial institution[s] shall establish anti-money laundering programs,"[37] in contrast to the BSA's provision requiring the filing of SARs, which provides that "any financial institution, *and any director, officer, employee, or agent of any financial institution*, [may be required] to report suspicious transactions relevant to a possible violation of law or regulation."[38] The court rejected this argument, reasoning that because the BSA's general civil penalty provision authorizes the imposition of money penalties against, among other individuals, "officer[s]" of financial institutions,[39] Haider could be held liable for violations of the BSA's AML program

---

[34] *Id.* at 3; *2015 Year-End Review of BSA/AML and Sanctions Developments and Their Importance to Financial Institutions*, *supra* note 14 at 7-10.

[35] *FinCEN Assesses $1 Million Penalty and Seeks to Bar Former MoneyGram Executive from Financial Industry*, FINANCIAL CRIMES ENFORCEMENT NETWORK (Dec. 8. 2014), https://www.fincen.gov/news/news-releases/fincenassesses-1-million-penalty-and-seeks-bar-former-moneygram-executive.

[36] *See* U.S. Dep't of Treasury v. Haider, No. 15-1518, 2016 WL 107940 at *3 (D. Minn. Jan. 8, 2016).

[37] 31 U.S.C. § 5318(h).

[38] *Haider*, 2016 WL 107940 at *2; 31 U.S.C. § 5318(g) (emphasis added).

[39] 31 U.S.C. § 5321(a)(1).

requirements.[40] Regulators have recently pursued a number of other BSA enforcement actions against individual compliance officers.[41]

This increased emphasis on individual prosecutions is broadly consistent with the approach outlined by the DOJ in the September 2015 "Yates Memo," which emphasized the importance of individual accountability for corporate wrongdoing.[42] Current Deputy Attorney General Rod Rosenstein has indicated that while he "generally agree[s] with the critique that motivated" the Yates Memo, the memo is currently under review.[43] Accordingly, it remains to be seen whether the DOJ under President Trump will maintain the previous Administration's emphasis on individual responsibility in white-collar enforcement actions and prosecutions.

---

[40] *Haider*, 2016 WL 107940 at *2-3.

[41] *See* Order Instituting Administrative and Cease-and-Desist Proceedings, Pursuant to Sections 15(b) and 21C of the Securities Exchange Act of 1934, Making Findings, and Imposing Remedial Sanctions and a Cease-and-Desist Order, In the Matter of Lia Yaffar-Pena, Release No. 79124, SECURITIES AND EXCHANGE COMMISSION (Oct. 19, 2016), https://www.sec.gov/litigation/admin/2016/34-79124.pdf; *FINRA Fines Raymond James $17 Million for Systemic Anti-Money Laundering Compliance Failures, Former AML Compliance Officer Fined and Suspended*, FINANCIAL INDUSTRY REGULATORY AUTHORITY (May 18, 2016), http://www.finra.org/newsroom/2016/finra-fines-raymond-james17-million-systemic-anti-money-laundering-compliance; Consent Order, In the Matter of Charles Sanders, AA-EC2015-92, OFFICE OF THE COMPTROLLER OF THE CURRENCY (Mar. 15, 2016), https://www.occ.gov/static/enforcementactions/ea2016-038.pdf. While these enforcement actions were not based on violations of the statutory provision at issue in *Haider*, they are consistent with a broader trend of increased risk of individual liability for BSA violations.

[42] Memorandum from Sally Quillian Yates, Deputy Att'y Gen., U.S. Dep't of Justice to All U.S. Att'ys et al., Individual Accountability for Corporate Wrongdoing (Sept. 9, 2015), https://www.justice.gov/archives/dag/file/ 769036/download.

[43] *Deputy Attorney General Rod Rosenstein Keynote Address on Corporate Enforcement Policy*, NYU PROGRAM ON CORPORATE COMPLIANCE & ENFORCEMENT (Oct. 6, 2017), https://wp.nyu.edu/compliance_enforcement/2017/10/06/nyu-program-on-corporate-compliance-enforcement-keynote-address-october-6-2017/.

In: Criminal Justice
Editor: Quincy Franks
ISBN: 978-1-53614-196-2

Chapter 4

MANDATORY MINIMUM SENTENCING OF FEDERAL DRUG OFFENSES*

Charles Doyle

ABSTRACT

As a general rule, federal judges must impose a minimum term of imprisonment upon defendants convicted of various controlled substance (drug) offenses and drug-related offenses. The severity of those sentences depends primarily upon the nature and amount of the drugs involved, the defendant's prior criminal record, any resulting injuries or death, and in the case of the related firearms offenses, the manner in which the firearm was used.

The drug offenses reside principally in the Controlled Substances Act or the Controlled Substances Import and Export Act. The drug-related firearms offenses involve the possession and use of firearms in connection with serious drug offenses and instances in which prior drug convictions trigger mandatory sentences for unlawful firearms possession.

---

* This is an edited, reformatted, and augmented version of a Congressional Research Service report, R45074, dated January 11, 2018.

The minimum sentences range from imprisonment for a year to imprisonment for life. Although the sentences are usually referred to as mandatory minimum sentences, a defendant may avoid them under several circumstances. Prosecutors may elect not to prosecute. The President may choose to pardon the defendant or commute his sentence. The defendant may qualify for sentencing for providing authorities with substantial assistance or under the so-called "safety valve" provision available to low-level, nonviolent, first-time offenders.

Over time, defendants, sentenced to mandatory terms of imprisonment for drug-related offenses, have challenged Congress's legislative authority to authorize them and the government's constitutional authority to enforcement. The challenges have met with scant success. Generally, courts have concluded that the provisions fall within congressional authority under the Commerce, Necessary and Proper, Treaty, and Territorial Clauses of the Constitution. By and large, courts have also found no impediment to imposition of mandatory minimum sentences under the Due Process, Equal Protection, or Cruel and Unusual Punishment Clauses, or the separation-of-powers doctrine.

Proposals to amend drug-related mandatory minimum sentence provisions surfaced during the 114th Congress. In the 115th Congress, Senator Grassley introduced the successor to those proposals for himself and a bi-partisan list of co-sponsors as S. 1917, the Sentencing Reform and Corrections Act of 2017. Many of the same issues are addressed in H.R. 4261 introduced by Representative Scott of Virginia. This is an overview of the law from which those proposals spring.

INTRODUCTION

This is a brief discussion of the law associated with the mandatory minimum sentencing provisions of federal controlled substance (drug) laws and drug-related federal firearms and recidivist statutes.[1] These mandatory

[1] The inventory includes: 21 U.S.C. §§ 841(a), 841(b) (manufacturing, distributing, dispensing, or possessing with the intent to do so various controlled substances); *id.* §§ 841(h), 841(b) (dispensing controlled substances by way of the Internet); *id.* §§ 844(a), 841(b) (simple possession of controlled substances by repeat offenders); *id.* §§ 846, 841(b) (attempt or conspiracy to commit an offense punishable by a mandatory minimum sentence); *id.* § 848 (continuing criminal enterprise (drug kingpin)); *id.* §§ 849, 841(b) (distribution of controlled substances as truck stops); 21 U.S.C. §§ 859, 841(b) (distribution of controlled substances to an individual under 21 years of age); *id.* §§ 860, 841(b) (distribution of controlled substances at in or near schools, playgrounds, public housing projects, etc.); *id.* §§ 861, 841(b) (use of children in drug operations); 21 U.S.C. §§ 861(f), 841(b) (distribution of controlled substances to pregnant individuals); *id.* §§ 952, 960 (importing

minimums, however, are not as mandatory as they might appear. The government may elect not to prosecute the underlying offenses. Federal courts may disregard otherwise applicable mandatory sentencing requirements at the behest of the government.[2] The federal courts may also bypass some of them for the benefit of certain low-level, nonviolent offenders with virtually spotless criminal records under the so-called "safety valve" provision.[3] Finally, in cases where the mandatory minimums would usually apply, the President may pardon offenders or commute their sentences before the minimum term of imprisonment has been served.[4] Be that as it may, sentencing in drug cases, particularly mandatory minimum drug sentencing, has contributed to an explosion in the federal prison

---

controlled substances into the U.S.); *id.* §§ 953, 960 (exporting controlled substances from the U.S.); *id.* §§ 955, 960 (possession of controlled substances aboard a ship arriving in or departing from the U.S.); *id.* §§ 959, 960 (possession abroad of controlled substances or listed substances for importation into the U.S. by vessel or plane); *id.* §§ 960a, 841(b) (narco-terrorism); *id.* §§ 963, 960 (attempt or conspiracy to commit an exporting or importing offense punishable by a mandatory minimum); 18 U.S.C. § 3261; 21 U.S.C. § 841(b) (military extraterritorial jurisdiction); 46 U.S.C. §§ 70503, 70506; 21 U.S.C. § 960 (maritime drug law enforcement act offenses). Here and throughout, the host of later amendments to the Controlled Substances Act and the Controlled Substances Import and Export Act counsel citation to the sections of those Acts as they appear in title 21 of the United States Code unless otherwise noted. 18 U.S.C. § 3559(c) (mandatory life imprisonment for defendants convicted of a serious violent felony who have a one or more prior serious drug convictions and one or more prior serious violent felony convictions); *id.* § 924(c) (mandatory minimum sentence for carrying a firearm in furtherance of a drug trafficking offense); *id.* § 924(e) (mandatory minimum sentence for conviction of unlawful possession of a firearm by a defendant with three or more prior violent felony or serious drug offense convictions). Here and throughout the terms "drug" and "controlled substance" are used interchangeably.

Various parts of the report are drawn from the author's earlier reports, principally CRS Report RL32040, *Federal Mandatory Minimum Sentencing Statutes*; CRS Report RL30281, *Federal Mandatory Minimum Sentencing Statutes: A List of Citations with Captions, Introductory Comments, and Bibliography*; CRS Report R42386, *Mandatory Minimum Sentencing for Federal Sex Offenses: An Overview*; CRS Report R41326, *Federal Mandatory Minimum Sentences: The Safety Valve and Substantial Assistance Exceptions*; CRS Report R41412, *Federal Mandatory Minimum Sentencing: The 18 U.S.C. 924(c) Tack-On in Cases Involving Drugs or Violence*; CRS Report R41461, *Three Strike Mandatory Sentencing (18 U.S.C. 3559(c)): An Overview*.

[2] 18 U.S.C. § 3553(e).

[3] *Id.* § 3553(f).

[4] U.S. CONST. art. II, § 2, cl. 1. E.g., President Obama Commutes Sentences of 95 Federal Drug Offenders, *The Washington Post*, Dec. 18, 2015, https://www.washingtonpost.com/world/national-security/president-obama-commutes-sentences-of-about-100-drug-offenders/2015/12/18/9b62c91c-a5a3-11e5-9c4e-be37f66848bb_story.html?utm_term=.19c2833a2a8c.

population and attendant costs. This, the federal inmate population at the end of 1976 was 23,566, and at the end of 1986 it was 36,042.5 On January 4, 2018, the federal inmate population was 183,493.[6] As of September 30, 2016, 49.1% of federal inmates were drug offenders and 72.3% of those were convicted of an offense carrying a mandatory minimum.[7] In 1976, federal prisons cost $183.914 million; in 1986, $550.014 million; and in 2016, $6.751 billion (est.).[8]

BACKGROUND

Federal mandatory minimum sentencing statutes have existed since the dawn of the Republic. When the first Congress assembled, it enacted several mandatory minimums, each of them a capital offense.[9] The drug mandatory minimums are of more recent origins. The first arrived in 1914, when Congress established a mandatory minimum of five years for the manufacture of opium for smoking purposes.[10] Shortly after mid-century, Congress began adding to the number of drug-related mandatory minimums. Prior to enactment of the Controlled Substances Act and the Controlled Substances Import and Export Act in 1970,[11] federal law included mandatory minimums for violations of the narcotics or marijuana

---

[5] U.S. Department of Justice, Bureau of Justice Statistics, SOURCEBOOK OF CRIMINAL JUSTICE STATISTICS – 1987, Table 6.52 (1987).

[6] Federal Bureau of Prisons, *Statistics*, https://www.bop.gov/about/statistics/population_statistics.jsp.

[7] U.S. Sentencing Commission, *Mandatory Minimum Penalties for Drug Offenses in the Federal Criminal Justice System*, 4 (Oct. 2017), https://www.ussc.gov/sites/default/files/pdf/research-and-publications/researchpublications/2017/20171025_Drug-Mand-Min.pdf.

[8] Budget of the U.S. Government: Appendix for Fiscal Years 1978, 1988, and 2017, respectively.

[9] The Act of April 30, 1790 declared that "persons ... adjudged guilty of treason against the United States ... shall suffer death," 1 Stat. 112; the same sentence awaited those who committed murder within the exclusive jurisdiction of the United States, *id.* at 113, or engaged in piracy, *id.* at 113-14, or counterfeiting, *id* . at 115.

[10] Act of January 17, 1914, 38 Stat. 278 (1914).

[11] The 1970 Comprehensive Drug Abuse Prevention and Control Act encompassed both the Controlled Substances Act and the Controlled Substances Import and Export Act, P.L. 91-513, 94 Stat. 1236 (1970).

tax regimes;[12] smuggling narcotics or marijuana;[13] distributing heroin to a child;[14] possession of narcotics aboard a U.S. vessel;[15] and violations of federal drug laws using communications facilities.[16] The 1970s legislation eliminated them all.[17] Left in their place were only the mandatory minimums in the continuing criminal enterprise (drug kingpin) section.[18]

Then, in 1984, Congress enacted the Sentencing Reform Act that created the United States Sentencing Commission and authorized it to promulgate then binding sentencing guidelines.[19] In many instances, the resulting Guidelines operated essentially, but briefly, to establish a mandatory minimum term of imprisonment where none had existed before.[20] Soon thereafter, Congress began to repopulate federal drug laws

---

[12] 26 U.S.C. § 7237 (1964 ed.) (imprisonment for not less than 2 years for the first offense, not less than 5 years for the second, and not less than 10 years for the third).

[13] 21 U.S.C. §§ 174, 176a (1964 ed.) (imprisonment for not less than 5 years for the first offense and not less than 10 years for the second).

[14] *Id.* § 176b (1964 ed.) (imprisonment for not less than 10 years for distributing heroin to a child).

[15] *Id.* § 184a (1964 ed.) (imprisonment for not less than 5 years for the first offense and not less than 10 years for the second).

[16] 18 U.S.C. § 1403 (1964 ed.) (imprisonment for not less than 2 years).

[17] Pub. L. No. 91-513, § 1101, 84 Stat. 1236, 1291-92 (1970).

[18] *Id.* § 408, 84 Stat. at 1265 (imprisonment for not less than 10 years for the first offense and not less than 20 years for the second).

[19] P.L. 98-473, title II, §§ 211, 217, 98 Stat. 1987, 2017 (1984). Although the Sentencing Guidelines still heavily influence the sentences imposed by federal courts, *see* Gall v. United States, 552 U.S. 38 (2007), the Guidelines are no longer binding, United States v. Booker, 543 U.S. 220 (2005).

[20] 18 U.S.C. § 3553(b) ("...The court shall impose a sentence ... within the range ... unless the court finds that an aggravating or mitigating circumstance exists that was not adequately taken into consideration by the Sentencing Commission..."). *See, e.g.*, United States v. Johnson, 908 F.2d 396, 399 (8th Cir. 1990) (sentencing under 18 U.S.C. § 1014, false statements on a loan application, no statutory mandatory minimum) ("Limiting appellate review of a district court's refusal to depart from the guidelines, 18 U.S.C. 3742(e) (1988) provides that a reviewing court must uphold a sentence unless it was : (1) imposed in violation of the law; (2) imposed because the court incorrectly applied the guidelines; (3) outside the range of the applicable guideline and was unreasonable; or (4) imposed for an offense with no applicable guideline and is plainly unreasonable. This circuit has determined that departures pursuant to section 3553(b) were intended by the Commission to be allowed only in rare cases."); United States v. Carey, 895 F.2d 318, 321, 326 (7th Cir. 1990) (sentencing under 18 U.S.C. § 1344, scheme to defraud a bank, no statutory mandatory minimum) ("At sentencing, the district court acknowledged that the pretrial service agency's calculation of the appropriate sentencing range at 12 to 18 months was accurate. The court, however, departed downward from the applicable range .... We share in the district court's apparent concern over any harshness the Guidelines create in the case at bar.... Nevertheless, the Guidelines seek to end the disparity in sentencing, *see* 28 U.S.C. §

with mandatory minimums, the bulk of which Congress inserted using the Anti-Drug Abuse Act of 1986.[21] The 1986 legislation, however, included substantial assistance provisions which allow the courts to disregard the mandatory minimums in the case of cooperative defendants.[22] In addition, shortly thereafter, Congress instructed the Sentencing Commission to provide it with a detailed report on federal mandatory minimum statutes.[23]

The Commission's 1991 report[24] observed that from 1984 to 1990 four drug-related statutes accounted for roughly 94 percent of the mandatory minimum offenses regularly prosecuted.[25] The Commission's initial report was quickly followed by a Department of Justice study that concluded that a substantial number of those sentenced under federal mandatory minimums were nonviolent, first-time, low-level drug offenders.[26] Congress responded with the safety valve provisions of 18 U.S.C. § 3553(f), under which the court may disregard various drug mandatory minimums and sentence an offender within the applicable sentencing guideline range as long as the offender was a low-level, nonviolent participant with no prior criminal record who has cooperated fully with the government.[27]

The hate crime legislation enacted in 2009 directed the U.S. Sentencing Commission to submit a second report on federal mandatory

---

991(b)(2)(B), and in doing so, mandate that departures be the exception and occur only when truly justified.").

[21] P.L. 99-570, 100 Stat. 3207 (1986). The Act established mandatory minimums in 21 U.S.C. §§ 841 (possession with intent to distribute controlled substances); 844 (simple possession); 845 (distribution of a person under 21 years of age); 845a (distribution near a school); 845b (use of child in a drug operation); 960 (controlled substance import or export offenses) (1988 ed.); and added drug offenses to the Armed Career Criminal Act (ACCA)'s predicate offense list, 18 U.S.C. § 924(e) (1988 ed.).

[22] P.L. 99-570, 100 Stat. 3207 (1986), 18 U.S.C. § 3553(e) (1988 ed.).

[23] P.L. 101-647, § 1703, 104 Stat. 4845 (1990).

[24] United States Sentencing Commission, *Mandatory Minimum Penalties in the Federal Criminal Justice System: Special Report to the Congress* (Aug. 1991) (*Commission Report I*).

[25] *Id.* at 10 ("[F]our statutes account for approximately 94 percent of the cases ... 21 U.S.C. § 841 (manufacture and distribution of controlled substances), 21 U.S.C. § 844 (possession of controlled substances), 21 U.S.C. § 960 (penalties for the importation/exportation of controlled substances), and 18 U.S.C. § 924(c) (minimum sentence enhancements for carrying a firearm during a drug or violent crime) ...").

[26] *United States Department of Justice: An Analysis of Non-Violent Drug Offenders with Minimal Criminal Histories*, *reprinted in*, 54 CRIM. L. REP. 2101 (1994).

[27] P.L. 103-322, § 80001(a), 108 Stat. 1985 (1994).

minimums.[28] The Commission presented its second report in October 2011.[29] A number of things had changed between the first and second Commission reports. Sentencing under the Guidelines had been in place for only a relatively short period of time when the first report was written. By the time of the second report, the number of defendants sentenced by federal courts had grown to almost three times the number sentenced under the Guidelines when the Commission wrote its first report.[30] The judicial landscape has changed as well. When the Commission issued its first report, the Guidelines were considered binding upon sentencing judges.[31] After the Supreme Court's *Booker* decision and its progeny, the Guidelines became but the first step in the sentencing process.[32] In addition, the Fair Sentencing Act, passed in 2010, reduced the powder cocaine-crack cocaine ratio from 100 to 10 to roughly 18 to 1.[33]

---

[28] The Matthew Shepard and James Byrd, Jr. Hate Crime Prevention Act, P.L. 111-84, § 4713, 123 Stat. 2843 (2009).

[29] United States Sentencing Commission, *Mandatory Minimum Penalties in the Federal Criminal Justice System: Report to the Congress* (Oct. 2011) (*Commission Report II*).

[30] *Id.* at 66 ("The total number of federal cases has almost tripled from 29,011 in fiscal year 1990 to 83,947 in fiscal year 2010"); *see also Commission Report I, supra* note 20 at 51 (noting that 29,011 defendants were sentenced under the Guidelines in fiscal year 1990). Moreover, although the second report noted that many of the mandatory minimum offenses were rarely prosecuted, it identified 195 mandatory minimum statutes. *Commission Report II, supra* note 26 at 348. The first report had identified 60. *Commission Report I, supra* note 20 at 11.

[31] 18 U.S.C. § 3553(b)(1) (" ... [T]the court shall impose a sentence of the kind, and within the range, [dictated by the Sentencing Guidelines,] unless the court finds that there exists an aggravating or mitigating circumstance of a kind, or to a degree, not adequately taken into consideration by the Sentencing Commission in formulating the guidelines that should result in a sentence different from that described.").

[32] In United States v. Booker, 543 U.S. 220 (2005), the Court held that Sixth Amendment right to jury trial precluded mandatory application of the Guidelines, but permitted their discretionary application. Thereafter, it explained that "a district court should begin all sentencing proceedings by correctly calculating the applicable Guidelines range.... [T]he district judge should then consider all of the § 3553(a) factors to determine whether they support the sentence requested by a party." United States v. Gall, 552 U.S. 38, 49-50 (2007). Thereafter, "the appellate court must review the sentence under the abuse of discretion standard. It must first ensure that the district court committed no significant procedural error, such as failing to calculate (improperly calculating) the Guidelines range.... " *id.* at 51.

[33] P.L. 111-220, § 2(a), 124 Stat. 2372 (2010). Prior to enactment, 5000 grams of powder cocaine or 50 grams of crack cocaine triggered the Controlled Substances Act's 10-year mandatory minimum, 21 U.S.C. §§ 841(b)(1)(A)(ii) and (iii) (2006 ed.), and 500 grams of powder or 5 grams of crack triggered its 5-year mandatory minimum. *Id.* §§ 841(b)(1)(B)(ii) and (iii) (2006 ed.). The FSA established a 5000 grams to 280 gram ratio for the 10-year mandatory

The second Commission report recommended that Congress consider expanding eligibility for the safety valve, and adjusting the scope, severity, and the prior offenses that trigger the recidivist provisions under firearm statute[34] and the two principal drug statutes, (21 U.S.C. § § 841 and 960).[35]

In October 2017, the Commission issued a third report devoted exclusively to mandatory minimum penalties for drug offenses, in which it made no recommendations.[36] Instead, the report provided an extensive statistical analysis, summarized in ten findings:

1) Drug mandatory minimum penalties continued to result in long sentences in the federal system.
2) Mandatory minimum penalties continued to have a significant impact on the size and composition of the federal prison population.
3) Offenses carrying a drug mandatory minimum penalty were used less often, as the number and percentages of offenders convicted of an offense carrying a mandatory minimum penalty has decreased since fiscal year 2010.
4) While fewer offenders were convicted of an offense carrying a mandatory minimum penalty in recent years, the offenses of those who were tended to be more serious.
5) Drug mandatory minimum penalties applied more broadly than Congress may have anticipated.
6) Statutory relief plays a significant role in the application and impact of drug mandatory minimum penalties, and results in significant reduced sentences when applied.

minimum, 21 U.S.C. §§ 841(b)(1)(A)(ii) and (iii), and a 500 grams to 28 gram ratio for the 5-year mandatory minimum. *Id.* §§ 841(b)(1)(B)(ii) and (iii).

[34] 18 U.S.C. § 924.

[35] *Commission Report II*, *supra* note 26 at 355, 356, 364.

[36] United States Sentencing Commission, *Mandatory Minimum Penalties for Drug offenses in the Federal Criminal Justice System* (Oct. 2017).

7) Additionally, drug mandatory minimum penalties appear to provide criminal defendants with a significant incentive to provide substantial assistance to the government pursuant to 18 U.S.C. § 3553(e) and the related guideline provisions of USSG §5K1.1.
8) However, neither the statutory safety valve provision at 18 U.S.C. § 3553(f), nor the substantial assistance provision of 18 U.S.C. § 3553(e) fully ameliorate the impact of drug mandatory minimum penalties on relatively low-level offenders.
9) There were significant demographic shifts in the data relating to mandatory minimum penalties.
10) Although likely due in part to an older age at release, drug trafficking offenders convicted of an offense carrying a drug mandatory minimum penalty had a lower recidivism rate than those drug trafficking offenders not convicted of such an offense.[37]

Although each house devoted considerable attention to mandatory minimum sentencing and associated issues, the 114th Congress ended without consensus.[38] Several proposals introduced in the 115th Congress address some of the same issues.[39]

MANDATORY MINIMUMS FOR DRUG CRIMES

Table 1 describes the mandatory minimum sentencing provisions for various drug and drug-related offenses.[40]

---

[37] *Id.* at 4-8.

[38] *See generally* CRS Legal Sidebar, WSGL 1713, *Sentencing Reform at the End of the 114th Congress*, by Charles Doyle.

[39] *E.g.*, S. 1917 ("Sentencing Reform and Corrections Act of 2017"); S. 1933 ("Smart Sentencing Act of 2017"); H.R. 3800 ("Mandatory Minimum Reform Act of 2017"); H.R. 4261 ("Safe, Accountable, Fair, Effective Justice Act"").

[40] For a chart listing the penalties for all federal controlled substance offenses see, CRS Report RL30722, *Drug Offenses: Maximum Fines and Terms of Imprisonment for Violation of the Federal Controlled Substances Act and Related Laws*, by Brian T. Yeh.

Table 1. Federal Drug Offenses: Mandatory Minimum Terms of Imprisonment

Substance	Minimum	Maximum
Trafficking 21 U.S.C. §841(b)(1)(A)/960(b)(1) substances (e.g.,1 kilo or more of heroin)	10 years	life
if death or serious injury results	20 years	life
with prior drug felony conviction	20 years	life
with prior drug felony conviction if death or serious injury results, or with two or more drug felony convictions	life	life
Trafficking 841(b)(1)(B)/960(b)(2) substances(*e.g.*, 100 grams or more of heroin)	5 years	40 years
if death or serious injury results	20 years	life
repeat offender	10 years	life
repeat offender if death or serious injury results	life	life
Trafficking lesser amounts of 841(b)(1)/960(b) substances; other Schedule I or II substances; analogues; or date rape drugs: if death or serious injury results	20 years	life
repeat offender if death or serious injury results	life	life
Simple possession of a controlled substance with 1 prior conviction	15 days	2 years
Simple possession of a controlled substance with 2 or more priors	90 days	3 years
Drug kingpin	20 years	life
repeat offender	30 years	life
large operation (e.g., gross $10 million + per year)	life	life
killing in furtherance	20 years	life/death
Unless a higher minimum applies, distribution of a controlled substance to a pregnant woman, or using a child	1 year	2x usual penalty
repeat offender	3 years	3x for repeat offenders
Unless a higher minimum applies, distribution of a controlled substance proximate to a school or other prohibited location	1 year	2x usual penalty
repeat offender	3 years	3x usual penalty
Narco-terrorism involving 841(b)(1) substances	2x usual minimum	life
Firearm possession in furtherance of drug trafficking(varying by use, firearm, recidivism)	7 years–life	life
Unlawful firearm possession with 3 or more prior serious drug or violent felony convictions	15 years	life
Serious violent felony with 2 or more prior serious drug and/or violent felony convictions	life	life

Source: CRS analysis of statutes cited below.

Note: The same minimum and maximum penalties generally apply to attempt, conspiracy, or aiding and abetting the offenses described above.

Features of Mandatory Minimum Drug Offenses

Domestic Manufacture or Distribution (21 U.S.C. § 841(a))

Section 841(a) outlaws knowingly or intentionally manufacturing, distributing, dispensing, or possessing with the intent to distribute or dispense controlled substances except as otherwise authorized by the Controlled Substances Act.

Knowingly or Intentionally

The government may establish the knowledge element of Section 841(a) in either of two ways. First, the "knowledge requirement may be met by showing that the defendant knew he possessed a substance listed on the [controlled substance] schedules."[41] Second, "[t]he knowledge requirement may also be met by showing that the defendant knew the identity of the substance he possessed. Take, for example, a defendant who knows that he is distributing heroin but does not know that heroin is listed on the schedules."[42] As long as the government proves the defendant knows he was dealing in heroin, it need not prove that the defendant knew the particular type or quantity of the controlled substance he intended to distribute.[43]

When a defendant claims no guilty knowledge, the circumstances may warrant a willful blindness instruction to the jury. The willful blindness instruction, sometimes called the deliberate ignorance or "ostrich head in the sand" instruction, is warranted if "(1) the defendant claims lack of knowledge; (2) the evidence would support an inference that the defendant

---

[41] McFadden v. United States, 135 S. Ct. 2298, 2304 (2015). *See also* United States v. Ways, 832 F.3d 887, 895 (8th Cir. 2016).

[42] *McFadden*, 135 S. Ct. at 2304; *Ways*, 832 F.3d at 895.

[43] United States v. Sanders, 668 F.3d 1298, 1310 (11th Cir. 2012) ("Although [for the mandatory minimums to apply] the jury must determine the quantity and type of drug involved, nothing in the statute, the Constitution, or *Apprendi* [*v. New Jersey*] requires the government to prove that the defendant had knowledge of the particular drug type or quantity for which a sentence is enhanced under § 841(b)"); *see also* United States v. Qattoum, 826 F.3d 1062, 1065 (8th Cir. 2016); United States v. Stanford, 823 F.3d 814, 834 (5th Cir. 2016); McPhearson v. United States, 675 F.3d 553, 561 (6th Cir. 2012); United States v. Branham, 515 F.3d 1268, 1275-76 (D.C. Cir. 2008); *cf.*, United States v. Gil-Cruz, 808 F.3d 274, 278-79 (5th Cir. 2015) (holding the same with respect to parallel provisions under the Controlled Substances Import and Export Act (21 U.S.C. § 960)).

consciously engaged in a course of deliberate ignorance; and (3) the proposed instruction, as a whole, could not lead the jury to conclude that an inference of knowledge is mandatory."[44]

Manufacture, Distribute, Dispense, or Possess

Manufacture

For purposes of Section 841(a), "'manufacture' means the production...or processing of a drug, and the term 'production' includes the manufacture, planting, cultivation, growing, or harvesting of a controlled substance."[45]

Distribute or Dispense

The Controlled Substances Act defines the term "distribute" broadly. The term encompasses any transfer of a controlled substance other than dispensing it.[46] It reaches both sales and transfers without compensation.[47] To "dispense" is "to deliver a controlled substance to an ultimate user ...by,

[44] United States v. Ford, 821 F.3d 63, 74 (1st Cir. 2016). *See also* United States v. Trejo, 831 F.3d 1090, 1095 (8th Cir. 2016) ("A willful blindness or deliberate indifference instruction is appropriate when there is evidence to support the inference that the defendant was aware of a high probability of the existence of the fact in question and purposely contrived to avoid learning all of the facts."); United States v. Haire, 806 F.3d 991, 998 (8th Cir. 2015) ("We reject Haire's contention that the willful blindness instruction lowered the government's burden of proof, because the district court instructed the jury that it could not find he acted knowingly if he was merely negligent, careless, or mistaken as to the fact that his suitcase contained rug proceeds."); United States v. Salinas, 763 F.3d 869, 880 (7th Cir. 2014) ("Deliberate avoidance is more than mere negligence; the defendant must have deliberately avoided acquiring knowledge of the crime being committed by cutting off his curiosity through an effort of the will. Evidence merely supporting a finding of negligence – that a reasonable person would have been strongly suspicious, or that a defendant should have been aware of criminal knowledge – does not support an inference that a particular defendant was deliberately ignorant.").

[45] United States v. Reveles-Espinoza, 522 F.3d 1044, 1047 (9th Cir. 2008) (citing 21 U.S.C. § 802(15), (22)). *See also* United States v. Bernitt, 392 F.3d 873, 879 (7th Cir. 2004).

[46] United States v. Soto, 794 F.3d 635, 659 (6th Cir. 2015) ("Title 21 U.S.C. § 802(11) defines 'distribute' as 'to deliver (other than by administering or dispensing) a controlled substance.' Subsection eight defines 'deliver' as 'the actual, constructive, or attempted transfer of a controlled substance.'").

[47] United States v. Bobadilla-Pagan, 747 F.3d 26, 32 (1st Cir. 2014) ("Nothing in the statute limits distribution to sale; rather it is well accepted that drugs may be distributed by giving them away for free.").

or pursuant to the lawful order of, a practitioner..."[48] The Controlled Substances Act outlaws practitioner's proscribing controlled substances for other than legitimate medical purposes.[49]

Possession with Intent to Distribute or Dispense

The government may satisfy the possession element with evidence of either actual or constructive possession.[50] "Actual possession is the knowing, direct, and physical control over a thing."[51] "Constructive possession exists when a person knowingly has the power and intention at a given time to exercise dominion and control over an object either directly or through others."[52]

The escalating mandatory minimums that apply to offenders with "a prior conviction for a felony drug offense" extend to those offenses classified as misdemeanors under state law, but punishable by imprisonment for more than a year.[53] They also apply even if the underlying state conviction has been expunged.[54] On the other hand, there is apparently at

---

[48] 21 U.S.C. § 802(10).

[49] United States v. Moore, 423 U.S. 122, 124 (1975) ("We ...hold that registered physicians can be prosecuted under § 841when their activities fall outside the usual course of professional practice."). *See also* United States v. Azmat, 805 F.3d 1018, 1034 (11th Cir. 2015).

[50] United States v. Ibarra-Diaz, 805 F.3d 908, 932 (10th Cir. 2015); United States v. Corrales-Portillo, 778 F.3d 823, 832 (8th Cir. 2015).

[51] *Id.*

[52] United States v. Apicelli, 839 F.3d 75, 79 (1st Cir. 2016). *See also* United States v. Simpson, 845 F.3d 1059-60 (10th Cir. 2017); United States v. Rebolledo-Delgadillo, 820 F.3d 870, 875 (7th Cir. 2016) ("Construction possession is a legal fiction hereby an individual is deemed to possess contraband items even when he does not actually have immediate, physical control of the objects...Constructive possession requires proof that the defendant had the power and intent to exercise ownership, dominion, authority, or control over the contraband."); United States v. Facen, 812 F.3d 280, 287 (2d Cir. 2016) (internal citations omitted) ("Mere presence at the location of contraband does not establish possession. However, presence under a particular set of circumstances whim from a reasonable jury could conclude that the defendant constructively possessed contraband located there can support a conviction. Courts have considered a number of actors in determining whether a person has the power and intention to exercise dominion and control over narcotics, including: the presence of documents pertaining to the defendant in the same location as the narcotics; the defendant's possession of a key to the location where the drugs are found; the defendant's reaction to the presence of police; whether the defendant has compete control over the narcotics; and whether the drugs are in plain view, suggesting that the defendant is a trusted member of the narcotics operation.").

[53] Burgess, v. United States, 553 U.S. 124, 126 (2008).

[54] United States v. Dyke, 718 F.3d 1282, 1292 (10th Cir. 2013).

least a division among the circuits over whether the government's failure to comply with the procedure for establishing a prior conviction,[55] and therefore to alert the defendant to the prospect of an enhanced mandatory minimum, precludes a sentencing court from taking prior conviction into account.[56]

Sentencing

Sentencing for violations of Section 841(a) is governed by the nature and volume of the substance involved, the defendant's criminal record, and injuries attributable to the offense.[57] The most severe penalties are reserved for high-volume trafficking of eight substances assigned to Controlled Substance Schedules I and II.[58]

The eight substances are heroin, powder cocaine, cocaine base (crack), PCP, LSD, fentanyl, methamphetamine, and marijuana. Criminal penalties related to each substance provide one set of mandatory minimums for trafficking in a very substantial amount listed in Section 841(b)(1)(A), and a second, lower set of mandatory minimums for trafficking in a lower but still substantial amount listed in Section 841(a)(1)(B). The first set (841(b)(1)(A) level) features the following thresholds:

- heroin - 1 kilogram;[59]
- powder cocaine - 5 kilograms;[60]

---

[55] 21 U.S.C. § 851.

[56] United States v, Isaac, 655 F.3d 148, 155-57 (3d Cir. 2011) (citing cases on either side of the divide).

[57] As noted later and in the chart above, the sentencing provisions for violations of the Controlled Substances Export and Import Act, 21 U.S.C. § 960(b), mirror those for violations of the Controlled Substances Act in Section 841(b).

[58] 21 U.S.C. § 812.

[59] *Id.* §§ 841(b)(1)(A)(i), 960(b)(1)(A) ("1 kilogram grams or more of a mixture or substance containing a detectable amount of heroin") (10 grams = .35 ounces; 1 kilogram (1,000 grams) = 2.2 lbs.).

[60] *Id.* §§ 841(b)(1)(A)(ii), 960(b)(1)(B) ("5 kilograms or more of a mixture or substance containing a detectable amount of- (I) coca leaves, except coca leaves and extracts of coca leaves from which cocaine, ecgonine, and derivatives of ecgonine or their salts have been removed; (II) cocaine, its salts, optical and geometric isomers, and salts of isomers; (III) ecgonine, its derivatives, their salts, isomers, and salts of isomers; or (IV) any compound, mixture, or preparation which contains any quantity of any of the substances referred to in subclauses (I) through (III)").

- crack - 280 grams;[61]
- PCP - 100 grams;[62]
- LSD - 10 grams;[63]
- fentanyl - 400 grams;[64]
- methamphetamine - 50 grams;[65]
- marijuana - 1,000 kilograms.[66]

The second set (841(b)(1)(B) level) has thresholds that are one-tenth of those of the higher set:

- heroin - 100 grams;[67]
- powder cocaine - 500 grams;[68]
- crack - 28 grams;[69]
- PCP - 100 grams;[70]

---

[61] *Id.* §§ 841(b)(1)(A)(iii), 960(b)(1)(C) ("280 grams or more of a mixture or substance described in clause (ii) which contains cocaine base").

[62] *Id.* §§ 841(b)(1)(A)(iv), 960(b)(1)(D) ("100 grams or more of phencyclidine (PCP) or 1 kilogram grams or more of a mixture or substance containing a detectable amount of phencyclidine (PCP)").

[63] *Id.* §§ 841(b)(1)(A)(v), 960(b)(1)(E) ("10 grams or more of a mixture or substance containing a detectable amount of lysergic acid diethylamide (LSD)").

[64] *Id.* §§ 841(b)(1)(A)(vi), 960(b)(1)(F) ("400 grams or more of a mixture or substance containing a detectable amount of N-phenyl-N- [1- (2-phenylethyl) -4-piperidinyl] propanamide or 10 grams or more of a mixture or substance containing a detectable amount of any analogue of N-phenyl-N-[1-(2-phenylethyl)-4-piperidinyl] propanamide").

[65] *Id.* §§ 841(b)(1)(A)(viii), 960(b)(1)(H) ("50 grams or more of methamphetamine, its salts, isomers, and salts of its isomers or 500 grams or more of a mixture or substance containing a detectable amount of methamphetamine, its salts, isomers, or salts of its isomers").

[66] *Id.* §§ 841(b)(1)(A)(vii), 960(b)(1)(G) ("1000 kilograms or more of a mixture or substance containing a detectable amount of marihuana, or 1000 or more marihuana plants regardless of weight").

[67] *Id.* §§ 841(b)(1)(B)(i), 960(b)(2)(A) ("100 grams or more of a mixture or substance containing a detectable amount of heroin") (10 grams = .35 ounces; 1 kilogram (1,000 grams) = 2.2 lbs.). *Id.* § § 841(b) and 960(b) use the same thresholds.

[68] *Id.* §§ 841(b)(1)(B)(ii), 960(b)(2)(B) ("500 grams or more of a mixture or substance containing a detectable amount of- (I) coca leaves, except coca leaves and extracts of coca leaves from which cocaine, ecgonine, and derivatives of ecgonine or their salts have been removed; (II) cocaine, its salts, optical and geometric isomers, and salts of isomers; (III) ecgonine, its derivatives, their salts, isomers, and salts of isomers; or (IV) any compound, mixture, or preparation which contains any quantity of any of the substances referred to in subclauses (I) through (III)").

[69] *Id.* §§ 841(b)(1)(B)(iii), 960(b)(2)(C) ("28 grams or more of a mixture or substance described in clause (ii) which contains cocaine base").

- LSD - 1 gram;[71]
- fentanyl - 40 grams;[72]
- methamphetamine - 5 grams;[73]
- marijuana - 100 kilograms.[74]

A Section 841(a) violation involving one of the eight drugs at the higher 841(b)(1)(A) level is punishable by imprisonment for:

- not less than 10 years;
- not less than 20 years if the offense results in death or serious bodily injury or if the offender has a prior felony drug conviction; and
- a mandatory term of life imprisonment if the offender has a prior felony drug conviction and the offense resulted in death or serious bodily injury or if the offender has two or more prior felony drug convictions.[75]

A Section 841(a) violation involving one of the eight drugs at the lower 841(b)(1)(B) level is punishable by imprisonment for:

- not less than 5 years;
- not less than 10 years, if the offender has a prior felony drug conviction;

---

[70] *Id.* §§ 841(b)(1)(B)(iv), 960(b)(2)(D) ("10 grams or more of phencyclidine (PCP) or 100 grams or more of a mixture or substance containing a detectable amount of phencyclidine (PCP)").

[71] *Id.* §§ 841(b)(1)(B)(v), 960(b)(2)(E) ("1 gram or more of a mixture or substance containing a detectable amount of lysergic acid diethylamide (LSD)").

[72] *Id.* §§ 841(b)(1)(B)(vi), 960(b)(2)(F) ("40 grams or more of a mixture or substance containing a detectable amount of N-phenyl-N- [1- (2-phenylethyl) -4-piperidinyl] propanamide or 10 grams or more of a mixture or substance containing a detectable amount of any analogue of N-phenyl-N-[1-(2-phenylethyl)-4-piperidinyl] propanamide").

[73] *Id.* §§ 841(b)(1)(B)(viii), 960(b)(2)(H) ("5 grams or more of methamphetamine, its salts, isomers, and salts of its isomers or 50 grams or more of a mixture or substance containing a detectable amount of methamphetamine, its salts, isomers, or salts of its isomers").

[74] *Id.* §§ 841(b)(1)(B)(vii), 960(b)(2)(G) ("100 kilograms or more of a mixture or substance containing a detectable amount of marihuana, or 100 or more marihuana plants regardless of weight.").

[75] *Id.* § 841(b)(1)(A).

- not less than 20 years if the offense results in death or serious bodily injury; and
- a mandatory term of life imprisonment if the offender has a prior felony drug conviction and the offense resulted in death or serious bodily injury.[76]

A Section 841(a) violation involving one of the eight drugs in lesser amounts, or some other Schedule I or II drug, or a date rape drug is punishable by imprisonment for:

- not less than 20 years if death or serious bodily injury results; and
- life if the offender has a prior felony drug conviction and death or serious bodily injury results.[77]

The felony drug convictions that trigger the sentencing enhancement include federal, state, and foreign convictions.[78] The "serious bodily injury" enhancement is confined to bodily injuries which involve "(A) a substantial risk of death; (B) protracted and obvious disfigurement; or (C) protracted loss or impairment of the function of a bodily member, organ, or mental faculty."[79] And, the "if death results" enhancement is available only if the drugs provided by the defendant were the "but-for" cause of death; it is not available if the drugs supplied were merely a contributing cause.[80] The same "but for" standard presumably applies with equal force to the "serious bodily injury" enhancement.

---

[76] *Id.* § 841(b)(1)(B).

[77] *Id.* § 841(b)(1)(C) ("In the case of a controlled substance in schedule I or II, gamma hydroxybutyric acid (including when scheduled as an approved drug product for purposes of section 3(a)(1)(B) of the Hillory J. Farias and Samantha Reid Date-Rape Drug Prohibition Act of 2000), or 1 gram of flunitrazepam, except as provided in subparagraphs (A), [or] (B) ...."). The penalty is imprisonment for not more 20 years and there is no mandatory minimum where neither death nor serious bodily injury result.

[78] *Id.*§ 802(44) ("The term 'felony drug offense' means an offense that is punishable by imprisonment for more than one year under any law of the United States or of a State or foreign country that prohibits or restricts conduct relating to narcotic drugs, marihuana, anabolic steroids, or depressant or stimulant substances.").

[79] *Id.* § 802(25).

[80] Burrage v. United States, 134 S. Ct. 881, 892 (2014); *see also* Santillana v. Upton, 846 F.3d 779, 781 (5th Cir. 2017); Krieger v. United States, 842 F.3d 490, 497 (7th Cir. 2016).

Attempt, Conspiracy, and Aiding and Abetting (21 U.S.C. § 846; 18 U.S.C. § 2)

The mandatory minimums of Section 841 apply with equal force to those who attempt to possess with intent to distribute;[81] who conspire to do so;[82] or who aid and abet a violation of Section 841 by others.[83]

Attempt

To prove an attempt to violate Section 841(a) "the government must establish beyond a reasonable doubt that the defendant (a) had the intent to commit the object crime and (b) engaged in conduct amounting to a substantial step towards its commission. For a defendant to have taken a substantial step, he must have engaged in more than mere preparation, but may have stopped short of the last act necessary for the actual commission of the substantive crime."[84]

Conspiracy

Conspiracy is an agreement to commit a crime.[85] "To establish that a defendant conspired to distribute drugs under 21 U.S.C. § 846, the government must prove: (1) that there was a conspiracy, i.e., an agreement to distribute the drugs; (2) that the defendant knew of the conspiracy; and (3) that the defendant intentionally joined the conspiracy."[86] The existence of the conspiracy need not be shown by written agreement or any other form of direct evidence, but may be inferred from the circumstances.[87]

---

[81] 21 U.S.C. §§ 856, 963.

[82] *Id.*

[83] 18 U.S.C. § 2.

[84] United States v. Anderson, 747 F.3d 51, 73-4 (2d Cir. 2014) (internal citations omitted). *See also* United States v. Stallworth, 656 F.3d 721, 728 (7th Cir. 2011); United States v. Hunt, 656 F.3d 906, 912 (9th Cir. 2011).

[85] United States v. Lyle, 856 F.2d 191, 207 (2d Cir. 2017).

[86] United States v. Jackson, 856 F.3d 1187, 1192 (8th Cir. 2017); *see also* United States v. Chapman, 851 F.3d 363,375 (5th Cir. 2017); United States v. Cardena, 842 F.3d 959, 994-95 (7th Cir. 2016); United States v. Williams, 827 F.3d 1134, 1162 (D.C. Cir. 2016).

[87] United States v. Garcia-Lagunas, 835 F.3d 479, 490 (4th Cir. 2016) ("[G]iven the clandestine and covert nature of conspiracies, the government can prove the existence of a conspiracy by circumstantial evidence alone."); *Jackson*, 856 F.3d at 1192; *Chapman*, 851 F.3d at 375; United States v. Trotter, 837 F.3d 864, 867-68 (8th Cir. 2016); *Williams*, 827 F.3d at 1162.

Moreover, each of the conspirators need not be fully aware of the roles or activities of all of their cohorts.[88] Each conspirator, however, is punishable for the foreseeable offenses committed in furtherance of the common scheme.[89]

Although it technically demonstrates an agreement to distribute a controlled substance, proof of a small, one-time sale of a controlled substance is ordinarily not considered sufficient for a conspiracy conviction. "[T]he factors that demonstrate a defendant was part of a conspiracy rather than in a mere buyer/seller relationship with that conspiracy include: (1) the length of affiliation between the defendant and the conspiracy; (2) whether there is an established method of payment; (3) the extent to which transactions are standardized; (4) whether there is a demonstrated level of mutual trust; (5) whether the transactions involved large amounts of drugs; and (6) whether the defendant purchased his drugs on credit."[90]

Aiding and Abetting

Accomplices who aid and abet the crime of another receive the same punishment as the offender they assist.[91] To prove, aiding and abetting, the government must show that the defendant knowingly embraced and assisted in the commission of the crime.[92]

---

[88] United States v. Bailey, 840 F.3d 99, 108 (3d Cir. 2016); United States v. Morales, 813 F.3d 1058, 1065 (8th Cir. 2016); United States v. Santos-Soto, 799 F.3d 49, 58 (1st Cir. 2015).

[89] Pinkerton v. United States, 328 U.S. 640, 64748 (1946); United States v. Hare, 820 F.3d 93, 105 (4th Cir. 2016); United States v. Gadson, 763 F.3d 1189, 1214 (9th Cir. 2014).

[90] *Bailey*, 840 F.3d at108. *See also Trotter*, 837 F.3d at 867-68 ("While proof of a conspiracy requires evidence of more than simply a buyer-seller relationship, we have limited the buyer-seller relationship cases to those involving only evidence of a single transient sales agreement and small amounts of drugs consistent with personal use."); United States v. Lyle, 856 F.3d 191, 207-208 (2d Cir. 2017).

[91] 18 U.S.C. § 2.

[92] United States v. Negron-Sostre, 790 F.3d 295, 311 (1st Cir. 2015) (internal citations omitted) ("[A] defendant may be held indirectly responsible as an aider and abettor if he associated himself with the venture ... participated in it as something that he wished to bring about, and ... sought by his actions to make the venture succeed."); United States v. Sanchez, 789 F.3d 827, 838 (8th Cir. 2015); United States v. Boykin, 785 F.3d 1352, 1359 (9th Cir. 2015).

Special Circumstances

Trafficking offenses that ordinarily do not trigger mandatory minimum sentences may do so if they involve special circumstances. Thus, trafficking to pregnant women,[93] children,[94] or in proximity of a school, playground, or other prohibited location,[95] or using a child to manufacture or traffic, are punishable with a one-year mandatory minimum term of imprisonment and in most instances a three-year mandatory minimum for repeat offenders.[96]

Import/Export Offenses

Sections 960 and 963 of the Controlled Substances Import and Export Act,[97] and by cross- reference Section 70506 of the Maritime Drug Law Enforcement Act (MDLEA),[98] largely track the penalties found in Section 841(b) of the Controlled Substances Act, including the mandatory minimum sentences of imprisonment.

---

[93] 21 U.S.C. § 861(f), (b), (c).

[94] *Id.* § 859.

[95] *Id.* § 860 ("(a) Any person who violates section 841(a)(1) of this title ... by distributing, possessing with intent to distribute, or manufacturing a controlled substance in or on, or within one thousand feet of, the real property comprising a public or private elementary, vocational, or secondary school or a public or private college, junior college, or university, or a playground, or housing facility owned by a public housing authority, or within 100 feet of a public or private youth center, public swimming pool, or video arcade facility, is (except as provided in subsection (b) of this section) subject to.... Except to the extent a greater minimum sentence is otherwise provided by section 841(b) of this title, a person shall be sentenced under this subsection to a term of imprisonment of not less than one year. The mandatory minimum sentencing provisions of this paragraph shall not apply to offenses involving 5 grams or less of marihuana. (b) Any person who violates section 841(a)(1) of this title by distributing, possessing with intent to distribute, or manufacturing a controlled substance in or on, or within one thousand feet of, ... or within 100 feet of a public or private youth center, public swimming pool, or video arcade facility, after a prior conviction under subsection (a) of this section has become final is punishable.... Except to the extent a greater minimum sentence is otherwise provided by section 841(b) of this title, a person shall be sentenced under this subsection to a term of imprisonment of not less than three years.... ").

[96] *Id.* § 861(a), (b), (c).

[97] *Id.* §§ 960, 963.

[98] 46 U.S.C. § 70506.

Section 960

Section 960 sets the penalties for three categories of offenses: (1) importing or exporting a controlled substance in violation of 21 U.S.C. § 825 (labeling and packaging), § 952 (importing controlled substances), § 953 (exporting controlled substances), or § 967 (smuggling controlled substances); (2) possession of a controlled substance aboard a vessel or aircraft in violation of 21 U.S.C. § 955; and (3) possession with intent to distribute in violation of 21 U.S.C. § 959.

Of these, violations of Sections 952 and 959 appear to be the most commonly prosecuted. "To sustain a conviction for the importation of a controlled substance[under Section 952], the government must prove: (1) the defendant played a role in bringing a quantity of a controlled substance into the United States; (2) the defendant knew the substance was controlled; and (3) the defendant knew the substance would enter the United States."[99] The government, however, need not prove that the defendant knew which controlled substance was being imported or its quantity.[100]

Section 959 proscribes two offenses: manufacturing or distributing a controlled substance for import purposes[101] and possession aboard an aircraft by a U.S. citizen or aboard a U.S. aircraft.[102] The section specifically states that it governs offenses committed outside the territory of the United States.[103]

Attempt, Conspiracy, and Aiding and Abetting

Section 963 outlaws attempts and conspiracies to violate the prohibitions covered by Section 960, and calls for the same penalties, including mandatory minimums, as apply to the underlying substantive offenses.

---

[99] United States v. Lopez-Monzon, 850 F.3d 202, 206 (5th Cir. 2017).

[100] United States v. Gil-Cruz, 808 F.3d 274, 278-79 (5th Cir. 2015); United States v. Jefferson, 791 Fl.3d 1013, 1016- 18 (9th Cir. 2015).

[101] 21 U.S.C. § 959(a); *e.g.*, United States v. Rojas, 812 F.3d 382, 399-400 (5th Cir. 2016); United States v. Romero-Padilla, 583 F.3d 126, 129-30 (2d Cir. 2009).

[102] 21 U.S.C. § 959(b), *e.g.*, United States v. Lawrence, 727 F.3d 386, 390-95 (5th Cir. 2013).

[103] 21 U.S.C. § 959(c).

Maritime Drug Law Enforcement Act (MDLEA) (46 U.S.C. §§ 70503, 70506)

MDLEA outlaws possession of a controlled substance aboard a vessel subject to U.S. jurisdiction or attempting or conspiring to do so.[104] Here too, violations carry the same penalties, including mandatory minimums, as the underlying substantive offenses.[105]

The term "vessel subject to the jurisdiction of the United States" includes vessels within U.S. territorial or customs waters, and vessels of foreign registration or vessels located in foreign territorial waters when the foreign nation has consented to application of U.S. law, as well as vessels for which no claim of registration or false claim of registration is presented.[106] Most of the lower federal appellate courts to consider the issue have held that the government need not establish any other nexus to the United States.[107] The type and volume of controlled substances ordinarily involved in MDLEA cases usually trigger the more severe mandatory minimum sentences.[108]

Narco-Terrorism (21 U.S.C. § 960a)

Section 960a doubles the otherwise applicable mandatory minimum sentence for drug trafficking (including an attempt or conspiracy to traffic) when the offense is committed in order to fund a terrorist activity or terrorist organization.[109] The merge of drug trafficking and terrorism offenses in Section 960a does not preclude conviction of the defendant for

---

[104] 46 U.S.C. §§ 70503, 70506(b).

[105] *Id.* § 70506(a).

[106] *Id.* § 70502(c).

[107] United States v. Wilchcombe, 838 F.3d 1179, 1186 (11th Cir. 2016) (citing United States v. Suerte, 291 F.3d 366, 369-72 (5th Cir. 2002); United States v. Cardales, 168 F.3d 548, 553 (1st Cir. 1999); United States v. Martinez-Hidalgo, 993 F.2d 1052, 1056 (3d Cir. 1993); contra, United States v. Klimavicius-Viloria, 144 F.3d 1249, 1257 (9th Cir. 1998)).

[108] *E.g.*, United States v. Trinidad, 839 F.3d 112, 114 (1st Cir. 2016) (114 kilograms of cocaine); *Wilchcombe*, 838 F.3d at 1183 (more than five kilograms of cocaine and more than 100 kilograms of marijuana); United States v. Cruickshank, 837 F.3d 1182, 1187 (11th Cir. 2016) (more than five kilograms of cocaine); United States v. Cruz-Mendez, 811 F.3d 1172, 1173 (9th Cir. 2016) (568 kilograms of marijuana); United States v. Pena-Santo, 809 F.3d 686, 691-92 (1st Cir. 2015) (more than 150 kilograms of cocaine).

[109] 21 U.S.C. §§ 960a, 963.

drug trafficking and terrorism offenses as well.[110] Here, too, the controlled substances involved ordinarily carry their own mandatory minimum term of imprisonment.[111]

Drug Kingpin (21 U.S.C. § 848)

Conviction of a Continuing Criminal Enterprise (CCE or Drug Kingpin) offense results in imposition of a 20-year mandatory minimum; the mandatory minimum for repeat offenders is 30 years.[112] Drug kingpins of enormous enterprises, however, face a mandatory sentence of life imprisonment.[113]

To secure a conviction, the government must establish, "1) a felony violation of the federal narcotics laws; 2) as part of a continuing series of three or more related felony violations of federal narcotics laws; 3) in concert with five or more other persons; 4) for whom [the defendant] is an organizer, manager or supervisor; [and] 5) from which [the defendant] derives substantial income or resources."[114]

The homicide mandatory minimum found in the drug kingpin statute sets a 20-year minimum term of imprisonment for killings associated with a kingpin offense or for killings of law enforcement officers associated

---

[110] United States v. Garavito-Garcia, 827 F.3d 242, 244, 249-50 (2d Cir. 2016) (conviction under 21 U.S.C. § 960a, as well as, 21 U.S.C. § 963 (conspiracy to import cocaine), 18 U.S.C. § 2339B (conspiracy to provide material support to a terrorist organization), and 18 U.S.C. § 2332g (conspiracy to traffic in anti-aircraft missiles); *cf.* United States v. Mohammed, 693 F.3d 192, 197 (D.C. Cir. 2012) (conviction under 21 U.S.C. § 960a and 21 U.S.C. § 959 (distribution of controlled substances with the intent to import into the United States).

[111] *E.g., Garavito-Garcia*, 827 F.3d at 244 ("ton-quantities" of cocaine), *Mohammed*, 693 F.3d at 195 (two kilograms of heroin).

[112] 21 U.S.C. § 848(a).

[113] *Id.* § 848(b) ("Any person who engages in a continuing criminal enterprise shall be imprisoned for life and fined in accordance with subsection (a), if - (1) such person is the principal administrator, organizer, or leader of the enterprise or is one of several such principal administrators, organizers, or leaders; and (2)(A) the violation referred to in subsection (c)(1) involved at least 300 times the quantity of a substance described in subsection 841(b)(1)(B) of this title, or (B) the enterprise, or any other enterprise in which the defendant was the principal or one of several principal administrators, organizers, or leaders, received $10 million dollars in gross receipts during any twelve-month period of its existence for the manufacture, importation, or distribution of a substance described in section 841(b)(1)(B).").

[114] United States v. Lee, 687 F.3d 935, 940 (8th Cir. 2012); *see also*, United States v. Bostick, 791 F.3d 127, 1490 (D.C. Cir. 2015); United States v. Isaac, 655 F.3d 148, 154 (3d Cir. 2011).

with certain other controlled substance offenses.[115] Neither prohibition requires the defendant to have been manufacturing or distributing controlled substances at the time of the killing.[116]

DRUG-RELATED MANDATORY MINIMUMS

Firearm Possession in Furtherance (18 U.S.C. § 924(c))

Mandatory minimums are found in two federal firearms statutes. One, the Armed Career Criminal Act, deals exclusively with recidivists.[117] The other, Section 924(c), attaches one of several mandatory minimum terms of imprisonment whenever a firearm is used or possessed during and in relation to a federal crime of violence or drug trafficking.[118]

---

[115] 21 U.S.C. § 848(e); United States v. Hager, 721 F.3d 167, 179-80 (4th Cir. 2013) (citing United States v. Aguilar, 585 F.3d 652, 657 (2d Cir. 2009) (internal citations and quotation marks omitted)("There are three prongs to this statue. The first prong covers those who intentionally kill someone while engaged in a CCE. The second prong concerns the one who intentionally kills another while working in furtherance of a CCE. And, the third prong envelops that person who intentionally kills another while engaged in an offense punishable under section 841(b)(1)(A) ... or section 960(b)(1)."). *Hager* and *Aguilar* describe 21 U.S.C. § 848(e)(1)(A). Section 848(e)(1)(B) establishes the same 20-year mandatory minimum for a killing of a police officer in the line of duty when committed in furtherance or to avoid punishment for any violation of the Controlled Substances or Controlled Substances Import and Export Acts.

[116] United States v. Barrett, 797 F.3d 1207, 1219 (10th Cir. 2015); United States v. Pierce, 785 F.3d 832, 839 (2d Cir. 2015) ("The government need only prove beyond a reasonable doubt that one motive for the killing ... was related to the drug conspiracy.").

[117] 18 U.S.C. § 924(e).

[118] *Id.* § 924(c). Section 924(c) has been the subject of repeated Supreme Court litigation and regular congressional amendment since its inception in 1968. However, the crime of violence prong of the section, rather than the drug trafficking prong, has been the scene of most of the activity. *See* United States v. O'Brien, 560 U.S. 218, 221 (2010) ("The Court must interpret, once again, §924(c) of Title 18 of the United States Code"); Dean v. United States, 137 S. Ct. 1170 (2017); Rosemond v. United States, 134 S. Ct. 1240 (2014); Alleyne v. United States, 133 S. Ct. 2151 (2013); United States v. Abbott, 562 U.S.18 (2010); Dean v. United States, 556 U.S. 568 (2009); Watson v. United States, 552 U.S. 74 (2007); Harris v. United States, 536 U.S. 545 (2002); Castillo v. United States, 530 U.S. 120 (2000); Mascarello v. United States, 524 U.S. 125 (1998); United States v. Gonzales, 520 U.S. 1 (1997); Bailey v. United States, 516 U.S. 137 (1995); Smith v. United States, 508 U.S. 223 (1993); Deal v. United States, 508 U.S. 129 (1993); P. L. 90-618, 82 Stat. 1223 (1968), 18 U.S.C. § 924(c)(1970 ed.); P. L. 91-644, §13, 84 Stat. 1889 (1971), 18 U.S.C. § 924(c) (1976 ed.); P. L. §1005, 98 Stat. 2138 (1984), 18 U.S.C. § 924(c) (1982 ed.) (Supp. II); P.L.

Section 924(c), in its current form, establishes one of several different minimum sentences when a firearm is used or possessed in furtherance of another federal crime of violence or drug trafficking. The mandatory minimums must be imposed in addition to any sentence imposed for the underlying crime of violence or drug trafficking and vary depending upon the circumstances:

- imprisonment for not less than five years, unless one of the higher mandatory minimums below applies;
- imprisonment for not less than seven years if a firearm is brandished;
- imprisonment for not less than 10 years if a firearm is discharged;
- imprisonment for not less than 10 years if a firearm is a short-barreled rifle or shotgun or is a semi-automatic weapon;
- imprisonment for not less than 15 years if the offense involves the armor piercing ammunition;
- imprisonment for not less than 25 years if the offender has a prior conviction for violation of Section 924(c);
- imprisonment for not less than 30 years if the firearm is a machine gun or destructive device or is equipped with a silencer; and
- imprisonment for life if the offender has a prior conviction for violation of Section 924(c) and if the firearm is a machine gun or destructive device or is equipped with a silencer.[119]

Features

Firearm

Section 924(c) outlaws possession of a firearm in furtherance of, or use of a firearm during and in relation to, a predicate offense. A "firearm" for

99-308, 100 Stat. 457 (1986), 18 U.S.C. § 924(c) (1982 ed.) (Supp. IV); P.L. 100-690, §6460, 102 Stat. 4373 (1988), 18 U.S.C. § 924(c) (1988 ed.); P.L. 101-647, §1101,104 Stat. 4829 (1990), 18 U.S.C. § 924(c) (1988 ed.) (Supp. II); P.L. 105-386, §1, 112 Stat. 3469 (1998), 18 U.S.C. § 924(c) (2000 ed.); P.L. 109-92, §6(b), 119 Stat. 2102 (2005), 18 U.S.C. § 924(c)(2000 ed.) (Supp. V).

[119] 18 U.S.C. § 924(c)(1), (5).

purposes of Section 924(c) includes not only guns ("weapons ... which will or [are] designed to or may readily be converted to expel a projectile by the action of an explosive"), but silencers and explosives as well.[120] It includes firearms that are not loaded or that are broken.[121] It does not include toys or imitations.[122] Nevertheless, the government need not produce the gun itself at trial. It need do no more than "present sufficient testimony, including the testimony of lay witnesses, in order to prove beyond a reasonable doubt that a defendant used, possessed or carried a 'firearm' as that term is defined for purposes of §924(c)."[123] Yet conviction must rest on some evidence of the presence of a firearm.[124]

Predicate Offenses

Section 924(c) is triggered when a firearm is used or possessed in furtherance of a predicate offense. The predicate offenses are crimes of violence and certain drug trafficking crimes. The drug trafficking predicates include any felony violation of the Controlled Substances Act, the Controlled Substances Import and Export Act, or the Maritime Drug Law Enforcement Act.[125] A defendant may be convicted under Section 924(c),

---

[120] *Id.* § 921(a)(3), (4) ("(3) The term 'firearm' means (A) any weapon (including a starter gun) which will or is designed to or may readily be converted to expel a projectile by the action of an explosive; ... (C) any firearm muffler or firearm silencer; or (D) any destructive device.... (4) The term 'destructive device' means - (A) any explosive, incendiary, or poison gas - (i) bomb, (ii) grenade, (iii) rocket having a propellant charge of more than four ounces, (iv) missile having an explosive or incendiary charge of more than one-quarter ounce, (v) mine, or (vi) device similar to any of the devices described in the preceding clauses ..."). *E.g.*, United States v. York, 600 F.3d 347, 354 (5th Cir. 2010) (Molotov cocktail constitutes a firearm for purposes of § 924(c)); United States v. Tomkins, 782 F.3d 338, 345 (7th Cir. 2015) (pipe bombs constitute firearms for purposes of § 924(c)).

[121] United States v. Cooper, 714 F.3d 873, 881 (5th Cir. 2013).

[122] United States v. Garrido, 596 F.3d 613, 617 (9th Cir. 2010) ("Possession of a toy or replica gun cannot sustain a conviction under § 924(c)"); *see also* United States v. Martinez-Armestica, 846 F.3d 436, 440 (1st Cir. 2017); United States v. Lawson, 810 F.3d 1032, 1039 (7th Cir. 2016).

[123] United States v. King, 751 F.3d 1268, 1274 (11th Cir. 2014); *see also Lawson*, 810 F.3d at 1039-40; United States v. Sherer, 770 F.3d 407, 412 (6th Cir. 2014); United States v. Kamahele, 748 F.3d 984, 1010 (10th Cir. 2014).

[124] United States v. Feliciano, 761 F.3d 1202, 1212 (11th Cir. 2014).

[125] 18 U.S.C. § 924(c)(2), referring to 21 U.S.C. §§ 801-904, 21 U.S.C. §§ 951-971, and 46 U.S.C. §§ 70501-70507, respectively. *See, e.g.*, United States v. Chapman, 851 F.3d 363, 372-73 (5th Cir. 2017); United States v. RiveraRuperto, 846 F.3d 417, 423 (1st Cir. 2017).

however, even though not convicted or even prosecuted for the predicate offense.[126]

Possession in Furtherance

Section 924(c) has two alternative firearm-nexus elements: (a) possession in furtherance and (b) carrying or use.[127] The possession-in-furtherance version of the offense requires that the defendant "(1) committed a drug trafficking crime; (2) knowingly possessed a firearm; and (3) possessed the firearm in furtherance of the drug trafficking crime [or other predicate offense]."[128] The "possession" component may take the form of either actual or constructive possession. "Constructive possession exists when a person does not have possession but instead knowingly has the power and the intention at a given time to exercise dominion and control over an object, either directly or through others."[129]

The "in furtherance" component compels the government to show some nexus between possession of a firearm and a predicate offense – that is, to show that the firearm furthered, advanced, moved forward, promoted, or in some way facilitated the predicate offense.[130] This requires more than proof of the presence of a firearm in the same location as the predicate

---

[126] United States v. Galati, 844 F.3d 152, 155 (3d Cir. 2016); Davila v. United States, 843 F.3d 729, 730-31 (7th Cir. 2016).

[127] United States v. Burnett, 773 F.3d 122, 134 (3d Cir. 2014) ("Section 924(c) has two separate prongs, the violation of either standing alone is sufficient to support a conviction under the statute: (1) 'us[ing] or carry[ing]' a firearm 'during and in relation to' the underlying offense; or (2) 'possess[ing] a firearm 'in furtherance' of the underlying offense.... By making this distinction, Congress may well have intended 'in furtherance' to impose a more stringent standard than 'in relation to.'").

[128] United States v. Bobadilla-Pagan, 747 F.3d 26, 35 (1st Cir. 2014); *see also* United States v. Ramos, 852 F.3d 747, 753 (8th Cir. 2017); United States v. Bailey, 840 F.3d 99, 112 (3d Cir. 2016); United States v. Perez, 661 F.3d 568, 576 (11th Cir. 2011).

[129] United States v. Taylor, 800 F.3d 701, 709(6th Cir. 2015); *see also* United States v. Fernandez-Santos, 856 F.3d 10, 20 (1st Cir. 2017); United States v. Webster, 775 F.3d 897, 905-906 (7th Cir. 2015); United States v. Booker, 774 F.3d 928, 929-31 (8th Cir. 2014).

[130] United States v. Green, 835 F.3d 844, 854 (8th Cir. 2016); United States v. Ray, 803 F.3d 244, 263 (6th Cir. 20150; United States v. Pineda, 770 F.3d 313, 317 (4th Cir. 2014); United States v. Renteria, 720 F.3d 1245, 1255 (10th Cir. 2013); United States v. Eller, 670 F.3d 762, 765 (7th Cir. 2012); United States v. Pena, 586 F.3d 105, 113 (1st Cir. 2009); United States v. London, 568 F.3d 553, 559 (5th Cir. 2009); United States v. Lopez-Garcia, 565 F.3d 1306, 1322 (11th Cir. 2009).

offense.[131] Most circuits have identified specific factors that commonly allow a court to distinguish guilty possession from innocent "possession at the scene," particularly in a drug case, they include "(1) type of criminal activity that is being conducted; (2) accessibility of the firearm; (3) the type of firearm; (4) whether the firearm is stolen; (5) the status of the possession (legitimate or illegal); (6) whether the firearm is loaded; (7) the time and circumstances under which the firearm is found; and (8) the proximity to the drugs or drug profits."[132]

Although the Supreme Court has determined that acquiring a firearm in an illegal drug transaction does not constitute "use" in violation of Section 924(c),[133] several of the circuits have found that such acquisition may constitute "possession in furtherance."[134]

Use or Carry

The "use" outlawed in the use or carriage branch of Section 924(c) requires that a firearm be actively employed "during and in relation to" a predicate offense – that is, either a crime of violence or a drug trafficking

---

[131] United States v. Russian, 848 F.3d 1239, 1250 (10th Cir. 2017); *Eller*, 670 F.3d at 765; United States v. Pena, 586 F.3d at 113; United States v. Penney, 576 F.3d 297, 315 (1st Cir. 2009).

[132] *Russian*, 848 F.3d at 1250; *see also* United States v. Amaya, 828 F.3d 518 (7th Cir. 2016); United States v. Holley, 831 F.3d 322, 329 (5th Cir. 2016); *Renteria*, 720 F.3d at 1255; United States v. Brown, 715 F.3d 985, 993-94 (6th Cir. 2013); United States v. Johnson, 677 F.3d 138, 143 (3d Cir. 2012); *Lopez-Garcia*, 565 F.3d at 1322; United States v. Perry, 560 F.3d 246, 254 (4th Cir. 2009); *see also* United States v. Chavez, 549 F.3d 119, 130 (2d Cir. 2008) (noting after quoting the factors that, "while no conviction would lie for a drug dealer's innocent possession of a firearm, ... a drug dealer may be punished under § 924(c)(1)(A) where the charged weapon is readily accessible to protect drugs, drug proceeds, or the drug dealer himself"); *but see* United States v. Hector, 474 F.3d 1150, 1157 (9th Cir. 2007) (internal citations omitted) ("Although the Fifth Circuit has developed a non-exclusive list of factors ... we have concluded that this approach is not particularly helpful in close cases.... In our most recent case addressing the 'in furtherance question,' we reiterated the importance of the factual inquiry. We declined once again to adopt a checklist approach to deciding this issue and held that it is the totality of the circumstances, coupled with a healthy dose of a jury's common sense when evaluating the facts in evidence, which will determine whether the evidence suffices to support a conviction.").

[133] Watson v. United States, 552 U.S. 74 (2007).

[134] United States v. Gurka, 605 F.3d 40, 44 (1st Cir. 2010) ("We join the ... circuits holding that *Watson* does not affect the prong of 18 U.S.C. § 924(c)(1)(A) concerned with 'possession in furtherance.'") (citing United States v. Gardner, 602 F.3d 97, 103 (2d Cir. 2010) and United States v. Mahan, 586 F.3d 1185, 1189 (9th Cir. 2009)); *see also* United States v. Miranda, 666 F.3d 1280, 1282-284 (11th Cir. 2012); United States v. Dickerson, 705 F.3d 683, 688-90 (7th Cir. 2013).

offense.[135] A defendant "uses" a firearm during or in relation to a drug trafficking offense when he uses it to acquire drugs in a drug deal;[136] when he uses it as collateral in a drug deal;[137] or when he sells both drugs and firearms;[138] but not when he accepts a firearm in exchange for drugs in a drug deal.[139] The "carry[ing]" that the section outlaws encompasses instances when a firearm is carried on the defendant's person as well as when it is simply readily accessible in a vehicle during and in relation to a predicate offense.[140]

A firearm is used or carried "during and in relation" to a predicate offense when it has "some purpose or effect with respect" to the predicate offense; "its presence or involvement cannot be the result of accident or coincidence."[141] The government must show that the availability of the firearm played an integral role in the predicate offense.[142] It need not show that the firearm was used "in furtherance" of the predicate offense.[143]

---

[135] Bailey v. United States, 516 U.S. 137, 143 (1995); United States v. Isnadin, 742 F.3d 1278, 1307 (11th Cir. 2014); United States v. Haynes, 582 F.3d 686, 704 (7th Cir. 2009); United States v. Combs, 369 F.3d 925, 932 (6th Cir. 2004).

[136] Smith v. United States, 508 U.S. 223, 228 (1993); *Bailey*, 516 U.S. at 148.

[137] United States v. Cox, 324 F.3d 77, 82 (2d Cir. 2003).

[138] United States v. Benitiz, 809 F.3d 243, 248 (5th Cir. 2015).

[139] *Watson*, 552 U.S. at 78.

[140] Muscarello v. United States, 524 U.S. 125, 126 (1998) ("The question before us is whether the phrase 'carries a firearm' is limited to the carrying of firearms on the person. We hold that it is not so limited. Rather, it also applies to a person who knowingly possesses and carries a firearm in a vehicle, including locked in a glove compartment or trunk of a car, which the person accompanies"); United States v. Franklin, 561 F.3d 398, 403 (5th Cir. 2009); United States v. Winder, 557 F.3d 1129, 1138-139 (10th Cir. 2009); United States v. Robinson, 390 F.3d 853, 878 (6th Cir. 2005); United States v. Williams, 344 F.3d 365, 370 (3d Cir. 2003).

[141] United States v. Henry, 819 F.3d 856, 865 (6th Cir. 2016); United States v. Mashek, 606 F.3d 922, 930 (8th Cir. 2010) (quoting Smith v. United States, 508 U.S. 223, 238 (1993)); United States v. Roberson, 459 F.3d 39, 48 (1st Cir. 2006); *Williams*, 344 F.3d at 371.

[142] United States v. Burkley, 513 F.3d 1183, 1189-90 (10th Cir,. 2008) ("A firearm is carried during and in relation to the underlying crime when the defendant avails himself of the weapon and ... the weapon plays an integral role in the underlying offense.... Thus, the government must prove that the defendant intended the firearm to be available for use in the offense.").

[143] United States v. Burnett, 773 F.3d 122, 134 (3d Cir. 2014); *cf.* United States v. Barnes, 822 F.3d 914, 918 (6th Cir. 2016) (noting that "possession in furtherance" or "using or carrying during and in relation to" are two distinct crimes).

Discharge and Brandish

The basic five-year mandatory minimum penalty for using, carrying, or possessing a firearm in the course of a predicate offense becomes a seven-year mandatory minimum if a firearm was brandished during the course of the offense and becomes a 10-year mandatory minimum if a firearm was discharged during the course of the offense.[144] The discharge provision applies even if the firearm was discharged inadvertently.[145] Whether a firearm is discharged or brandished is a question that after *Alleyne v. United States* must be presented to the jury and proven beyond a reasonable doubt.[146] A firearm is brandished for these purposes when (1) it is displayed or its presence made known (2) in order to intimidate another.[147] Intimidation is a necessary feature of brandishing, but it is no less present when the fear is induced by using a gun as a club rather than merely displaying it.[148]

Short Barrels, Semiautomatics, Machine Guns, and Bombs

For some time, Section 924(c) consisted of a single long paragraph with brandishing, discharging, short barrels, semiautomatics, machine

---

[144] 18 U.S.C. § 924(c)(1)(A)(ii), (iii).

[145] Dean v. United States, 556 U.S. 568, 574 (2009); United States v. Mann, 786 F.3d 1244, 1251 (10th Cir. 2015).

[146] Alleyne v. United States, 133 S. Ct. 2151, 2163 (2013) ("Because the finding of brandishing increased the penalty to which the defendant was subjected, it was an element, which had to be found by the jury beyond a reasonable doubt"). *Alleyne* overruled *Harris*, which had held that brandishing was a sentencing factor that might be entrusted to the judge to find by a preponderance of the evidence (Harris v. United States, 535 U.S. 545, 556 (2002)); United States v. Cardena, 842 F.3d 959, 1000-1001 (7th Cir. 2016); United States v. Lewis, 802 F3.d 449, 454 (3d Cir. 2015); United States v. Hackett, 762 F.3d 493, 502 (6th Cir. 2014); United States v. King, 751 F.3d 1268, 1278-280 (11th Cir. 2014). The fact of a second or subsequent conviction, however, remains a sentencing factor, because the Supreme Court's holding in Almendarez-Torres v. United States, 523 U.S. 224 (1998), to that effect has not been withdrawn, *King*, 751 F.3d at 1280 (citing Alleyne v. United States, 133 S. Ct. at 2160 n.1); *Cardena*, 842 F.3d at 1000.

[147] 18 U.S.C. § 924(c)(4) ("For purposes of this subsection, the term 'brandish' means, with respect to a firearm, to display all or part of the firearm, or otherwise make the presence of the firearm known to another person, in order to intimidate that person, regardless of whether the firearm is directly visible to that person"); *Cardena*, 842 F.3d at 1001; United States v. Gonzales, 841 F.3d 339, 353 (5th Cir. 2016); United States v. Carter, 560 F.3d 1107, 1114 (9th Cir. 2009); United States v. Payne, 763 F.3d 1301, 1304-1305 (11th Cir. 2014).

[148] United States v. Bowen, 527 F.3d at 1075 (10th Cir. 2008).

guns, and bombs all in the same paragraph. When Congress added the "possession in furtherance" language, it parsed the section. Now, the general, brandish, and discharge mandatory penalties provisions appear in one part.[149] The provisions for offenses involving a short-barreled rifle or shotgun, a semiautomatic assault weapon, a silencer, a machine gun, or explosives appear in a second part.[150] The provisions for second and consequent convictions appear in a third part.[151]

The circuits are apparently divided over the question of whether the government must show that the defendant knew that the firearm at issue was of a particular type (i.e., short-barreled rifle or shotgun, machine gun, or bomb).[152]

Prior to the division, the Supreme Court had identified as an element of a separate offense (rather than a sentencing factor) the question of whether a machine gun was the firearm used during and in relation to a predicate offense.[153] The use of a short-barreled rifle, semiautomatic assault weapon, silencer, machine gun, or bomb is not a sentencing factor, but an element of a separate offense to be charged and proved to the jury beyond a

---

[149] 18 U.S.C. § 924(c)(1) (emphasis added) ("(A) Except to the extent that a greater minimum sentence is otherwise provided by this subsection or by any other provision of law, any person who, during and in relation to any crime of violence or drug trafficking crime (including a crime of violence or drug trafficking crime that provides for an enhanced punishment if committed by the use of a deadly or dangerous weapon or device) for which the person may be prosecuted in a court of the United States, uses or carries a firearm, or who, in furtherance of any such crime, possesses a firearm, shall, in addition to the punishment provided for such crime of violence or drug trafficking crime - *(i) be sentenced to a term of imprisonment of not less than 5 years; (ii) if the firearm is brandished, be sentenced to a term of imprisonment of not less than 7 years; and (iii) if the firearm is discharged, be sentenced to a term of imprisonment of not less than 10 years* ...").

[150] 18 U.S.C. § 924(c)(1)(B) ("If the firearm possessed by a person convicted of a violation of this subsection - (i) is a short-barreled rifle, short-barreled shotgun, or semiautomatic assault weapon, the person shall be sentenced to a term of imprisonment of not less than 10 years; or (ii) is a machinegun or a destructive device, or is equipped with a firearm silencer or firearm muffler, the person shall be sentenced to a term of imprisonment of not less than 30 years.... ").

[151] Id. § 924(c)(1)(C) ("In the case of a second or subsequent conviction under this subsection, the person shall - (i) be sentenced to a term of imprisonment of not less than 25 years; and (ii) if the firearm involved is a machinegun or a destructive device, or is equipped with a firearm silencer or firearm muffler, be sentenced to imprisonment for life.").

[152] United States v. Burwell, 690 F.3d 500, 510-11 (D.C. Cir. 2012) (citing cases evidencing a split).

[153] Castillo v. United States, 530 U.S. 120, 121 (2000).

reasonable doubt.[154] The question of whether a second or subsequent conviction has occurred, however, remains a sentencing factor.[155]

Aiding, Abetting, and Conspiracy

As a general rule, anyone who commands, counsels, aids, or abets the commission of a federal crime by another is punishable as though he had committed the crime himself.[156] "In order to aid and abet another to commit a crime it is necessary that a defendant in some sort associate himself with the venture that he participate in it as in something that he wishes to bring about, that he seek by his action to make it succeed."[157]

The Supreme Court has said in *Rosemond v. United States* that to aid or abet a violation of Section 924(c), the assistance may be shown to have advanced either the predicate offense or the firearm use.[158] However, the defendant must be shown to have intended his efforts contribute to the success of the Section 924(c) violation – that is, commission of a predicate offense while armed.[159] Thus, the defendant must be shown to have known before the commission of the predicate offense that his confederate was armed.[160]

---

[154] United States v. O'Brien, 560 U.S. 218, 235 (2010).

[155] United States v. Rivera-Rivera, 555 F.3d 277, 291 (1st Cir. 2009); United States v. Mejia, 545 F.3d 179, 207-208 (2d Cir. 2008). This is true even after *Alleyne*, because the Court continues to recognize a recidivist exception to the *Apprendi* rule, *see, e.g.*, Alleyne v. United States, 133 S. Ct. 2151, 2160 n.1 ("In *Almendarez-Torres v. United States*, 523 U.S. 224 (1998), we recognized a narrow exception to this general rule for the fact of a prior conviction. Because the parties do not contest that decision's vitality, we do not revisit it for purposes of our decision today.").

[156] 18 U.S.C. § 2.

[157] Nye & Nissen v. United States, 336 U.S. 613, 619 (1949); *see also* United States v. Centeno, 793 F.3d 378, 387 (3d Cir. 2015); United States v. Sosa, 777 F.3d 1279, 1292 (11th Cir. 2015) ("Thus, to convict under a theory of aiding and abetting, the government must prove that (1) someone committed the substantive offense; (2) the defendant contributed to and furthered the offense; and (3) the defendant intended to aid in its commission.").

[158] Rosemond v. United States, 134 S. Ct. 1240, 1247 (2014)("Rosemond therefore could assist in § 924(c)'s violation by facilitating either the drug transaction or the firearms use (or of course both.").

[159] *Id.* at 1248("[A] person aids and abets a crime when (in addition to taking the requisite act) he intends to facilitate that offense's commission.... [T]he intend must go to the specific and entire crime charged—so here, to the full scope (predicate crime plus gun use) of § 924(c).").

[160] *Id.* at 1249; United States v. Diaz-Rodriguez, 853 F.3d 540, 544-45 (1st Cir. 2017); United States v. Gooch, 850 F.3d 285, 287 (6th Cir. 2017).

In similar manner, conspirators are liable for any foreseeable crimes committed by any of their co-conspirators in furtherance of the conspiracy.[161] The rule applies when a defendant's coconspirator has committed a violation of Section 924(c).[162]

Sentencing Considerations

The penalties under Section 924(c) were once flat sentences. For example, the penalty for use of a firearm during the course of a predicate offense was a five-year term of imprisonment.[163] Now, they are simply mandatory minimums, each carrying an unspecified maximum term of life imprisonment.[164]

A court may not avoid the mandatory minimums called for in Section 924(c)(1) by imposing a probationary sentence,[165] or by ordering that a Section 924(c)(1) minimum mandatory sentence be served concurrently with some other sentence.[166] A court may, however, take Section 924(c)'s mandatory minimum into account when calculating the appropriate sentence for the underlying predicate offense.[167]

If a criminal episode involves more than one predicate offense, more than one violation of Section 924(c) may be punished.[168] Moreover, the

---

161 Pinkerton v. United States, 328 U.S. 640, 646 (1946); Smith v. United States, 133 S. Ct. 718, 719 (2013).

162 United States v. Bailey, 784 F.3d 99, 112 (3d Cir. 2016); United States v. Hare, 8120 F.3d 93, 105 (4th Cir. 2016); United States v. Soto, 794 F.3d 635, (6th Cir. 2015); United States v. Adams, 789 F.3d 713, 715 (7th Cir. 2015); United States v. Reed, 780 F.3d 272, 272 (4th Cir. 2015) ("A defendant may be convicted on a § 924(c) charge on the basis of a coconspirator's use of a gun if the use was in furtherance of the conspiracy and was reasonable foreseeable to the defendant.").

163 18 U.S.C. § 924(c) (1976 ed.).

164 United States v. Lara-Ruiz, 781 F.3d 919, 924 (8th Cir. 2015); United States v. Diaz-Bermudez, 778 F.3d 309, 313 14 (1st Cir. 2015); United States v. Shabazz, 564 F.3d 280, 289 (3d Cir. 2009) (citing United States v. Johnson, 507 F.3d 793, 798 (2d Cir. 2007); United States v. Dare, 425 F.3d 634, 642 (9th Cir. 2005); United States v. Avery, 295 F.3d 1158, 1170 (10th Cir. 2002); United States v. Cristobal, 293 F.3d 134, 147 (4th Cir. 2002); United States v. Sandoval, 241 F.3d 549, 551 (7th Cir. 2001); United States v. Pounds, 230 F.3d 1317, 1319 (11th Cir. 2000); United States v. Silas, 227 F.3d 244, 246 (5th Cir. 2000).

165 18 U.S.C. § 924(c)(1)(D)(i).

166 *Id.* § 924(c)(1)(D)(ii). Dean v. United States, 137 S. Ct. 1170, 1174 (2017).

167 *Id.* at 1178.

168 United States v. Sandstrom, 594 F.3d 634, 658 (8th Cir. 2010) ("... [M]ultiple underlying offenses support multiple §924(c) convictions"); United States v. Catalan-Roman, 585 F.3d 453, 472 (1st Cir. 2009); United States v. Penny, 576 F.3d 297, 316 (6th Cir. 2009)

second or subsequent convictions which trigger enhanced mandatory minimum penalties need not be the product of separate trials, but may be part of the same verdict. Thus, a defendant charged and convicted in a single trial on several counts may be subject to multiple, consecutive, mandatory minimum terms of imprisonment.[169]

A number of defendants have sought refuge in the clause of Section 924(c), which introduces the section's mandatory minimum penalties with an exception: "[e]xcept to the extent that a greater minimum sentence is otherwise provided by this subsection or by any other provision of law." Defendants at one time argued that the mandatory minimums of Section 924(c) become inapplicable when the defendant was subject to a higher mandatory minimum under the predicate drug trafficking offense under the Armed Career Criminal Act (18 U.S.C. § 924(e)), or some other provision of law.[170] The Supreme Court rejected the argument in *Abbott v. United States*.[171] Thus, the clause means that the standard five-year minimum applies except in cases where the facts trigger one of Section 924(c)'s higher minimums.[172]

Armed Career Criminal Act (18 U.S.C. § 924(e))

> In the case of a person who violates section 922(g) of this title and has three previous convictions by any court referred to in section

("[W]hen two separate predicate offenses for triggering §924(c)(1) are charged and proved, a defendant may be convicted and sentenced for two separate crimes, even if both offenses were committed in the course of the same event"); United States v. Looney, 532 F.3d 392, 396 (5th Cir. 2008).

169 Deal v. United States, 508 U.S. 129, 132 (1993); United States v. Gooch, 850 F.3d 285, 290 (6th Cir. 2017); United States v. Buck, 847 F.3d 267, 278 (5th Cir. 2017); United States v. Davis, 841 F.3d 1253, 1260 n. 9 (11th Cir. 2016); United States v. Cardena, 842 F.3d 959, 999 (7th Cir. 2016); United States v. Arline, 835 F.3d 277, 281-82 (2d Cir. 2016); United States v. Washington, 714 F.3d 962, 969-70 (6th Cir. 2013) (noting, however, that the stacking should be governed by the rule of lenity, so that, for example, the 25-year mandatory minimums for second offenses should be stacked starting with a seven-year brandishing sentence rather than a 10-year discharge sentence).

170 United States v. Almany, 598 F.3d 238, 241-42 (6th Cir. 2010); United States v. Whitley, 529 F.3d 150, 153-56 (2d Cir. 2008).

171 562 U.S. 8, 13 (2010).

172 *Id.*; United States v. Robles, 709 F.3d 98, 100-101 (2d Cir. 2013).

> 922(g)(1) of this title for a violent felony or a serious drug offense, or both, committed on occasions different from one another, such person shall be fined under this title and imprisoned not less than fifteen years....
> 18 U.S.C. § 924(e)(1).

Section 922(g) outlaws the possession of firearms by felons, fugitives, and various other categories of individuals.[173] The Armed Career Criminal Act (ACCA), quoted above, visits a 15 year mandatory minimum term of imprisonment upon anyone who violates Section 922(g), having been convicted three times previously of a violent felony or serious drug offense.[174] As the cases below suggest, the section most often ensnarls felons found in possession of a firearm who have three qualifying prior convictions. More often than not, the prior convictions are for violations of state law.[175]

Features

Section 924(e) begins with unlawful possession of a firearm ("a person who violates section 922(g)"). The threshold possession offense need not itself involve a drug or violent crime.[176] Section 924(e)'s 15-year mandatory minimum term of imprisonment instead flows as a consequence

---

[173] The disqualified categories cover felons, fugitives, drug addicts, mental defectives, unlawful aliens, dishonorably discharged members of the Armed Forces, individuals who have renounced their U.S. citizenship, those under a domestic violence restraining order, and those convicted of misdemeanor domestic violence, 18 U.S.C. § 922(g)(1)-(9).

[174] The ACCA is not to be confused with the federal three-strikes statute, 18 U.S.C. § 3559(c), which establishes a mandatory term of life imprisonment upon a third serious violent felony conviction, or with its two-strike counterpart in 18 U.S.C. § 3559(e), relating to mandatory life imprisonment for repeated child sex offenders.

[175] The vast majority of the Supreme Court's Section 924(e) cases involved at last one prior state conviction, *see, e.g.,* Mathis v. United States, 136 S. Ct. 2243 (2016); Welch v. United States, 136 S. Ct. 1257 (2016); Johnson v. United States, 135 S. Ct. 2551 (2015); Descamps v. United States, 570 U.S. 254 (2013); Sykes v. United States, 564 U.S. 1 (2011), overruled by *Johnson*, 135 S. Ct. 2551 (2015); McNeill v. United States v. 563 U.S. 816 (2011); Johnson v. United States, 559 U.S. 133 (2010); Chambers v. United States, 555 U.S. 122 (2009), overruled by *Johnson*, 135 S. Ct. 2551 (2015); United States v. Rodriquez, 553 U.S. 377 (2008); Begay v. United States, 553 U.S. 137 (2008), overruled by *Johnson*, 135 S. Ct. 2551 (2015); Logan v. United States, 552 U.S. 23 (2007); James v. United States, 550 U.S. 192 (2007), overruled by *Johnson*, 135 S. Ct. 2551 (2015); Shepard v. United States, 544 U.S. 13 (2005); Custis v. United States, 511 U.S. 485 (1994); Taylor v. United States, 495 U.S. 575 (1990).

[176] United States v. Raymond, 778 F.3d 716, 717 (8th Cir. 2015).

of the offender's prior criminal record ("three prior convictions ... referred to in section 922(g)(1)...for a violent felony or a serious drug offense").[177] Not all violent felonies or serious drug offenses count. Certain convictions, principally those which have been overturned, pardoned, or otherwise set aside as a matter of state law, are exempt by definition.[178]

Moreover, qualifying violent felonies or serious drug offenses must have been committed on different occasions.[179] "[T]o trigger a sentence enhancement under the ACCA, a defendant's prior felony convictions must involve separate criminal episodes. However, offenses are considered distinct criminal episodes if they occurred on occasions different from one another," one court has observed.[180] And "two offenses are committed on occasions different from one another if it is possible to discern the point at which the first offense is completed and the second offense begins."[181]

---

[177] The statutory mandatory minimum takes precedence over a plea agreement calling for a sentence beneath the mandatory minimum. United States v. Symington, 781 F.3d 1308, 1313 (11th Cir. 2015) (citing United States v. Davis, 689 F.3d 349, 354 (4th Cir. 2012), and United States v. Moyer, 282 F.3d 1311, 1314 (10h Cir. 2002)).

[178] 18 U.S.C. § 921(20) ("The term 'crime punishable by imprisonment for a term exceeding one year' does not include- (A) any Federal or State offenses pertaining to antitrust violations, unfair trade practices, restraints of trade, or other similar offenses relating to the regulation of business practices, or (B) any State offense classified by the laws of the State as a misdemeanor and punishable by a term of imprisonment of two years or less. What constitutes a conviction of such a crime shall be determined in accordance with the law of the jurisdiction in which the proceedings were held. Any conviction which has been expunged, or set aside or for which a person has been pardoned or has had civil rights restored shall not be considered a conviction for purposes of this chapter, unless such pardon, expungement, or restoration of civil rights expressly provides that the person may not ship, transport, possess, or receive firearms."). *See* United States v. Sellers, 784 F.3d 876, 881-87 (2d Cir. 2015) (A New York youthful offender conviction set aside as a matter of New York law does not qualify as a predicate offense) (citing United States v. Collins, 61 F.3d 1379, 1382 (9th Cir. 1995), and United States v. Clark, 993 F.2d 402, 403 (4th Cir. 1993); and distinguishing, United States v. Ellis, 619 F.3d 72,75 (1st Cir. 2010) ("'It was not blatant error for the sentencing court to take [a defendant's] juvenile adjudication into consideration for the purpose of applying the ACCA' because 'juvenile adjudications [under Massachusetts law] are not "set aside" for the purpose of imposing sentence in later criminal proceedings.'")).

[179] 18 U.S.C. § 924(e)(1).

[180] United States v. Martin, 526 F.3d 926, 938-39 (6th Cir. 2008) (internal citations omitted).

[181] *Id. See also* United States v. Morris, 821 F.3d 877, 880 (7th Cir. 2016); United States v. Limney, 819 F.3d 747, 751 (4th Cir. 2016) (internal citations omitted) ("We have come to rely on five factors to determine whether predicate ACCA offenses were committed on different occasions: (1) whether the offenses arose in different geographic locations; (2) whether the nature of each offense was substantively different; (3) whether each offense involved different victims; (4) whether such offense involved different criminal objectives;

Thus, separate drug deals on separate days will constitute offenses committed on different occasions though they involve the same parties and location.[182] The fact that two crimes occurred on different occasions, however, must be clear on the judicial record; recourse to police records will not do.[183]

There is "no authority to ignore [an otherwise qualified] conviction because of its age or its underlying circumstances. Such considerations are irrelevant...under the Act."[184] Moreover, application of Section 924(e) provides no opportunity to challenge the validity of the underlying predicate offenses.[185]

The section defines serious drug offenses as those violations of state or federal drug law punishable by imprisonment for 10 years or more.[186]

---

and (5) whether the defendant had the opportunity after committing the first-in-time offense to make a conscious and knowing decision to engage in the next-in-time offense. Importantly, these five factors may be considered together or independently and the strong presence of any one factor can dispositively segregate an extended criminal episode into a serious of separate and distinct episodes."); United States v. Weeks, 711 F.3d 1255, 1261 (11th Cir. 2013) (internal citations omitted) ("To satisfy the ACCA's different-occasions requirement, a defendant must have at least three prior convictions for crimes that are temporally distinct. So long as the predicate crimes are successive rather than simultaneous, they constitute separate criminal episodes for purposes of the ACCA.").

[182] United States v. Abbott, 794 F.3d 896, 898 (8th Cir. 2015) ("We have repeatedly held that convictions for separate drug transactions on separate days are multiple AWCCA predicate offenses, even if the transactions were sales to the same victim or informant.").

[183] United States v. King, 853 F.3d 267, 279 (6th Cir. 2017); *Limney*, 819 F.3d at 751-52 (4th Cir. 2016); United States v. McCloud, 818 F.3d 591, 595-96 (11th Cir. 2016) (each citing Shepard v. United States, 544 U.S. 13 (2005)).

[184] United States v. Moody, 770 F.3d 577, 580 (7th Cir. 2014).

[185] Custis v. United States, 511 U.S. 485, 487 (1994) ("[A] defendant has no such right (with the sole exception of convictions obtained in violation of the right to counsel) to collaterally attack prior convictions."); Daniels v. United States, 532 U.S. 374, 378-82 (2001); United States v. Coleman, 655 F.3d 480, 485 (6th Cir. 2011); United States v. Greer, 607 F.3d 559, 565 (8th Cir. 2010); United States v. Dean, 604 F.3d 169, 174-75 (4th Cir. 2010); United States v. Covington, 565 F.3d 1336, 1345 (11th Cir. 2009); United States v. Buie, 547 F.3d 401, 403-404 (2d Cir. 2008); United States v. Krejcarek, 453 F.3d 1290, 1297 (10th Cir. 2006).

[186] 18 U.S.C. § 924(e)(2)(A) ("[T]he term 'serious drug offense' means - (i) an offense under the Controlled Substances Act (21 U.S.C. 801 et seq.), the Controlled Substances Import and Export Act (21 U.S.C. 951 et seq.), or chapter 705 of title 46, for which a maximum term of imprisonment of ten years or more is prescribed by law; or (ii) an offense under State law, involving manufacturing, distributing, or possessing with intent to manufacture or distribute, a controlled substance (as defined in section 102 of the Controlled Substances Act (21 U.S.C. 802)), for which a maximum term of imprisonment of ten years or more is prescribed by law.").

Conviction under a statute which carries a 10-year maximum for repeat offenders qualifies, even though the maximum term for first-time offenders is five years.[187] It is the maximum permissible term which determines qualification, even when discretionary sentencing guidelines call for a term of less than 10 years,[188] or when the defendant was in fact sentenced to a lesser term of imprisonment.[189] To qualify as a predicate drug offense, the crime must have been at least a 10-year felony at the time of conviction for the predicate offense.[190]

The term "serious drug offense" includes attempts or conspiracies to commit a serious drug offense, as long as the attempt or conspiracy is punishable by imprisonment for 10 years or more.[191] By the same token, there is no need to prove that the defendant knew of the illicit nature of the controlled substance involved in his predicate serious drug offense if the serious drug offense satisfied the 10-year requirement and, in the case of state law predicate, involved the manufacture, distribution, or possession with intent to distribute a controlled substance.[192]

The Supreme Court in *Johnson v. United States* found unconstitutionally vague Section 924(e)'s violent felony residual clause ("the term 'violent felony' means any crime punishable by imprisonment for a term exceeding one year ... that ... involves conduct that presents a serious

---

[187] United States v. Rodriquez, 533 U.S. 377, 380 (2008). The record must make it clear, however, that the defendant was subject to any recidivist provision needed to reach the 10-year threshold, United States v. Lockett, 782 F.3d 349, 352-53 (7th Cir. 2015) ("Rodriquez requires the government to provide evidence from the record that the defendant was in fact subject to the enhanced recidivist penalties that could elevate his sentence past the ten-year mark.").

[188] United States v. Rodriquez, 533 U.S. at 390; United States v. Mayer, 560 F.3d 948, 963(9th Cir. 2009).

[189] United States v. Buie, 547 F.3d 401, 404 (2d Cir. 2008); United States v. Williams, 508 F.3d 724, 728 (4th Cir. 2007); United States v. Henton, 473 F.3d 467, 470 (7th Cir. 2004).

[190] McNeill v. United States, 563 U.S. 816, 817-18 (2011); United States v. Faust, 853 F.3d 39, 57 (1st Cir. 2017); United States v. Seabrooks, 839 F.3d 1326, 1347 (11th Cir. 2016); Rivera v. United States, 716 F.3d 685, 688-89 (2d Cir. 2013).

[191] United States v. Trent, 767 F.3d 1046, 1057 (10th Cir. 2014) (citing United States v. Bynum, 669 F.3d 880, 887 (8th Cir. 2012); United States v. Williams, 488 F.3d 1004, 1009 (D.C. Cir. 2007); and United States v. McKinney, 450 F.3d 39, 44 (1st Cir. 2006)).

[192] United States v. Smith, 775 F.3d 1262, 1266-67 (11th Cir. 2014).

potential risk of physical injury to another.").[193] The decision raises no question as to the validity of the mandatory minimum sentences imposed under the serious drug offense prong of Section 924(e).[194]

SAFETY VALVE

Low-level drug offenders can escape some of the mandatory minimum sentences for which they qualify under the safety valve found in 18 U.S.C. § 3553(f). Congress created the safety valve after it became concerned that the mandatory minimum sentencing provisions could have resulted in equally severe penalties for both the more and the less culpable offenders.[195] The safety valve is available to qualified offenders convicted of violations of the possession-with-intent, simple possession, attempt, or conspiracy provisions of the Controlled Substances or Controlled Substances Import and Export Acts.[196]

The safety valve is not available to avoid the mandatory minimum sentences that attend other offenses, even those closely related to the covered offenses. Section 860 (21 U.S.C. § 860), which outlaws violations of Section 841 near schools, playgrounds, or public housing facilities and sets the penalties for violation at twice what they would be under Section 841, is not covered. Those charged with a violation of Section 860 are not

---

[193] Johnson v. United States, 135 S. Ct. 2551, 2563 (2015) (construing 18 U.S.C. § 924(e)(2)(B)(ii)).

[194] *Cf. In re* Davis, 929 F.3d 1297, 1298 (11th Cir. 2016).

[195] H. R. REP. NO. 103-460, at 4 (1994); United States v. Carillo-Ayala, 713 F.3d 82, 88 (11th Cir. 2013).

[196] 18 U.S.C. § 3553(f) ("Notwithstanding any other provision of law, in the case of an offense under section 401, 404, or 406 of the Controlled Substances Act (21 U.S.C. 841, 844, 846) or section 1010 or 1013 of the Controlled Substances Import and Export Act (21 U.S.C. 960, 963), the court shall impose a sentence pursuant to guidelines promulgated by the United States Sentencing Commission under section 994 of title 28 without regard to any statutory minimum sentence, if the court finds at sentencing ... ").

eligible for relief under the safety valve provisions.[197] In addition, safety valve relief is not available to those convicted under the Maritime Drug Law Enforcement Act, even though the act proscribes conduct closely related to the smuggling and trafficking activities punished under Sections 960 and 963 (21 U.S.C. §§ 960, 963).[198]

For the convictions to which the safety valve does apply, the defendant must convince the sentencing court by a preponderance of the evidence that he satisfies each of the safety valve's five requirements.[199] He may not have more than one criminal history point.[200] He may not have used violence or a dangerous weapon in connection with the offense.[201] He may not have been an organizer or leader of the drug enterprise.[202] He must have provided the government with all the information and evidence at his disposal.[203] Finally, the offense may not have resulted in serious injury or death.[204]

---

[197] United States v. Phillips, 382 F.3d 489, 499-500 (5th Cir. 2004); United States v. Koons, 300 F.3d 985, 993 (8th Cir. 2002); United States v. Kakatin, 214 F.3d 1049, 1050-51 (9th Cir. 2000); United States v. Anderson, 200 F.3d 1344, 1346-348 (11th Cir. 2000); United States v. McQuilkin, 78 F.3d 105, 108 (3d Cir. 1996).

[198] United States v. Gamboa-Cardenas, 508 F.3d 491, 496-503 (9th Cir. 2007).

[199] United States v. Syms, 846 F.3d 230, 235 (7th Cir. 2017); United States v. Claxton, 766 F.3d 280, 305 (3d Cir. 2014); United States v. Schmitt, 765 F.3d 841, 842 (8th Cir. 2014); United States v. Rodriguez, 676 F.3d 183, 191 (D.C. Cir. 2012); United States v. Aidoo, 670 F.3d 600, 606-607 (4th Cir. 2012); United States v. Pena, 598 F.3d 289, 292 (6th Cir. 2010); United States v. Larios, 593 F.3d 82, 89 (1st Cir. 2010); United States v. Altamirano-Quintero, 511 F.3d 1087, 1098 (10th Cir. 2007); United States v. Mejia-Pimental, 477 F.3d 1100, 1104 (9th Cir. 2007).

[200] 18 U.S.C. § 3553(f)(1) ("[T]he defendant does not have more than 1 criminal history point, as determined under the sentencing guidelines.").

[201] *Id.* § 3553(f)(2) ("[T]he defendant did not use violence or credible threats of violence or possess a firearm or other dangerous weapon (or induce another participant to do so) in connection with the offense.").

[202] *Id.* § 3553(f)(4) ("[T]he defendant was not an organizer, leader, manager, or supervisor of others in the offense, as determined under the sentencing guidelines and was not engaged in a continuing criminal enterprise, as defined in section 408 of the Controlled Substances Act").

[203] *Id.* § 3553(f)(5) ("[N]ot later than the time of the sentencing hearing, the defendant has truthfully provided to the Government all information and evidence the defendant has concerning the offense or offenses that were part of the same course of conduct or of a common scheme or plan, but the fact that the defendant has no relevant or useful other information to provide or that the Government is already aware of the information shall not preclude a determination by the court that the defendant has complied with this requirement.").

[204] *Id.* § 3553(f)(3) ("[T]he offense did not result in death or serious bodily injury to any person.").

One Criminal History Point

More than one "criminal history point" is safety valve disqualifying.[205] The criminal history point qualification refers to the defendant's criminal record. The Sentencing Guidelines assign criminal history points based on a defendant's past criminal record. Two or more points are assigned for every prior sentence of imprisonment or juvenile confinement of 60 days or more, or for offenses committed while the defendant was in prison, was an escaped prisoner, or was on probation, parole, or supervised release.[206] A single point is assigned for every other federal or state prior sentence of conviction, subject to certain exceptions.[207]

Foreign sentences of imprisonment are not counted;[208] nor are sentences imposed by tribal courts;[209] nor summary court martial sentences;[210] nor sentences imposed for expunged, reversed, vacated, or invalidated convictions;[211] nor sentences for certain petty offenses or minor misdemeanors.[212] The Sentencing Guidelines list two classes of these minor misdemeanor or petty offenses that are not counted for criminal history purposes and thus for safety valve purposes. One class consists of eight types of minor offenses, like hunting and fishing violations or juvenile truancy that are not counted regardless of the sentence imposed.[213] The other class consists of arguably more serious offenses, such as gambling or prostitution, that are excused only if the offender was sentenced no more severely than to imprisonment for 30 days or less or to

---

[205] *Id.* § 3553(f)(2); United States v. Monzo, 852 F.3d 1343, 1351 (11th Cir. 2017).

[206] U.S.S.G. §§ 4A1.1(a), (b), (d); 4A1.2(d). United States v. Yepez, 704 F.3d 1087, 1089-90 (9th Cir. 2012) (a federal crime committed while the offender is on state probation is no less so because a state court subsequently terminates the probationary term as of the time it was originally ordered (*i.e.*, before the federal crime was committed)).

[207] U.S.C.G. §§ 4A1.1(c); 4A1.2.

[208] *Id.* § 4A1.2(h).

[209] *Id.* § 4A1.2(i).

[210] *Id.* § 4A1.2(g). Sentences imposed by general and special courts martial are counted, *id.*

[211] *Id.* §§ 4A1.2(j); 4A1.2, cmt. n.6.

[212] *Id.* § 4A1.2(c).

[213] The full list includes: "fish and game violations, hitchhiking, juvenile status offenses and truancy, local ordinance violations (except those violations that are also violations under state criminal law), loitering, minor traffic infractions (e.g., speeding), public intoxication, [and] vagrancy." *Id.* § 4A1.2(c)(2).

probation for less than a year.[214] Both classes also include similar offenses to those listed "by whatever name they are known."[215]

Only the Nonviolent

The safety valve has two disqualifications designed to reserve its benefits to the nonviolent. One involves instances in which the offense resulted in death or serious bodily injury. The other involves the use of violence, threats, or the possession of weapons. The weapon or threat of violence disqualification turns upon the defendant's conduct or the conduct of those he "aided or abetted, counseled, commanded, induced, procured, or willfully caused."[216] It is not triggered by the conduct of a co-conspirator unless the defendant "aided, abetted, [or] counsel ..." the co-

---

[214] Again, the full list consists of: "careless or reckless driving, contempt of court, disorderly conduct or disturbing the peace, driving without a license or with a revoked or suspended license, false information to a police officer, gambling, hindering or failure to obey a police officer, insufficient funds check, leaving the scene of an accident, non-support, prostitution, resisting arrest, [and] trespassing." *Id.* § 4A1.2(c)(1).

[215] *Id.* §§ 4A1.2(c)(1), (c)(2). The Sentencing Guidelines suggest a number of factors to assist in the determination of whether an unlisted offense may be consider "similar" for purposes of Section 4A1.2(c): " (i) a comparison of punishments imposed for the listed and unlisted offenses; (ii) the perceived seriousness of the offense as indicated by the level of punishment; (iii) the elements of the offense; (iv) the level of culpability involved; and (v) the degree to which the commission of the offense indicates a likelihood of recurring criminal conduct." *Id.* § 4A1.2, cmt. n.12(A). *See, e.g.*, United States v. Foote, 705 F.3d 305, 307-308 (8th Cir. 2013) (possession of small amount of marijuana punishable by a small fine is not a similar offense to a similarly fined traffic offense); United States v. Burge, 683 F.3d 829, (7th Cir. 2012) (abandonment of a llama in violation of state wildlife code is sufficient similar to fish and game violations); United States v. DeJesus-Concepcion, 607 F.3d 303, 305-306 (2d Cir. 2010) (third degree unauthorized use of a vehicle is not a similar offense to careless or reckless driving); United States v. Calderon Espinosa, 569 F.3d 1005, 1008 (9th Cir. 2009)(offense of loitering for drug activities is loitering "by whatever name it is known"); United States v. Russell, 564 F.3d 200, 206 (3d Cir. 2009) (misdemeanor marijuana possession is not similar to public intoxication); United States v. Pando, 545 F.3d 682, 684 (8th Cir. 2008) (driving while intoxicated is not similar to careless or reckless driving, citing U.S.S.G. § 4A1.2, cmt. n.5); United States v. McKenzie, 539 F.3d 15, 17-18 (1st Cir. 2008) (shoplifting is not similar to "insufficient funds check"); United States v. Garrett, 528 F.3d 525, 527-29 (7th Cir. 2008) (bail jumping is similar to contempt of court); United States v. Sanchez-Cortez, 530 F.3d 357, 359-60 (5th Cir. 2008) (military AWOL offense was not similar to truancy); United States v. Cole, 418 F.3d 592, 599-600 (6th Cir. 2005) (underage (over 18 but under 21) possession of alcohol was similar to a juvenile status offense).

[216] U.S.S.G. § 5C1.2, cmt., n.4.

conspirator's violence or possession.[217] Disqualifying firearm possession may be either actual or constructive.[218] Constructive possession is the dominion or control over a firearm or the place where one is located.[219] Disqualification requires that the threat of violence or possession of a firearm be "in connection with the offense,"[220] and may include threats against witnesses.[221] In many instances, possession of a firearm in a location where drugs are stored or transported, or where transactions occur, will be enough to support an inference of possession in connection with the drug offense of conviction.[222]

The Sentencing Guidelines define "serious bodily injury" for purposes of Section 3553(f)(3) as an "injury involving extreme physical pain or the protracted impairment of a function of a bodily member, organ, or mental faculty; or requiring medical intervention such as surgery, hospitalization, or physical rehabilitation."[223] On its face, the definition would include

---

[217] United States v. Denis, 560 F.3d 872, 873 (8th Cir. 2009); United States v. Figueroa-Encarnacion, 343 F.3d 23, 34 (1st Cir. 2003); United States v. Sarabia, 297 F.3d 983, 989 (10th Cir. 2002).

[218] United States v. Leanos, 827 F.3d 1167, 1170 (8th Cir. 2016); United States v. Jackson, 552 F.3d 908, 909-10 (8th Cir. 2009) (citing United States v. Matias, 465 F.3d 169, 173-74 (5th Cir. 2006); United States v. Herrera, 446 F.3d 283, 287 (2d Cir. 2006); United States v. McLean, 409 F.3d 492, 501 (1st Cir. 2005); United States v. Gomez, 431 F.3d 818, 820-22 (D.C. Cir. 2005); United States v. Stewart, 306 F.3d 295, 327 n.19 (6th Cir. 2002), but noting in apparent disagreement United States v. Zavalza-Rodriguez, 379 F.3d 1182, 1186-187 (10th Cir. 2004)).

[219] United States v. Stewart, 306 F.3d 295, 326 (6th Cir. 2002).

[220] 18 U.S.C. 3553(f)(2). United States v. Sandoval-Sianuqui, 632 F.3d 438, 443 (8th Cir. 2011) (the disqualifying violence or threat of violence extends to efforts to avoid detection or conviction). *But see* United States v. CarilloAyala, 713 F.3d 82, 91 (11th Cir. 2013) ("At least one of our sister circuits appears to hold that imposition of the enhancement under [U.S.S.G] § 2D1.1(b)(1) [(enhancement under the drug conviction guideline for *possession* of a dangerous weapon without explicitly requiring that it be *possessed in connection* with the offense)] necessarily precludes safety valve relief ... See United States v. Ruiz, 621 F.3d 390, 397 (5th Cir. 2010).... We hold that not all defendants who receive the enhancement under § 2D1.1(b)(1) are precluded from relief under subsection (a)(2) of the safety valve. Where 'a firearm was possessed' by the defendant personally, and yet the defendant also seeks the protection of the safety valve, the district court must determine whether the facts of the case show that a 'connection' between the firearm and the offense, though possible, is not probable.").

[221] United States v. Ortiz, 775 F.3d 964, 968-69 (7th Cir. 2015).

[222] United States v. Carillo-Ayala, 713 F.3d at 92; United States v. Jackson, 552 F.3d 908, 910 (8th Cir. 2009); United States v. Stark, 499 F.3d 72, 80 (1st Cir. 2007); United States v. Stewart, 306 F.3d 295, 327 (6th Cir. 2002).

[223] U.S.S.G. § 5C1.2, cmt. n.2; § 1B1.1, cmt. n.1(L).

serious bodily injuries, such as one that requires hospitalization, suffered by the defendant as a result of the offense.[224] Unlike the gun and violence disqualification in Section 3553(f)(2), the serious injury disqualification in Section 3553(f)(3) may be triggered by the conduct of a coconspirator.[225]

Only Single or Low Level Offenders

The Guidelines disqualify anyone who acted as a manager of the criminal enterprise or who receives a Guideline level increase for his aggravated role in the offense.[226] Thus, by implication, it does not disqualify a defendant to have received a Guideline decrease based on his minimal or minor participation in a group offense or a defendant who acted alone.[227]

Tell All

The most heavily litigated safety valve criterion requires full disclosure on the part of the defendant. The requirement extends not only to information concerning the crimes of conviction, but also to information

---

[224] The Eleventh Circuit in a nonbinding opinion seems to have come to same conclusion. United States v. ValenciaVergara, 264 F.App'x. 832, 836 (11th Cir. 2008) ("The district court did not clearly err in denying Valencia-Vergara a reduction under the safety valve provisions. The evidence shows that both he and one of his codefendants sustained second and third degree burns on their bodies, for which they had to be treated at a hospital.").

[225] *Cf.* United States v. Grimmett, 150 F.3d 958, 960-61(8th Cir. 1998).

[226] U.S.S.G. §§ 5C1.2(a)(4), cmt. n.5; United States v. Syms, 846 F.3d 230, 235-36 (7th Cir. 2017); ("'Organizer ... supervisor of others in the offense, as determined under the sentencing guidelines' as used in subsection (a)(4), means a defendant who receives an adjustment for an aggravating role under § 3B1.1 (Aggravating Role*)"). E.g.,* United States v. Gonzalez-Mendoza, 584 F.3d 726, 729 (7th Cir. 2009); United States v. Bonilla-Filomeno, 579 F.3d 852, 858 (8th Cir. 2009); United States v. Nobari, 574 F.3d 1065, 1083-84 (9th Cir. 2009); United States v. Rendon, 354 F.3d 1320, 1333 (11th Cir. 2003).

[227] The Sentencing Guidelines recommend a sentencing increase for offenders who acted as organizers, leaders, managers, or supervisors of a criminal enterprise with multiple participants and a sentencing reduction for offenders who acted as minimal or minor participants in such an enterprise. U.S.S.G. §§ 3B1.1, 3B1.2.

concerning other crimes that "were part of the same course of conduct or of a common scheme or plan," including uncharged related conduct.[228]

Neither Section 3553(f) nor the Sentencing Guidelines explains what form the defendant's full disclosure must take. At least one court has held that under rare circumstances disclosure through the defendant's testimony at trial may suffice.[229] The stipulation of facts in a plea bargain without more ordinarily will not qualify.[230] Most often, the defendant provides the information during an interview with prosecutors or by a proffer.[231] The defendant must disclose the information to the prosecutor, however. Disclosure to the probation officer during preparation of the presentence report is not sufficient.[232] Moreover, a defendant does not necessarily qualify for relief merely because he has proffered a statement and invited the prosecution to identify any additional information it seeks; for "the government is under no obligation to solicit information from a defendant."[233] A defendant's proffer must be "truthful."[234] On the other

---

228 United States v. Ceballos, 605 F.3d 468, 472 (8th Cir. 2010); United States v. Altamirano-Quintero, 511 F.3d 1087, 1096 (10th Cir. 2007) (citing United States v. Montes, 381 F.3d 631, 635-36 (7th Cir. 2004); United States v. Johnson, 375 F.3d 1300, 1302-303 (11th Cir. 2004); United States v. Salgado, 250 F.3d 438, 459 (6th Cir. 2001); United States v. Cruz, 156 F.3d 366, 371 (2d Cir. 1998); United States v. Miller, 151 F.3d 957, 958 (9th Cir. 1998); and United States v. Sabir, 117 F.3d 750, 753 (3d Cir. 1997)).

229 United States v. DeLaTorre, 599 F.3d 1198, 1206 (10th Cir. 2010); United States v. Delgrosso, 852 F.3d 821, 829 (8th Cir. 2017) (citing and contrasting United States v. Hinojosa, 728 F.3d 787, 790 (8th Cir. 2013) where the trial court granted safety valve relief for a defendant who argued ignorance of co-defendant's misconduct but admitted he unreasonably failed to take the steps to investigate).

230 *E.g.*, United States v. Cruz-Romero, 848 F.3d 399, 402 (5th Cir. 2017).

231 *E.g.*, United States v. Rebolledo-Delgadillo, 820 F.3d 870, 879 (7th Cir. 2016).

232 United States v. Cervantes, 519 F.3d 1254, 1257 (10thCir. 2008) ("In making this determination, we join the First, Second, Fourth, Fifth, Seventh, and Ninth Circuits in ruling that a probation officer is not the government for the purposes of the safety valve.") (citing United States v. Wood, 378 F.3d 342, 351 (4th Cir. 2004); Emezuo v. United States, 357 F.3d 703, 706 n.2 (7th Cir. 2004); United States v. Contreras, 136 F.3d 1245, 1246 (9th Cir. 1998); United States v. Jimenez Martinez, 83 F.3d 488, 495-66 (1st Cir. 1996); United States v. Rodriguez, 60 F.3d 193, 195-96 (5th Cir. 1995); and United States v. Smith, 174 F.3d 52, 56 (2d Cir. 1999)).

233 United States v. Milkintas, 470 F.3d. 1339, 1345 (11th Cir. 2006) (citing United States v. O'Dell, 247 F.3d 655, 675 (6th Cir. 2001); United States v. Ortiz, 136 F.3d 882, 884 (2d Cir. 1997); United States v. Flanagan, 80 F.3d 143, 146- 47 (5th Cir. 1996); and United States v. Ivester, 75 F.3d 182, 185-86 (4th Cir. 1996)); United States v. Cruz-Romero, 848 F.3d 399, 402 (5th Cir. 2017) (plea bargain fact stipulation standing alone is insufficient); United States v. Claxton, 766 F.3d 280, 306 (3d Cir. 2014) ("The mere fact that the

hand, past lies do not render a defendant ineligible for relief under the truthful disclosure criterion of the safety valve, although they may undermine his credibility.[235]

Substantial Assistance

> Upon motion of the Government, the court shall have the authority to impose a sentence below a level established by statute as a minimum sentence so as to reflect a defendant's substantial assistance in the investigation or prosecution of another person who has committed an offense. Such sentence shall be imposed in accordance with the guidelines and policy statements issued by the Sentencing Commission pursuant to section 994 of title 28, United States Code.[236]

The substantial assistance provision was enacted with little fanfare in the twilight of the 99th Congress as part of the wide-ranging Anti-Drug

---

investigators did not ask the 'right' questions for purposes of Claxton's safety valve claim did not relieve him of his burden under the safety valve provision.").

[234] 18 U.S.C. § 3553(f)(5); *Rebolledo-Delgadillo*, 820 F.3d at 879-80.

[235] United States v. Rodriguez, 676 F.3d 183, 190-91 (D.C. Cir. 2012) ("The provision does not distinguish between defendants who provide the authorities only with truthful information and those who provide false information before finally telling the truth."); United States v. Wu, 668 F.3d 882, 888 (7th Cir. 2011) ("Here, in contrast, the district court denied the reduction. It believed that Wu's credibility had been undermined by inconsistencies in his statements and his ultimate retraction."); United States v. Padilla-Colon, 578 F.3d 23, 31-2 (1st Cir. 2009) ("Inconsistencies between statements made during the proffer and statements made to the authorities on other occasions are not necessarily disqualifying. But the court may legitimately consider such inconsistencies in deciding on the truthfulness of the proffer."); United States v. Mejia-Pimental, 477 F.3d 1100, 1108 (9th Cir. 2007) ("The district court therefore erred, as a matter of law, in finding Mejia-Pimental ineligible for safety valve relief on the basis of the lies and delays that preceded his final proffer."); United States v. Jeffers, 329 F.3d 94, 99-100 (2d Cir. 2003) ("[A] sentencing court may not disqualify a defendant at the threshold from eligibility for safety valve relief based solely on his commission of perjury at trial, where the defendant otherwise fulfills the statutory criteria under 18 U.S.C. § 3553(f)(1)-(5). To do so would contradict the plain language of the statute and contravene the statutory deadline for full compliance with its criteria at the time of the commencement of the sentencing hearing. A court may, of course, consider the relevance of the prior perjury or other obstructive behavior in making a factual finding as to whether the defendant has made a complete and truthful proffer in compliance with 18 U.S.C. § 3553(f)(5).").

[236] 18 U.S.C. § 3553(e).

Abuse Act of 1986, legislation that established or increased a number of mandatory minimum sentencing provisions.[237] The section passed between the date authorizing the Sentencing Guidelines and the date the Guidelines became effective. Rather than replicate the language of Section 3553(e), the Guidelines contain an overlapping section which authorizes a sentencing court to depart from the minimum sentence called for by the Guidelines.[238] A motion asking the court to sentence a defendant beneath the statutory mandatory minimum must be filed under Section 3553(e); a motion under Section 5K1.1 of the Guidelines alone is insufficient.[239] The government has at least a year to file its motion for substantial assistance.[240]

---

[237] Section 1007(a) of P.L. 99-570, 100 Stat. 32-07-7 (1986).

[238] U.S.S.G. § 5K1.1 ("Upon motion of the government stating that the defendant has provided substantial assistance in the investigation or prosecution of another person who has committed an offense, the court may depart from the guidelines. (a) The appropriate reduction shall be determined by the court for reasons stated that may include, but are not limited to, consideration of the following: (1) the court's evaluation of the significance and usefulness of the defendant's assistance, taking into consideration the government's evaluation of the assistance rendered; (2) the truthfulness, completeness, and reliability of any information or testimony provided by the defendant; (3) the nature and extent of the defendant's assistance; (4) any injury suffered, or any danger or risk of injury to the defendant or his family resulting from his assistance; (5) the timeliness of the defendant's assistance."); *see also* FED. R. CRIM. P. 35(b) (quoted below).

[239] Melendez v. United States, 518 U.S. 120, 123-24 (1996) ("[T]he Courts of Appeals disagree as to whether a Government motion attesting to the defendant's substantial assistance and requesting that the district court depart below the minimum of the applicable sentencing range under the Guidelines also permits the district court to depart below any statutory minimum ... We now hold that such a motion does not authorize a departure below a lower statutory minimum.").

[240] FED. R. CRIM. 35(b) (captions omitted) ("(1) Upon the government's motion made within one year of sentencing, the court may reduce a sentence if the defendant, after sentencing, provided substantial assistance in investigating or prosecuting another person. (2) Upon the government's motion made more than one year after sentencing, the court may reduce a sentence if the defendant's substantial assistance involved: (A) information not known to the defendant until one year or more after sentencing; (B) information provided by the defendant to the government within one year of sentencing, but which did not become useful to the government until more than one year after sentencing; or (C) information the usefulness of which could not reasonably have been anticipated by the defendant until more than one year after sentencing and which was promptly provided to the government after its usefulness was reasonably apparent to the defendant. (3) In evaluating whether the defendant has provided substantial assistance, the court may consider the defendant's presentence assistance. (4) When acting under Rule 35(b), the court may reduce the sentence to a level below the minimum sentence established by statute.").

Upon the Motion of the Government

As a general rule, a defendant is entitled to a sentence below an otherwise applicable statutory minimum under the provisions of § 3553(e) only if the government agrees.[241] The courts have acknowledged that due process, equal protection, or other constitutional guarantees may provide a narrow exception.[242] For instance, a defendant is entitled to relief if the government's refusal constitutes a breach of its plea agreement.[243] A defendant is also "entitled to relief if the prosecutor's refusal to move was not rationally related to any legitimate Government end."[244] Some courts have suggested that a defendant is entitled to relief if the prosecution refuses to move under circumstances that "shock the conscience of the court," or that demonstrate bad faith, or for reasons unrelated to substantial assistance.[245]

The court is under no obligation to grant the government's substantial assistance motion and the defendant is not entitled to be heard on the issue.[246]

---

[241] *Melendez*, 518 U.S. at 125-26 ("We believe that § 3553(e) requires a government motion requesting or authorizing the district court to impose a sentence below a level established by statute as a[a] minimum sentence before the court may impose such a sentence."); United States v. Massey, 663 F.3d 852, 860 (6th Cir. 2011).

[242] Wade v. United States, 504 U.S. 181, 185-86 (1992); United States v. Patton, 847 F.3d 883, 885 (7th Cir. 2017); United States v. Gomez, 705 F.3d 68, 79 (2d Cir. 2013).

[243] United States v. Doe, 741 F.3d 359, 362-63 (2d Cir. 2013); United States v. Barnes, 730 F.3d 456, 457 (4th Cir. 2013); United States v. Motley, 587 F.3d 1153, 1159 (D.C. Cir. 2009); United States v. Smith, 574 F.3d 521, 525 (8th Cir. 2009).

[244] *Wade*, 504 U.S. at 186; *Patton*, 847 F.3d at 885.

[245] United States v. Freemont, 513 F.3d 884, 889 (8th Cir. 2008) ("The district court may review the government's refusal to make a motion in limited circumstances. First, the district court may review the government's decision for an unconstitutional motive ... Second, a district court can compel a § 3553(e) motion if the government acknowledges the defendant provided substantial assistance, but refuses to make a motion expressly because the defendant engaged in unrelated misconduct – a reason unrelated to the quality of the defendant's assistance ... Third, the district court may be able to compel a motion if the government acted in bad faith by refusing to make a motion."); *but see* United States v. Perez, 526 F.3d 1135, 1138 (8th Cir. 2008) (citing cases evidencing a split within the circuit over whether bad faith provides a sufficient based to compel a government motion); United States v. Doe, 865 F.3d 1295 (10th Cir. 2017) (noting a split between the circuits and within the circuit on the question).

[246] United States v. McMahan, 872 F.3d 717, 719-21 (5th Cir. 2017) (declining to be guided by a contrary conclusion in United States v. Gangi, 45 F.3d 28 (2d Cir. 1995), announced before Rule 35(b) was amended).

To Reflect a Defendant's Substantial Assistance

Any sentence imposed below the statutory minimum by virtue of Section 3553(e) must be based on the extent of the defendant's assistance; it may not reflect considerations unrelated to such assistance.[247] It has been suggested that a court may use the factors found in Section 5K1.1 of the Sentencing Guidelines for that determination.[248] District courts appear to have some latitude as to the method used to calculate the reduction for substantial assistance e.g., "offense-level-based reductions, month-based reductions, and percentage-based reductions."[249]

The substantial assistance exception makes possible convictions that might otherwise be unattainable. Yet, it may also lead to "inverted sentencing," that is, a situation in which "the more serious the defendant's crimes, the lower the sentence – because the greater his wrongs, the more information and assistance he had to offer to a prosecutor"; while in

---

[247] United States v. Spinks, 770 F. 3d 285, 287 (4th Cir. 2014); United States v. Lee, 725 F.3d 1159, 1168 (9th Cir. 2013); United States v. Williams, 687 F.3d 283, 286 (6th Cir. 2012); United States v. Span, 682 F.3d 565, 566 (7th Cir. 2012); United States v. Winebarger, 664 F.3d 388, 392-93 (3d Cir. 2011) ("Congress's chosen language explicitly indicates that the reduction below the statutory minimum is to 'reflect' a defendant's assistance to the government in investigating and prosecuting other offenders. This language does not give a court carte blanche to sentence a defendant below a statutory minimum sentence based on non-assistance-related factors once it is established that the defendant provided assistance to the government"); United States v. Burns, 577 F.3d 887, 894 (8th Cir. 2009) (en banc) ("Where a court has authority to sentence below a statutory minimum only by virtue of a government motion under § 3553(e), the reduction below the statutory minimum must be based exclusively on assistance-related considerations"); United States v. Jackson, 577 F.3d 1032, 1036 (9th Cir. 2009); United States v. Hood, 556 F.3d 226, 234 n.2 (4th Cir. 2009) (citing United States v. Richardson, 521 F.3d 149, 159 (2d Cir. 2008) and United States v. Desselle, 450 F.3d 179, 182 (5th Cir. 2006)).

[248] United States v. Gabbard, 586 F.3d 1046, 1051 (6th Cir. 2009) (citing United States v. Richardson, 521 F.3d at 159). U.S.S.G. § 5K1.1(a) ("The appropriate reduction shall be determined by the court for reasons stated that may include, but are not limited to, consideration of the following: (1) the court's evaluation of the significance and usefulness of the defendant's assistance, taking into consideration the government's evaluation of the assistance rendered; (2) the truthfulness, completeness, and reliability of any information or testimony provided by the defendant; (3) the nature and extent of the defendant's assistance; (4) any injury suffered, or any danger or risk of injury to the defendant or his family resulting from his assistance; [and] (5) the timeliness of the defendant's assistance.").

[249] United States v. Marroquin-Medina, 817 F. 3d 1285, 1289 (11th Cir. 2016).

contrast the exception is of no avail to the peripheral offender who can provide far less substantial assistance.[250]

CONSTITUTIONAL CONSIDERATIONS

Defendants sentenced to mandatory minimum terms of imprisonment have challenged their sentences on a number of constitutional grounds beginning with Congress's legislative authority and ranging from cruel and unusual punishment through ex post facto and double jeopardy to equal protection and due process. Each constitutional provision defines outer boundaries that a mandatory minimum sentence and the substantive offense to which it is attached must be crafted to honor.

Legislative Authority

The federal government is a creature of the Constitution; it enjoys only such powers as can be traced to the Constitution.[251] Among the powers which the Constitution bestows upon Congress are the powers to define and punish felonies committed upon the high seas, to exercise exclusive legislative authority over certain federal territories and facilities, to make rules governing the Armed Forces, to regulate interstate and foreign commerce, and to enact legislation necessary and proper for the execution of those and Congress's other constitutionally granted powers.[252] It also grants Congress authority to enact legislation necessary and proper to the

---

[250] United States v. Brigham, 977 F.2d 317, 318 (7th Cir. 1992) ("Mandatory minimum penalties, combined with a power to grant exceptions, create a prospect of inverted sentencing. The more serious the defendant's crimes, the lower the sentence – because the greater is wrongs, the more information and assistance he has to offer to the prosecutor. Discounts for the top dogs have the virtue of necessity, because rewards for assistance are essential to the business of detecting and punishing crime. But what makes the post-discount sentencing structure topsy-turvy is the mandatory minimum, binding only for the hangers one.").

[251] U.S. CONST. amend. X.

[252] *Id.* art. I, § 8, cls.10, 17, 14, 3, and 18, respectively.

execution of those powers which it vests in any officer or department of the federal government.[253]

Many of the federal laws with mandatory minimum sentencing requirements were enacted pursuant to Congress's legislative authority over crimes occurring on the high seas or within federal enclaves,[254] or to its power to regulate commerce.[255] When a statute falls for want of legislative authority, the penalties it would impose fall with it. This has yet to occur in the area of mandatory minimum sentences relating to controlled substances.

Commerce Clause

"The Congress shall have Power ... To regulate Commerce with Foreign Nations, and among the several States, and with Indian Tribes."[256] This clause vests Congress with authority to regulate three broad categories of interstate commerce. In the words of *United States v. Lopez*, "[f]irst, Congress may regulate the use of the channels of interstate commerce.... Second, Congress is empowered to regulate and protect the instrumentalities of interstate commerce, or persons or things in interstate commerce, even though the threat may come only from intrastate activities.... Finally, Congress's commerce authority includes the power to regulate those activities having a substantial relation to interstate commerce."[257]

Applying these standards, the *Lopez* Court concluded that the Commerce Clause did not authorize Congress to enact a particular statute which purported to outlaw possession of a firearm on school property. Because the statute addressed neither the channels nor instrumentalities of interstate commerce, its survival turned upon whether it came within

---

[253] *Id.* art. I, § 8, cl.18; *see generally* United States v. Comstock, 560 U.S. 126 (2010).

[254] *E.g.,* 18 U.S.C. § 2241(a) ("Whoever, in the special maritime and territorial jurisdiction of the United States ... knowing causes another person to engage in a sexual act – (1) by using force against that other person ... shall be ... imprisoned for any term of years or life ... ").

[255] *E.g., Id.* § 2251(a), (e) ("(a) Any person ... who transports any minor in or affecting interstate or foreign commerce ... with the intent that such minor engage in any sexually explicit conduct for the purpose of producing any visual depiction of such conduct.... (e) Any individual who violates ... this section shall be ... imprisoned not less than 15 years.... ").

[256] U.S. CONST. art. I, § 8, cl. 3.

[257] United States v. Lopez, 514 U.S. 549, 558-59 (1995).

Congress's power to regulate activities that have a substantial impact on interstate commerce.[258] Here, the statute was found wanting. "[B]y its terms" it had "nothing to do with commerce or any sort of economic enterprise."[259] It "contain[ed] no jurisdictional element which would ensure, through case-by-case inquiry, that the firearm possession in question affect[ed] interstate commerce."[260] Its impact on commerce was so remote that to credit it would envision a virtually boundless power and one reserved to the states, the Court explained.[261]

A few years later, the Court in *United States v. Morrison*[262] reiterated "that Congress may [not] regulate noneconomic, violent criminal conduct based solely on that conduct's aggregate effect on interstate commerce. The Constitution requires a distinction between what is truly national and what is truly local."[263] Yet purely intrastate activities may have a sufficient impact on interstate commerce to bring them within the reach of Congress's Commerce Clause power. So it is in the case of the Controlled Substances Act. The Court concluded in *Gonzales v. Raich* that:

> Given the enforcement difficulties that attend distinguishing between marijuana cultivated locally and marijuana grown elsewhere and concerns about diversion into illicit channels, we have no difficulty concluding that Congress had a rational basis for believing that failure to regulate the

---

258 *Id.* at 559.
259 *Id.* at 561.
260 *Id.*
261 *Id.* at 563-64 ("The Government argues that possession of a firearm in a school zone may result in violent crime and that violent crime can be expected to affect the functioning of the national economy in two ways. First, the costs of violent crime are substantial, and, through the mechanism of insurance, those costs are spread throughout the population. Second, violent crime reduces the willingness of individuals to travel to areas within the country that are perceived to be unsafe. The Government also argues that the presence of guns in schools poses a substantial threat to the educational process by threatening the learning environment. A handicapped educational process, in turn, will result in a less productive citizenry. That, in turn, would have an adverse effect on the Nation's economic well-being.... Thus, if we were to accept the Government's arguments, we are hard pressed to posit any activity by an individual that Congress is without power to regulate. "); *id.* at 567 ("To uphold the Government's contentions here, we would have to pile inference on inference in a manner that would bid fair to convert congressional authority under the Commerce Clause to a general police power of the sort retained by the States.").
262 529 U.S. 598 (2000).
263 *Id.* 617-18.

intrastate manufacture and possession of marijuana would leave a gaping hole in the CSA [Controlled Substances Act]. Thus ... when it enacted comprehensive legislation to regulate the interstate market in a fungible commodity, Congress was acting well within its authority to 'make all Laws which shall be necessary and proper' to 'regulate Commerce ... among the several States.' That the regulation ensnares some purely intrastate activity is of no moment."[264]

Treaty Power

The Constitution grants the President authority to negotiate treaties and the Senate the authority to approve them in the exercise of its advice and consent prerogatives.[265] Almost a century ago, the Court observed that "[i]f the treaty is valid there can be no dispute about the validity of the statute under Article I, § 8, as a necessary and proper means to execute the powers of the Government."[266] The Controlled Substances Act might be considered implementation of various treaties of the United States relating to controlled substances.[267] In fact, the Controlled Substances Act begins with the congressional finding and declaration that "[t]he United States is a party to the Single Convention on Narcotic Drugs, 1961, and other international conventions designed to establish effective control over international and domestic traffic in controlled substances."[268] Congress was even more explicit in the Psychotropic Substances Act of 1978 when it declared, "[i]n implementing the Convention on Psychotropic Substances, the Congress intends that, consistent with the obligations of the United States under the Convention, control of psychotropic substances in the United States should be accomplished within the framework of the procedures and criteria for classification of substances provided in the Comprehensive Drug Abuse Prevention and Control Act of 1970."[269]

---

[264] 545 U.S. 1, 22 (2005) (internal citations omitted).

[265] U.S. CONST. art. II, § 2, cl. 2.

[266] Missouri v. Holland, 252 U.S. 416, 432 (1920).

[267] *E.g.*, SINGLE CONVENTION ON NARCOTIC DRUGS, Mar. 30, 1961, 18 U.S.T. 1407, 520 U.N.T.S. 204; CONVENTION ON PSYCHOTROPIC SUBSTANCES, Feb. 21, 1971, 32 U.S.T. 543, 1019 U.N.T.S. 175.

[268] 21 U.S.C. § 801(7).

[269] *Id.* § 801a(3). At least one court has held that extraterritorial application of the Controlled Substances Export and Import Act's prohibitions, and by implication its mandatory

Territorial and Maritime Jurisdiction

The Constitution empowers Congress "to define and punish Piracies and Felonies committed on the high Seas, and Offenses against the Law of Nations."[270] The courts have held that the Maritime Drug Law Enforcement Act (MDLEA), which includes mandatory minimum sentencing requirements, constitutes a valid exercise of Congress's authority under the High Seas Felonies Clause.[271]

Necessary and Proper

"The Congress shall have Power ... To make all Laws which shall be necessary and proper for carrying into Execution the foregoing Powers, and all other Powers vested by this Constitution in the Government of the United States, or in any Department or Officer thereof."[272] It has never been thought that the Necessary and Proper Clause empowers only those laws that are absolutely necessary. Instead, "[l]et the end be legitimate, let it be within the scope of the constitution, and all means which are appropriate, which are plainly adapted to that end, which are not prohibited, but consist[ent] with the letter and spirit of the constitution, are constitutional."[273] Thus, the Necessary and Proper Clause makes possible those statutes that are rationally related to the implementation of another constitutional power.[274]

The Court in *United States v. Comstock* provided a hint of the scope of Necessary and Proper Clause.[275] The statute there authorized the Attorney General to continue to hold a federal inmate, pending a civil commitment

---

minimum penalties, constitute a permissible exercise of "Congress' treaty-making power under the Necessary and Proper Clause." United States v. Lawrence, 727 F.3d 386, 397 (5th Cir. 2013).

[270] U.S. CONST. art. I, § 8, cl. 10.

[271] United States v. Hernandez, 864 F.3d 1292, 1303 (11th Cir. 2017) (citing United States v. Campbell, 743 F.3d 802, 809-12 (11th Cir. 2014)); United States v. Ballestas, 795 F.3d 138, 146-47 (D.C. Cir. 2015). The Eleventh Circuit had previous held, however, that the MDLEA rests beyond the reach of the *Law of Nations Clause*. United States v. Bellaizac-Hurtado, 700 F.3d 1245, 1253-58 (11th Cir. 2012).

[272] U.S. CONST. art. I, § 8, cl. 18.

[273] McCulloch v. Maryland, 4 Wheat. (17 U.S.) 316, 421 (1819).

[274] Sabri v. United States, 541 U.S. 600, 605 (2004) ("*McCulloch v. Maryland* ... establish[es] review for means-ends rationality under the Necessary and Proper Clause.").

[275] United States v. Comstock, 560 U.S. 126 (2010).

determination, after his scheduled date of release.[276] The Court analyzed the breadth of the power without any explicit reference to any other constitutional power, deciding that:

> [T]he statute is a "necessary and proper" means of exercising the federal authority that permits Congress to create federal criminal laws, to punish their violation, to imprison violators, to provide appropriately for those imprisoned, and to maintain the security of those who are not imprisoned but who may be affected by the imprisonment of others.[277]

Justice Scalia, in his *Raich* concurrence, saw the Necessary and Proper Clause as a necessary Commerce Clause supplement for legislation like the Controlled Substances Act that purports to regulate purely in-state activity.[278] Moreover, as noted above, at least one lower federal appellate court considers the Necessary and Proper Clause the implementing vehicle for enactment of the Maritime Drug Law Enforcement Act under Congress's treaty-making powers.[279]

Limits on Legislative Authority

The Constitution both grants and limits Congress's legislative authority. In the area of mandatory minimum sentences for controlled substance violations, the constitutional challenges have arisen largely under the Eighth Amendment's Cruel and Unusual Punishment Clause; the equal protection element of the Fifth Amendment; the Fifth and Sixth Amendment components awakened by *Apprendi v. New Jersey* and its progeny; and the separation-of- powers doctrine.

---

[276] 18 U.S.C. § 4248.

[277] *Comstock*, 560 U.S. at 149.

[278] Gonzales v. Raich, 545 U.S. 1, 34 (Scalia, J., concurring in the judgment) ("Congress's regulatory authority over intrastate activities that are not themselves part of interstate commerce (including activities that have a substantial effect on interstate commerce) derives from the Necessary and Proper Clause.").

[279] United States v. Lawrence, 727 F.3d 386, 397 (5th Cir. 2013).

Cruel and Unusual Punishment

Mandatory minimums implicate considerations under the Eighth Amendment's Cruel and Unusual Punishment Clause.[280] The clause bars mandatory capital punishment statutes[281] and mandatory imposition on a juvenile of life imprisonment without the possibility of parole.[282] Although the case law is somewhat uncertain, it seems to condemn punishment that is "grossly disproportionate" to the misconduct for which it is imposed,[283] a standard which a sentence imposed under a mandatory minimum statute might breach only under extreme circumstances.

The Supreme Court decision in *Harmelin v. Michigan*[284] seems to make a defendant's Eighth Amendment arguments in a controlled substances case more difficult. The defendant in *Harmelin* was a first-time offender convicted of possession of 672 grams of cocaine, enough for possibly as many as 65,000 individual doses. Under the laws of the State of Michigan, the conviction carried with it a mandatory sentence of life imprisonment without the possibility of parole. The Court splintered over the question of whether Harmelin's mandatory sentence offended the Eighth Amendment because it was grossly disproportionate to his offense.

Five members of the Court concluded that it did not. Two members, Justice Scalia and Chief Justice Rehnquist, simply refused to recognize an Eighth Amendment proportionality requirement, at least in noncapital cases.[285] Justices Kennedy, O'Connor, and Souter concluded the Eighth Amendment does in fact forbid "extreme sentences that are grossly

---

[280] The Eighth Amendment to the United States Constitution states in its entirety, "[e]xcessive bail shall not be required, nor excessive fines imposed, nor cruel and unusual punishments inflicted."

[281] Woodson v. North Carolina, 428 U.S. 280, 305-306 (1976).

[282] Miller v. Alabama, 567 U.S. 460, 489 (2012). Virtual all contemporary convictions for federal offenses are convictions without the possibility of parole, because Congress abolished parole in the case of federal crimes over three decades ago. Section 212(a), P.L. 98-473, 98 Stat. 1987 (1984).

[283] Ewing v. California, 538 U.S. 11, 31-32 (2003).

[284] 501 U.S. 957 (1991).

[285] *Id.* at 994 (Scalia, J., with Rehnquist, Ch.J.) (citations omitted) ("Proportionality review is one of several respects in which we have held that 'death is different', and have imposed protections that the Constitution nowhere else provides. We would leave it there, but will not extend it further.").

disproportionate to the crime."[286] They explained, however, that Harmelin's sentence was not grossly disproportionate to the severity of his crime – that is, a crime whose "pernicious effects ... demonstrate that the ... legislature could with reason conclude that the threat posed to the individual and society by possession of this large an amount of cocaine—in terms of violence, crime, and social displacement—is momentous enough to warrant the deterrence and retribution of a life sentence without parole."[287]

Decisions of the lower federal courts seem to confirm that the Eighth Amendment precludes a mandatory term of imprisonment in drug trafficking cases only in those exceptionally rare cases when the punishment is grossly disproportionate to the offense.[288]

---

[286] *Id.* at 1001 (Kennedy, J., with O'Connor & Souter, J.J., concurring in part and concurring the judgment).

[287] *Id.* at 1003.

[288] See, e.g., United States v. Syms, 846 F.3d 230, 236 (7th Cir. 2017) (151-month sentence for conspiracy to distribute cocaine) (citations omitted) ("Only extreme sentences that are 'grossly disproportionate' to the crime will be deemed cruel and unusual. Additionally, 'eighth amendment challenges to sentences that are both prescribed by the [sentencing] guidelines, and within the statutory maximums established by Congress, are not looked on with disfavor.'"); United States v. Camberos-Villapuda, 832 F.3d 948, 953 (8th Cir. 2016) ("This court has ruled on numerous occasions that the imposition of a mandatory life sentence under that statute [21 U.S.C. § 841(b)(1)(A)] does not violate the Eighth Amendment's prohibition on cruel and unusual punishment."); United States v. Law, 806 F.3d 1103, 1107 (D.C. Cir. 2015) (quoting Miller v. Alabama, 567 U.S. 460, 481 (2012)) ("Law also contends ... that the life sentence the court imposed ... violates the Eight Amendment because it constitutes cruel and unusual punishment. This contention is foreclosed by precedent. The Supreme Court rejected it in Harmelin v. Michigan ... In its recent opinion in Miller v. Alabama, the Supreme Court left Harmelin undisturbed ... '[L]ife without parole is permissible for nonhomicide offenses – except ... for children ... Our reading thus neither overrules nor undermines nor conflicts with Harmelin.'"); United States v. Flores-Alvarado, 779 F.3d 250, 257 n.3 (4th Cir. 2015) (life sentence for recidivist trafficker); United States v. Gay, 771 F.3d 681, 686-87 (10th Cir. 2014) (262-month sentence for crack trafficker) (citing Harmelin); United States v. Adams, 768 F.3d 219, 224-25 (2d Cir. 2014) (210-month sentence for marijuana trafficker) ("Lengthy prison sentences, moreover, even those that exceed any conceivable life expectancy of a convicted defendant, do not violate the Eighth Amendment's prohibition against cruel and unusual punishment when based on a proper application of the Sentencing Guidelines or statutory mandated consecutive terms. We have also recognized that in a noncapital case it is exceedingly rare to uphold a claim that a sentence within the statutory limits is disproportionately severe.").

Equal Protection

The Equal Protection Clause of the Fourteenth Amendment condemns statutory classifications invidiously based on race, or constitutionally suspect factors. Moreover, "[d]iscrimination on the basis of race odious in all aspects is especially pernicious in the administration of justice."[289] These prohibitions apply with equal force under the equal protection component of the Fifth Amendment's Due Process Clause.[290] An explicit racial classification scheme can survive only under the most exceptional circumstances.[291] A statute, racially neutral on its face but discriminatory in its impact, cannot survive if racially motivated.[292] The circumstances surrounding the passage of a legislative measure with discriminatory impact may provide evidence of improper racial motivation.[293]

At one time, possession with intent to distribute crack cocaine (cocaine base) was punished 100 times more severely than possession with intent to distribute cocaine in powdered form.[294] Defendants claimed the distinction had a racially disparate impact. The claim was almost universally rejected.[295]

---

[289] *Pena-Rodriquez*, 137 S. Ct. 855, 868 (2017).

[290] Buckley v. Valeo, 424 U.S. 1, 93 (1976).

[291] Personnel Administrator v. Feeney, 442 U.S. 256, 272 (1979).

[292] Arlington Heights v. Metropolitan Housing Corp., 429 U.S. 252, 264-66 (1977).

[293] *Id.* at 267-68.

[294] At one time, for example, the same mandatory minimum sentence applied to 5000 grams of powder cocaine as applied to 50 grams of crack cocaine. 21 U.S.C. § 841(b)(1)(A) (2006 ed.).

[295] *E.g.*, United States v. Dumas, 64 F.3d 1427, 1429 (9th Cir. 1995) (citing United States v. Harding, 971 F.2d 410 (9th Cir. 1992)) ("We have previously considered and rejected 'as enacted' equal protection challenges to 21 U.S.C. § 841(b) and USSG § 2D1.1... [W]e refused to apply a strict level of scrutiny to the sentencing distinction between crack and powder cocaine. We noted that, on its fact, section 841(b) implicates neither a suspect class nor a fundamental right. Therefore, we reviewed the distinction only under the rational basis test, the lowest level of scrutiny applicable to equal protection challenges. We held that the crack/powder cocaine distinction survived rationality review because, although crack and powder cocaine are different forms of the same drug, Congress reasonably could have considered that crack's differing physiological and psychological effects, and its greater marketability, made crack a greater societal problem meriting more severe punishment."); United States v. Fenner, 600 F.3d 1014, 1024-25 (8th Cir. 2010); United States v. Wimbley, 553 F.3d 455, 463 (6th Cir. 2009); United States v. Eirby, 262 F.3d 31, 41 (1st Cir. 2001); United States v . Matthews, 168 F.3d 1234, 1250-51 (11th Cir. 1999); United States v. Holton, 116 F.3d 1536, 1548 (D.C. Cir. 1997); United States v. Perkins, 108 F.3d 512, 518 (4th Cir. 1997); United States v. Teague, 93 F.3d 81, 84-5 (2d Cir. 1996); United States v. Reddrick, 90 F.3d 1276, 1282 (7th Cir. 1996); United States v. McKinney, 53 F.3d 664, 678

Juries, Grand Juries, and due Process

The Constitution demands that no person "be held to answer for a capital or otherwise infamous crime, unless on a presentment or indictment of a grand jury" and that "[i]n all criminal prosecutions, the accused shall enjoy the right to a speedy and public trial, by an impartial jury."[296]

Moreover the Supreme Court's *In re Winship* decision explained that due process requires that the prosecution prove beyond a reasonable doubt "every fact necessary to constitute the crime" with which an accused is charged.[297] After *Winship*, the question arose whether a statute might authorize or require a more severe penalty for a particular crime based on a fact—not included in the indictment, not found by the jury, and not proven beyond a reasonable doubt. Pennsylvania passed a law under which various serious crimes (rape, robbery, kidnapping, and the like) were subject to a mandatory minimum penalty of imprisonment for five years, if the judge after conviction found by a preponderance of the evidence that the defendant had been in visible possession of a firearm during the commission of the offense.[298] Had the Pennsylvania statute created a new series of crimes? For example, had it supplemented its crime of rape with a new crime of rape while in visible possession of a firearm? And if so, did the fact of visible possession have to be proven to the jury beyond a reasonable doubt?[299]

The Supreme Court concluded that visible possession of a firearm under the statute was not an element of a new series of crimes, but was instead a sentencing consideration that had been given a legislatively

---

(5th Cir. 1995); United States v. Williamson, 1500, 1503 (10th Cir. 1995); United States v. Frazier, 981 F.3d 92, 95 (3d Cir. 1992); *contra* United States v. Clary, 846 F. Supp. 768, 796-97 (E.D. Mo. 1994) (holding that the 100 to 1 sentencing ratio found in the 21 U.S.C. § 841(b) and the implementing U.S. Sentencing Commission Sentencing Guidelines constitute a violation of the Constitution's equal protection guarantees), rev'd, 34 F.3d 710 (8th Cir. 1994).

[296] U.S. CONST. amends. V, VI.

[297] *In re* Winship, 397 U.S. 358, 364 (1970).

[298] 42 Pa.Cons.Stat. 9712 (1982), reprinted in McMillan v. Pennsylvania, 477 U.S. 79, 81-2 n.1 (1986).

[299] The right to grand jury indictment was not implicated since the Sixth Amendment right to grand jury indictment applies only to federal prosecutions, Alexander v. Louisiana, 405 U.S. 625, 633 (1972).

prescribed weight.[300] As such, the Pennsylvania statutory scheme neither offended due process nor triggered any right to a separate jury finding.[301]

There followed a number of state and federal statutes under which facts that might earlier have been treated as elements of a new crime were simply classified as sentencing factors. In some instances, the new sentencing factor permitted imposition of a penalty far in excess of that otherwise available for the underlying offense. For instance, the Supreme Court found no constitutional defect in a statute which punished a deported alien for returning to the United States by imprisonment for not more than 2 years, but which permitted the alien to be sentenced to imprisonment for not more than 20 years upon a post-trial, judicial determination that the alien had been convicted of a serious crime following deportation.[302]

Perhaps uneasy with the implications, the Court soon made it clear in *Apprendi* that, "under the Due Process Clause of the Fifth Amendment and the notice and jury trial guarantees of the Sixth Amendment, any fact (other than prior conviction) that increases the *maximum* penalty for a crime must be charged in an indictment, submitted to a jury, and proven beyond a reasonable doubt."[303] Side opinions questioned the continued vitality of *McMillan*'s mandatory minimum determination in light of the *Apprendi*.[304]

Initially unwilling to extend *Apprendi* to mandatory minimums in *Harris v. United States*,[305] the Court did so in *Alleyne v. United States*.[306]

---

[300] McMillan v. Pennsylvania, 477 U.S. 79 (1986).

[301] *Id.* at 84, 93.

[302] Almendarez-Torres v. United States, 523 U.S. 224, 247 (1998).

[303] Apprendi v. New Jersey, 530 U.S. 466, 476 (2000) (emphasis added).

[304] "Thus, the Court appears to hold that any fact that increases or alters the range of penalties to which a defendant is exposed – which, by definition, must include increases or alterations to either the minimum or maximum penalties – must be proved to a jury beyond a reasonable doubt. In *McMillan*, however, we rejected such a rule to the extent it concerned those facts that increase or alter the minimum penalty to which a defendant is exposed. Accordingly, it is incumbent on the Court not only to admit that it is overruling *McMillan*, but also to explain why such a course of action is appropriate under normal principles of *stare decisis*." *Id.* at 533 (O'Connor, with Kennedy, Breyer, JJ., and Rehnquist, Ch.J., dissenting) (referring to *McMillan v. Pennsylvania*, 477 U.S. 79 (1986). *See also id.* at 518, 521-22 (Thomas, J., concurring); *Rethinking Mandatory Minimums After Apprendi*, 96 NW. U. L. REV. 811 (2002); Levine, *The Confounding Boundaries of "Apprendi-land": Statutory Minimums and the Federal Sentencing Guidelines*, 29 AMER. J. CRIM. L. 377 (2002).

[305] Harris v. United States, 536 U.S. 545, 568 (2002).

Alleyne was convicted under the statute that imposes a series of mandatory minimum penalties upon defendants who carry a firearm during and in furtherance of a crime of violence (5 years for carrying; 7 years for brandishing; 10 years for discharging).[307] The jury found him guilty of carrying; the trial court judge concluded the gun had been brandished.[308] The Sixth Amendment requires that the question of brandishing had to be found by the jury, the Court declared:

> *Harris* drew a distinction between facts that increase the statutory maximum and facts that increase only the mandatory minimum. We conclude that this distinction is inconsistent with our decision in *Apprendi* and with the original meaning of the Sixth Amendment. Any fact that, by law, increases the penalty for a crime is an element that must be submitted to the jury and found beyond a reasonable doubt. Mandatory minimum sentences increase the penalty for a crime. It follows, then, that any fact that increases the mandatory minimum is an element that must be submitted to the jury.[309]

Neither *Apprendi* nor *Alleyne* limits Congress's authority to establish mandatory minimum sentences or limits the authority of the courts to impose them. They simply dictate the procedural safeguards that must accompany the exercise of that authority. Thus, the lower federal appellate courts have held that the neither the Fifth nor Sixth Amendment requires that "facts that determine whether a defendant is eligible under the safety valve for a sentence below the statutory minimum" need be found by the jury beyond a reasonable doubt.[310]

---

[306] 133 S. Ct. 2151 (2013).

[307] 18 U.S.C. § 924(c).

[308] *Alleyne*, 133 S. Ct. at 2156.

[309] *Id.* at 2155.

[310] United States v. Leanos, 827 F.3d 1167, 1169-70 (8th Cir. 2016) (citing United States v. King, 773 F.3d 48, 55 (5th Cir. 2014); United States v. Lizarraga-Carrizales, 757 F.3d 955, 997-99 (9th Cir. 2014); and United States v. Harakaly, 734 F.3d 88, 97 (1st Cir. 2013)).

Separation of Powers

While “it remains a basic principle of our constitutional scheme that one branch of the Government may not intrude upon the central prerogatives of another,”[311] the Supreme Court has observed that “Congress has the power to define criminal punishments without giving the courts any sentencing discretion.”[312] Thus, the lower federal courts have regularly upheld mandatory minimum statutes when challenged on separation-of-powers grounds,[313] and the Supreme Court has denied any separation-of-powers infirmity in the federal sentencing guideline system, which at the time might have been thought to produce its own form of mandatory minimums.[314]

---

[311] Loving v. United States, 517 U.S. 748, 757 (1996).

[312] United States v. Chapman, 500 U.S. 453, 467 (1991).

[313] United States v. Carpenter, 819 F.3d 880, 892 (6th Cir. 2016); United States v. Major, 676 F.3d 803, 811 (9th Cir. 2012); United States v. Nigg, 667 F.3d 929, 934-35 (7th Cir. 2012); United States v. Page, 604 F.3d 1268, 1274 (11th Cir. 2010); United States v. Walker, 473 F.3d 71,76 (3d Cir. 2007); United States v. Rasco, 123 F.3d 222, 226-27 (5th Cir. 1997); United States v. Prior, 107 F.3d 654, 660 (8th Cir. 1997).

[314] Mistretta v. United States, 488 U.S. 361 (1989). Mistretta, sentenced under the guidelines to 18 months' imprisonment for conspiracy to distribute cocaine, argued that the guidelines constituted an unconstitutional delegation of Congress's legislative authority and that the service of judges upon the Commission constituted extrajudicial service at odds with the separation of powers doctrine. The Court rejected both arguments concluding “that in creating the Sentencing Commission ... Congress neither delegated excessive legislative power nor upset the constitutionally mandated balance of powers among the coordinate Branches,” *Id.* at 412.

In: Criminal Justice
Editor: Quincy Franks

ISBN: 978-1-53614-196-2

Chapter 5

THE STATE DEPARTMENT'S TRAFFICKING IN PERSONS REPORT: SCOPE, AID RESTRICTIONS, AND METHODOLOGY*

Liana W. Rosen

ABSTRACT

The State Department's annual release of the Trafficking in Persons report (commonly referred to as the TIP Report) has been closely monitored by Congress, foreign governments, the media, advocacy groups, and other foreign policy observers. The 109th Congress first mandated the report's publication in the Trafficking Victims Protection Act of 2000 (TVPA; Div. A of the Victims of Trafficking and Violence Protection Act of 2000, P.L. 106-386).

Over time, the number of countries covered by the TIP Report has grown, peaking at 188 countries, including the United States. In the 2017 TIP Report, the State Department categorized 187 countries. Countries were placed into one of several lists (or tiers) based on their respective

* This is an edited, reformatted, and augmented version of a Congressional Research Service report, R44953, dated September 19, 2017.

governments' level of effort to address human trafficking between April 1, 2016, and March 31, 2017. An additional category of special cases included three countries that were not assigned a tier ranking because of ongoing political instability (Libya, Somalia, and Yemen).

Its champions describe the TIP Report as a keystone measure of government efforts to address and ultimately eliminate human trafficking. Some U.S. officials refer to the report as a crucial tool of diplomatic engagement that has encouraged foreign governments to elevate their own antitrafficking efforts. Its detractors question the TIP Report's credibility as a true measure of antitrafficking efforts, suggesting at times that political factors distort its country assessments. Some foreign governments perceive the report as a form of U.S. interference in their domestic affairs.

Continued congressional interest in the TIP Report and its country rankings has resulted in several key modifications to the process. Such modifications have included the creation of the special watch list, limiting the length of time a country may remain on a subset of the special watch list, expanding the list of criteria for determining whether countries are taking serious and sustained efforts to eliminate trafficking, establishing a list of governments that recruit and use child soldiers, and prohibiting the least cooperative countries on antitrafficking matters from participating in authorized trade negotiations. These modifications were often included as part of broader legislative efforts to reauthorize the TVPA, whose current authorization for appropriations expires at the end of FY2017.

Recent Developments

On June 27, 2017, the U.S. Department of State released the 17th edition of the TIP Report—the first for the Administration of President Donald J. Trump. In spite of State Department efforts to alleviate congressional concerns that the report's methodology is susceptible to political pressure, several Members in the 115th Congress have introduced legislation to further modify key aspects of the annual country ranking and reporting process.

The most significant changes to the TIP Report methodology are contained in H.R. 2200, the Frederick Douglass Trafficking Victims Prevention and Protection Reauthorization Act of 2017, which passed the House on July 12, 2017. If enacted, the changes could reduce State Department flexibility and discretion in assigning tier rankings to countries and increase the number of countries that would fall into the worst category (Tier 3)—while also making it potentially more difficult for countries to attain the best category (Tier 1). Other proposed changes to the TIP Report methodology are contained in S. 377, S. 952, H.R. 436, H.R. 1191, and H.R. 2219.

While some observers may anticipate that changes to the TIP Report's methodology will improve its overall credibility and country ranking process, others may question whether such changes will confuse foreign governments and be perceived as too complex. The reputational harm of a poor ranking in the TIP Report has motivated some countries to improve their antitrafficking efforts. It is not clear, however, if this scenario will hold true indefinitely. If the prospect of achieving a top ranking in the TIP Report begins to appear unattainable, could the TIP Report's ability to motivate countries to improve their antitrafficking efforts—and thus its value as a policy tool for international engagement to combat human trafficking—diminish?

INTRODUCTION

Congress has led both U.S. and international efforts to eliminate severe forms of trafficking in persons, particularly with its enactment of the Victims of Trafficking and Violence Protection Act of 2000 (P.L. 106-386). Division A of that act, the Trafficking Victims Protection Act of 2000 (TVPA), established U.S. antitrafficking policy to (1) *prevent* trafficking, (2) *protect* trafficking victims, and (3) *prosecute* and punish traffickers (known as the three Ps).

A key element of the TVPA's foreign policy objectives involved a new requirement for the Secretary of State to produce an annual report on human trafficking and to rank foreign governments based on their antitrafficking efforts. In the ensuing reports, which the State Department titled as *Trafficking in Persons* (TIP) reports, the department developed a ranking system in which the best countries were identified as Tier 1 and the worst Tier 3. Moreover, the TVPA stipulated that the worst performers (Tier 3 countries) in the TIP Report could be subject to potential restrictions on certain types of U.S. foreign aid and other U.S. and multilateral funds—a policy that is intended to motivate countries to avoid Tier 3 by prioritizing antitrafficking efforts.

The TIP Report's annual release remains a topic of widespread interest among international and domestic stakeholders, including Congress. Since the TVPA's enactment 17 years ago, Congress has continued to adjust the requirements associated with how countries are ranked in the TIP Report, as well as the policy consequences of such rankings. (See Figure 1 below.) These changes were often the result of congressional dissatisfaction with some aspect of the TIP Report:

- Due to difficulty discerning differences among Tier 2 countries, Congress modified the TVPA in 2003 to create a special watch list, composed of countries that deserve enhanced scrutiny.[1]
- Out of concern that countries were listed for too many consecutive years on the special watch list, Congress modified the TVPA in 2008 to limit the number of years a country may remain on it.[2]
- In response to the plight of children exploited in armed conflict, Congress modified the TVPA in 2008 to require the State Department to identify countries whose governments recruit and use child soldiers.[3]
- With the objective of linking U.S. trade policy to antitrafficking outcomes, Congress in 2015 prohibited Tier 3 countries from participating in authorized trade negotiations.[4]
- As a result of greater awareness of antitrafficking best practices, Congress has incrementally expanded its expectations for governments to conduct *serious and sustained efforts* to address human trafficking.

In light of ongoing congressional scrutiny of the State Department's TIP Report and its country ranking process, several bills in the 115th

[1] §6 of the Trafficking Victims Protection Reauthorization Act of 2003 (2003 TVPRA; P.L. 108-193) amended §110 of the Trafficking Victims Protection Act of 2000 (TVPA); 22 U.S.C. 7107.

[2] §107 of the William Wilberforce Trafficking Victims Protection Reauthorization Act of 2008 (2008 TVPRA; P.L. 110-457) amended §110 of the TVPA; 22 U.S.C. 7107.

[3] See Title IV of P.L. 110-457, the Child Soldiers Prevention Act of 2008 (CSPA); 22 U.S.C. 2370c et seq.

[4] §106 of the Bipartisan Congressional Trade Priorities and Accountability Act of 2015 (TPA; Title I of P.L. 114-26) added this statutory restriction; it was subsequently amended to allow for a waiver by §914 of the Trade Facilitation and Trade Enforcement Act of 2015 (P.L. 114-125); 19 U.S.C. 4205.

Congress have been introduced to further modify requirements associated with the TIP Report. Some of these proposed changes could significantly change—and at least temporarily complicate—the current TIP Report's methodology.[5] A critical question is whether further changes to the TIP Report's methodology will incentivize countries to boost their antitrafficking efforts or, in contrast, may erode the legitimacy of the TIP Report as a credible tool to advocate for human trafficking concerns.

This chapter describes the legislative provisions that govern the U.S. Department of State's production of the annual TIP Report, reviews country ranking trends in the TIP Report, and identifies recent congressional oversight of and legislative activity to modify the TIP Report. Answers to selected frequently asked questions (FAQs) are included throughout the report

TIP Report Scope

The contents of each annual TIP Report are governed by two provisions, one in the TVPA, as amended, and a second in the Child Soldiers Prevention Act of 2008 (CSPA).[6] In addition, current law requires the President and the Secretary of State to prepare related follow-on documentation for certain categories of countries. These include reporting requirements that were added to the TVPA as part of TVPA reauthorization acts, as well as requirements contained in the Bipartisan Congressional Trade Priorities and Accountability Act of 2015 (TPA), as amended.

Reporting Requirements in the TVPA

The TVPA, as amended, establishes the core contents of the TIP Report. Specifically, it requires the Secretary of State to submit to

[5] For further discussion, see "Legislative Oversight and Outlook" section, below.

[6] §110 of the TVPA (22 U.S.C. 7107) and §404 of the CSPA (22 U.S.C. 2370c-1).

appropriate congressional committees an annual report, due not later than June 1 each year, which describes, on a country-by-country basis:[7]

- government efforts to eliminate severe forms of trafficking in persons;
- the nature and scope of trafficking in persons in each country; and
- trends in each government's efforts to combat trafficking.

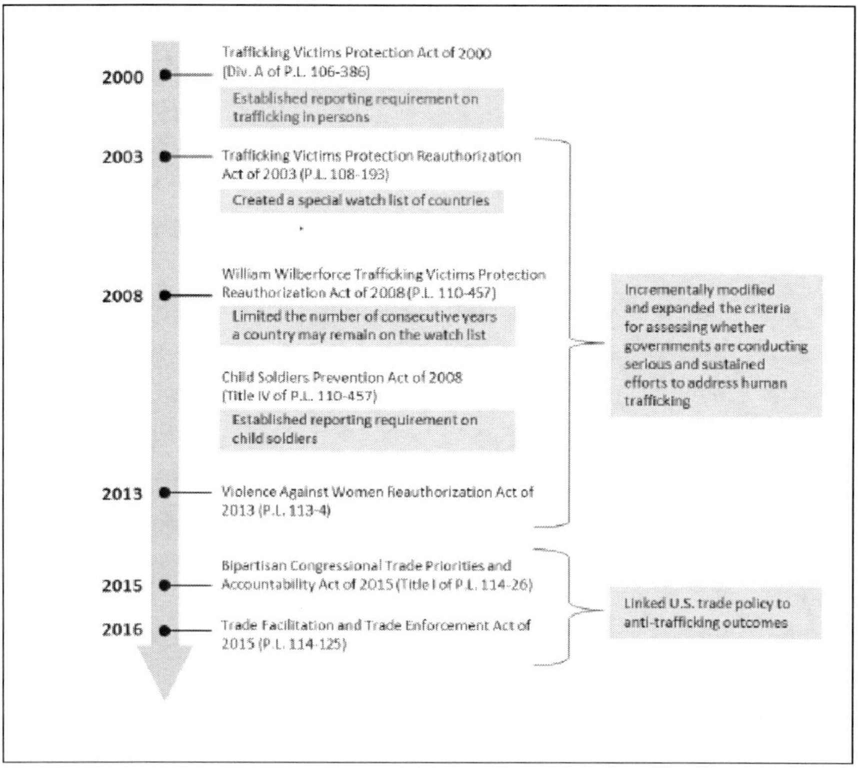

Source: CRS, based on Congress.gov.

Figure 1. Key Legislative Changes to the TIP Report, 2000-2016.

[7] *Appropriate congressional committees* in the TVPA refer to the Senate Foreign Relations Committee (SFRC), the Senate Judiciary Committee (SJUD), the House Foreign Affairs Committee (HFAC), and the House Judiciary Committee (HJUD). See §103 of the TVPA; 22 U.S.C. 7102.

FAQ: What Are Severe Forms of Trafficking in Persons?

The TVPA defines severe forms of trafficking in persons to mean:

a) sex trafficking in which a commercial sex act is induced by force, fraud, or coercion, or in which the person induced to perform such act has not attained 18 years of age; or
b) the recruitment, harboring, transportation, provision, or obtaining of a person for labor or services, through the use of force, fraud, or coercion for the purpose of subjection to involuntary servitude, peonage, debt bondage, or slavery.[8]

This definition is largely consistent with the definition of trafficking in persons contained in the United Nations Protocol to Prevent, Suppress and Punish Trafficking in Persons, Especially Women and Children[9] (adopted by the U.N. in 2000)—and TIP Reports use the terms trafficking in persons, severe forms of trafficking in persons, and human trafficking interchangeably. TIP Reports have also described human trafficking as modern slavery.[10]

The 2017 TIP Report illustratively describes common manifestations of human trafficking to include sex trafficking, child sex trafficking, forced labor, bonded labor (also known as debt bondage), domestic servitude, forced child labor, and unlawful recruitment and use of child soldiers.[11] Some government and nongovernmental entities may apply different definitions to refer to human trafficking, sometimes conflating human trafficking with human smuggling, illegal adoptions, international trade in human organs, child pornography, and prostitution.

---

[8] §103 of the TVPA; 22 U.S.C. 7102.

[9] For the treaty's current status, see United Nations Treaty Collection, *Protocol to Prevent, Suppress and Punish Trafficking in Persons, Especially Women and Children, supplementing the United Nations Convention against Transnational Organized Crime*, https://treaties.un.org/Pages/ViewDetails.aspx?src=IND&mtdsg_no=XVIII-12-a&chapter=18&lang=en.

[10] See U.S. Department of State, *Trafficking in Persons*, report (TIP Report), June 28, 2017.

[11] Ibid.

Required Country Lists in the TIP Report

Central to the TVPA's reporting requirements is a set of country lists, based on whether governments are achieving four minimum standards that the law prescribes for the elimination of severe forms of trafficking in persons. Specifically, the TVPA requires the report to include[12]

- a list of countries whose governments *fully comply* with the minimum standards for the elimination of severe forms of trafficking in persons; although the TVPA does not use the *tier* nomenclature, TIP Reports describe this list as Tier 1. (See Table 1 below.)
- a list of countries whose governments *do not fully comply* with the minimum standards but are making *significant efforts* to become compliant; TIP Reports describe this list as Tier 2. (See Table 2 below.)
- a list of countries whose governments do not fully comply and are not making significant efforts to become compliant; TIP Reports describe this list as Tier 3. (See Table 3 below.)

Table 1. Tier 1 Countries in the 2017 TIP Report

Armenia	Denmark	Korea, South	St. Maarten
Australia	Finland	Lithuania	Slovakia
Austria	France	Luxembourg	Slovenia
The Bahamas	Georgia	Netherlands	Spain
Belgium	Germany	New Zealand	Sweden
Canada	Guyana	Norway	Switzerland
Chile	Ireland	Philippines	Taiwan
Colombia	Israel	Poland	United Kingdom
Czechia	Italy	Portugal	United States

Source: U.S. Department of State, *TIP Report*, June 28, 2017, p. 46.

[12] §110 of the TVPA; 22 U.S.C. 7107.

In accordance with the 2003 amendments to the TVPA, which required the creation of a new "special watch list," the 2004 TIP Report introduced a new category of country ranking, called the Tier 2 Watch List.[13] For further discussion, see section on "Reporting Requirements Related to the Special Watch List."

Table 2. Tier 2 Countries in the 2017 TIP Report

Afghanistan	Ecuador	Lesotho	St. Vincent and the Grenadines
Albania	Egypt	Macedonia	Seychelles
Angola	El Salvador	Malawi	Sierra Leone
Argentina	Estonia	Malaysia	Singapore
Aruba	Ethiopia	Maldives	Solomon Islands
Azerbaijan	Fiji	Malta	South Africa
Bahrain	Greece	Mauritius	Sri Lanka
Barbados	Honduras	Mexico	Tajikistan
Bhutan	Iceland	Micronesia	Tanzania
Bosnia and Herzegovina	India	Mongolia	Timor-Leste
Botswana	Indonesia	Morocco	Togo
Brazil	Jamaica	Namibia	Tonga
Brunei	Japan	Nepal	Trinidad and Tobago
Cambodia	Jordan	Palau	Tunisia
Costa Rica	Kazakhstan	Panama	Turkey
Cote D'Ivoire	Kenya	Paraguay	Uganda
Croatia	Kosovo	Peru	Ukraine
Curaçao	Kyrgyz Republic	Qatar	United Arab Emirates
Cyprus	Latvia	Romania	Uruguay
Dominican Republic	Lebanon	St. Lucia	Vietnam

Source: U.S. Department of State, *TIP Report*, June 28, 2017, p. 46.

[13] §6 of the 2003 TVPRA amended §110 of the TVPA; 22 U.S.C. 7107.

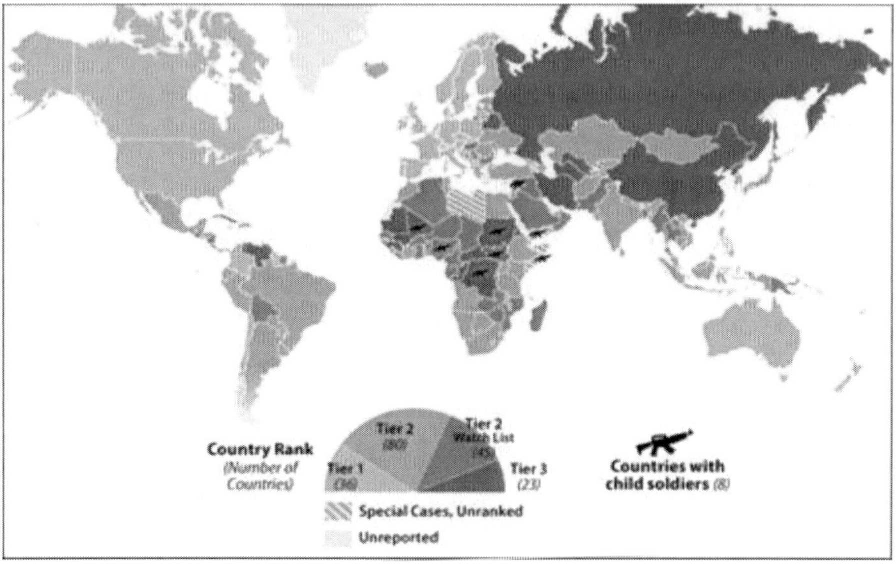

Source: CRS, based on U.S. Department of State, *TIP Report*, June 28, 2017, pp. 20, 46.

Figure 2. 2017 TIP Report: Country Rankings.

Table 3. Tier 3 Countries in the 2017 TIP Report

Belarus	Congo, Democratic Republic of	Iran	Sudan
Belize	Congo, Republic of	Korea, North	Syria
Burundi	Equatorial Guinea	Mali	Turkmenistan
Central African Republic	Eritrea	Mauritania	Uzbekistan
China	Guinea	Russia	Venezuela
Comoros	Guinea-Bissau	South Sudan	

Source: U.S. Department of State, *TIP Report*, June 28, 2017, p. 46.

Other Required Information in the TIP Report

In addition to the required country lists, the TVPA requires the State Department to include other information in the annual TIP Report. This includes[14]

[14] §110 of the TVPA, as amended; 22 U.S.C. 7107.

- information on what the United Nations, Organization for Security and Cooperation in Europe, North Atlantic Treaty Organization, and other multilateral organizations, as appropriate, are doing to prevent their employees, contractors, and peacekeeping forces from engaging in human trafficking or exploiting victims of trafficking;
- information on changes in the global patterns of human trafficking, including prevalence data, disaggregated by source, transit, and destination countries, as well as nationality, gender, and age;
- information on emerging human trafficking issues; and
- information on "promising practices in the eradication of trafficking in persons."[15]

Reporting Requirements in the CSPA

Congress enacted the Child Soldiers Prevention Act of 2008 (CSPA) as part of its 2008 reauthorization of the TVPA.[16] A key element of the CSPA is the requirement to include in the annual TIP Report an additional list of foreign governments that recruit and use child soldiers in their armed forces or in government-supported armed groups. Government-supported armed groups include paramilitaries, militias, and civil defense forces. The 2017 TIP Report identified eight countries on the CSPA list: the Democratic Republic of Congo, Mali, Nigeria, Somalia, South Sudan, Sudan, Syria, and Yemen.

[15] §1205 of the Violence Against Women Reauthorization Act of 2013 (2013 VAWRA; P.L. 113-4) added this requirement to §110 of the TVPA; 22 U.S.C. 7107. The 2014 TIP Report contained a section entitled "Promising Practices in the Eradication of Trafficking in Persons." Although the phrase *promising practices* is used in the 2015 Report, subsequent TIP Reports do not contain a section on "Promising Practices in the Eradication of Trafficking in Persons." Moreover, the 2016 and 2017 TIP Reports do not contain the phrase *promising practices*.

[16] Title IV of the 2008 TVPRA; 22 U.S.C. 2370c et seq.

FAQ: Who is a *child soldier*?

The CSPA of 2008 defines child solider (including those "serving in any capacity, including in a support role such as a cook, porter, messenger, medic, guard, or sex slave") to mean children:

i. under 18 years who take direct part in hostilities as a member of government armed forces;
ii. under 18 years who are compulsorily recruited into governmental armed forces;
iii. under 15 years who are voluntarily recruited into governmental armed forces; or
iv. under 18 years who are recruited or used in hostilities by non-state armed forces.

Reporting Requirements Related to the Special Watch List

Apart from the TIP Report, the TVPA, as amended, requires the Secretary of State to submit to appropriate congressional committees a special watch list composed of countries determined by the Secretary of State to require special scrutiny during the following year. This requirement to develop a special watch list was first enacted in the TVPA reauthorization of 2003.[17]

The TVPA mandates that this list be composed of three types of countries: (1) countries upgraded in most recent TIP Report and now assessed to be fully compliant with the minimum standards (from Tier 2 to Tier 1); (2) countries upgraded in the most recent TIP Report and now assessed to be making significant efforts toward compliance with the minimum standards (from Tier 3 to Tier 2); and (3) a subset of Tier 2 countries in which

[17] This criterion was added by §6 of the 2003 TVPRA and amended by §1205 of the 2013 VAWRA; 22 U.S.C. 7107. The 2004 TIP Report was the first TIP Report to include the "special watch list." Beginning with the 2005 TIP Report, the State Department termed the special watch list countries that were not upgraded as "Tier 2 Watch List." For further discussion, see subsection on "Relationship to the Tier 2 Watch List."

- the absolute number of victims is very significant or significantly increasing;
- there is a failure to provide evidence of increasing efforts to combat severe forms of trafficking in persons, compared to the previous year; or
- the determination that significant efforts are being made to become compliant is based on government commitments to take additional future steps over the next year.

Relationship to the Tier 2 Watch List

Although the TVPA, as amended, authorizes the special watch list to be submitted separately from the TIP Report, the State Department introduced it as a feature in the 2004 TIP Report.[18] Beginning with the 2004 TIP Report, the department included a fourth list of countries in its annual TIP Report, called the Tier 2 Watch List. This Tier 2 Watch List is composed of the special watch list countries whose governments would otherwise be listed on Tier 2, except that the absolute number of victims is large or growing, or antitrafficking efforts appear to have stalled or have yet to be implemented. (See Table 4 below.)

Mid-Year Interim Assessment

Due on February 1 each year, the TVPA, as amended, requires the Secretary of State to submit to appropriate congressional committees an interim assessment of the progress made by each special watch list country since the last TIP Report.[19] These mid-year assessments are typically brief, stating both positive and negative developments in each special watch list country. Readers are unable to predict, based solely on these reports,

---

[18] §110 of the TVPA, as amended, specifically requires the special watch list to be submitted to appropriate congressional committees no later than the date when the President submits a notification and determination regarding which countries will be barred or waived from certain categories of foreign assistance due to their failure to comply with the minimum standards and make significant efforts toward compliance. The latter notification and determination is required to be made not less than 45 days or more than 90 days after submission of the TIP Report (due June 1) or an "Interim Report" pursuant to §110(b)(2) of the TVPA, which may be referring to a provision that was struck by §1205(2) of the 2013 VAWRA.

[19] §110 of the TVPA, as amended by §6 of the 2003 TVPRA; 22 U.S.C. 7107.

whether a country's ranking will improve, remain the same, or decline in the next TIP Report.

Watch List Downgrades

The TVPA, as amended, requires that a country on the special watch list (in practice, the Tier 2 Watch List) for two consecutive years be subsequently listed among those whose governments do not fully comply and are not making significant efforts to become compliant (Tier 3). The requirement to limit the length of time a country may remain on the watch list was enacted in the TVPA reauthorization of 2008.[20] The first year in which it came into effect was 2009 and the first year in which a Tier 2 Watch List country was downgraded for its duration in this tier category was 2013.

Table 4. Tier 2 Watch List Countries in the 2017 TIP Report

Algeria	Djibouti	Macau	Rwanda
Antigua and Barbuda	Gabon	Madagascar	Saudi Arabia
Bangladesh	The Gambia	Marshall Islands	Senegal
Benin	Ghana	Moldova	Serbia
Bolivia	Guatemala	Montenegro	Suriname
Bulgaria	Haiti	Mozambique	Swaziland
Burkina Faso	Hong Kong	Nicaragua	Thailand
Burma	Hungary	Niger	Zambia
Cabo Verde	Iraq	Nigeria	Zimbabwe
Cameroon	Kuwait	Oman	
Chad	Laos	Pakistan	
Cuba	Liberia	Papua New Guinea	

Source: U.S. Department of State, *TIP Report*, June 28, 2017, p. 46.

In the 2017 TIP Report, a total of five countries were downgraded to Tier 3 after two or more consecutive years on the Tier 2 Watch List:

- China (downgraded after three consecutive years on the Tier 2 Watch List);

[20] §110 of the TPVA, as amended by §107 of the 2008 TVPRA; 22 U.S.C. 7107.

- Democratic Republic of Congo (downgraded after two consecutive years);
- Republic of Congo (downgraded after two consecutive years);
- Guinea (downgraded after four consecutive years); and
- Mali (downgraded after four consecutive years).

FAQ: How Is Congress Notified of Watch List Downgrade Waivers?

Credible evidence in support of downgrade waivers is to be submitted to the Senate Foreign Relations and the House Foreign Affairs Committees. Within 30 days after such congressional notification, the TVPA, as amended, also requires the Secretary of State to provide a detailed description of such evidence on a publicly available website maintained by the State Department.[21]

Watch List Downgrade Waivers

Pursuant to the TVPA, as amended, the President may waive downgrades for up to two years if the President determines and reports credible evidence justifying a waiver because

- the country has a written plan to begin making significant efforts to become compliant with the minimum standards for the elimination of trafficking in persons;
- the written plan, if implemented, would constitute significant efforts to become compliant with the minimum standards; and

---

[21] §110 of the TPVA, as amended by §107 of the 2008 TVPRA and §1205 of the 2013 VAWRA; 22 U.S.C. 7107. The 2013 VAWRA added the public notice provision. A December 2016 U.S. Government Accountability Office (GAO) report found that the State Department had not posted the requisite detailed description online until September 2016. See GAO, *Human Trafficking: State Has Made Improvements in Its Annual Report but Does Not Explicitly Explain Certain Tier Rankings or Changes*, GAO-17-56, December 2016. For the 2017 public notification, see State Department, Office to Monitor and Combat Trafficking in Persons, "Memorandum of Justification Consistent with Section 110(B)(2)(D) of the Trafficking Victims Protection Act of 2000," webpage, July 18, 2017, https://www.state.gov/j/tip/rls/reports/2017/272651.htm.

- the country is devoting sufficient resources to implement the plan.[22]

In the 2017 TIP Report, a total of nine countries received waivers to stay on Tier 2 Watch List for more than two consecutive years. (See Table 5.)

Table 5. Tier 2 Watch List Countries for More than Two Consecutive Years Country Rank Outcomes in the 2014-2017 TIP Reports

Country	2014 TIP Report	2015 TIP Report	2016 TIP Report	2017 TIP Report
Antigua and Barbuda	Tier 2 Watch List	Tier 2 Watch List	Tier 2 Watch List	Tier 2 Watch List
Bolivia	Tier 2 Watch List	Tier 2 Watch List	Tier 2 Watch List	Tier 2 Watch List
Bulgaria	Tier 2	Tier 2 Watch List	Tier 2 Watch List	Tier 2 Watch List
Cuba	Tier 3	Tier 2 Watch List	Tier 2 Watch List	Tier 2 Watch List
Gabon	Tier 2	Tier 2 Watch List	Tier 2 Watch List	Tier 2 Watch List
Ghana	Tier 2	Tier 2 Watch List	Tier 2 Watch List	Tier 2 Watch List
Laos	Tier 2 Watch List	Tier 2 Watch List	Tier 2 Watch List	Tier 2 Watch List
Pakistan	Tier 2 Watch List	Tier 2 Watch List	Tier 2 Watch List	Tier 2 Watch List
Saudi Arabia	Tier 3	Tier 2 Watch List	Tier 2 Watch List	Tier 2 Watch List

Source: U.S. Department of State, *TIP Reports*, 2014-2017, pp. 58, 54, 56, and 46, respectfully.

Reporting Requirements in the TPA

The President is required to submit to appropriate congressional committees additional information on countries upgraded from Tier 3 in the prior year's TIP Report. Pursuant to the Bipartisan Congressional Trade Priorities and Accountability Act of 2015 (TPA), as amended, the President must submit detailed descriptions of credible evidence supporting these upgrades.[23] The detailed descriptions may be accompanied by copies of documents providing such evidence.

---

[22] Ibid. The President delegated this waiver authority to the Secretary of State. See 75 FR 67023.

[23] The TPA is Title I of P.L. 114-26, the Defending Public Safety Employees' Retirement Act. The TIP Report-related provision in the TPA was amended by §914 of the Trade

In the 2017 TIP Report, nine countries were upgraded from Tier 3 in the 2016 TIP Report: Algeria, Burma, Djibouti, The Gambia, Haiti, Marshall Islands, Papua New Guinea, Suriname, and Zimbabwe.

EXPECTATIONS FOR THE ELIMINATION OF TRAFFICKING

As discussed above, a central and required element of each TIP Report is the evaluation of each government's commitment to eliminating severe forms of trafficking in persons. Countries are assessed on the basis of four *minimum standards* and 12 *criteria* prescribed by the TVPA, as amended.[24] While the four minimum standards have not been amended since the TVPA was first enacted, the criteria for evaluating what constitutes *serious and sustained efforts* to eliminate trafficking have been modified and expanded through multiple reauthorizations of the TVPA since 2000.[25] Although these provisions prescribe the means through which the State Department evaluates the efforts of foreign governments, country-specific considerations often leave State Department officials considerable discretion in categorizing countries (for further discussion, see section on "Ranking Dispute Resolution" below).

Four Minimum Standards

The TVPA identifies four *minimum standards* for the elimination of trafficking, which governments are expected to achieve:[26]

Facilitation and Trade Enforcement Act of 2015. See 19 U.S.C. 4205. The President delegated this reporting requirement to the Secretary of State. See 81 FR 35579.

[24] §108 of the TVPA, as amended; 22 U.S.C. 7106.

[25] Although the four minimum standards have not been amended since the TVPA was first enacted, §106 of the 2008 TVPRA revised a prefatory provision that specified the types of countries, which would be evaluated in TIP Reports for compliance with the minimum standards. Originally, §108 of the TVPA stated that the minimum standards were "applicable to the government of a country of origin, transit, or destination for a significant number of victims of severe forms of trafficking." §106 of the 2008 TVPRA removed from §108 of the TVPA the phrase *a significant number of*— a phrase that the State Department had previously used to limit the number of countries subject to rankings in the TIP Report.

[26] §108 of the TVPA; 22 U.S.C. 7106.

1) Governments should prohibit severe forms of trafficking in persons and punish such acts.
2) Governments should prescribe punishment commensurate with that of grave crimes for the knowing commission of any act involving sex trafficking induced by force, fraud, or coercion; sex trafficking involving a child; or any act that includes rape, kidnapping, or which causes death.
3) Governments should prescribe punishment for the knowing commission of any severe form of trafficking in persons that is sufficiently stringent to deter future acts and adequately reflect the heinous nature of the offense.
4) Governments should make *serious and sustained efforts* to eliminate severe forms of trafficking in persons.

Twelve Criteria for Serious and Sustained Efforts

In assessing whether governments are achieving the fourth minimum standard, that of making *serious and sustained efforts* to eliminate severe forms of trafficking in persons, the TVPA initially included seven criteria, or indicative factors.[27] Subsequent TVPA reauthorizations amended the TVPA to modify some of the original criteria and expand the list. There are currently 12 criteria:

1) *Enforcement and prosecution*—whether governments vigorously investigate and prosecute acts of severe forms of traffickin[28] in

[27] The Conference Report accompanying the TVPA clarified that countries are not required to meet all the listed criteria. Specifically it states: "The conferees do not expect that a government would be required to fulfill all the criteria... in order to be making 'serious and sustained efforts' to eliminate severe forms of trafficking in persons. Rather, the subsection requires only that the Secretary consider these factors in determining whether the government is making such efforts." See Conference Report to Accompany H.R. 3244, Victims of Trafficking and Violence Protection Act of 2000, H.Rept. 106-939, October 5, 2000, p. 96.

[28] This criterion was amended by §6 of the 2003 TVPRA and §106 of the 2008 TVPRA.

persons, including convicting and sentencing those responsible for such acts.

2) *Victim protection*—whether governments protect victims of severe forms of trafficking in persons, encourage their assistance in the investigation and prosecution of such trafficking, and ensure that victims are not inappropriately incarcerated, filed, or otherwise penalized for unlawful acts resulting directly from having been trafficked.[29]
3) *Trafficking prevention*—whether governments have adopted measures to prevent severe forms of trafficking in persons.[30]
4) *International cooperation*—whether governments cooperate with other governments in the investigation and prosecution of severe forms of trafficking in persons and whether governments have entered into bilateral, multilateral, or regional law enforcement cooperation and coordination arrangements with others.[31]
5) *Extradition*—whether governments extradite those charged with acts of severe forms of trafficking in persons on terms and to an extent similar to those charged with other serious crimes.
6) *Trafficking patterns and human rights protections*—whether governments monitor migration patterns for evidence of severe forms of trafficking in persons and whether law enforcement responses to such evidence are both consistent with the vigorous investigation and prosecution of acts of such trafficking and with the protection of a victim's human rights.
7) *Enforcement and prosecution of public officials*—whether governments vigorously investigate, prosecute, convict, and sentence public officials who participate in or facilitate severe forms of trafficking in persons, as well as whether governments

---

[29] This criterion was amended by §106 of the 2008 TVPRA.

[30] This criterion was amended by §104 of the 2005 TVPRA (P.L. 109-164), §106 of the 2008 TVPRA, and §1204 of the VAWRA of 2013.

[31] This criterion was amended by §1204 of the 2013 VAWRA.

take all appropriate measures against officials who condone such trafficking.[32]

8) *Foreign victims*—whether noncitizen victims of severe forms of trafficking in persons are insignificant as a percentage of all victims in a country.[33]
9) *Partnerships*—whether governments have entered into effective and transparent partnerships, cooperative arrangements, or agreements that have resulted in concrete and measurable outcomes with the United States or other external partners.[34]
10) *Self-monitoring*—whether governments systematically monitor their efforts to satisfy certain above-listed criteria and publicly share periodic assessments of such efforts.[35]
11) *Progress*—whether governments achieve appreciable progress in eliminating severe forms of trafficking in persons, compared to the previous year's assessment.[36]
12) *Demand reduction*—whether governments have made serious and sustained efforts to reduce demand for commercial sex acts and international sex tourism.[37]

ACTIONS AGAINST GOVERNMENTS FAILING TO MEET MINIMUM STANDARDS

The TVPA established that certain types of foreign assistance may not be provided to governments that are not committed to meeting the

---

[32] This criterion was amended by §6 of the 2003 TVPRA, §104 of the 2005 TVPRA, and §1204 of the 2013 VAWRA.

[33] This criterion was added by §6 of the 2003 TVPRA.

[34] This criterion was added by §1204 of the 2013 VAWRA.

[35] This criterion was added by §6 of the 2003 TVPRA (and moved by §1204 of the 2013 VAWRA).

[36] Ibid.

[37] Key elements of this criterion had previously been included in the third criterion, as added by §104 of the 2005 TVPRA. It was later moved and modified by §106 of the 2008 TVPRA and then moved again by §1204 of the 2013 VAWRA.

minimum standards for the elimination of severe forms of trafficking in persons (Tier 3 countries).

> It is the policy of the United States not to provide nonhumanitarian, non-trade-related foreign assistance to any government that—
>
> (1) does not comply with minimum standards for the elimination of trafficking; and
>
> (2) is not making significant efforts to bring itself into compliance with such standards.[38]

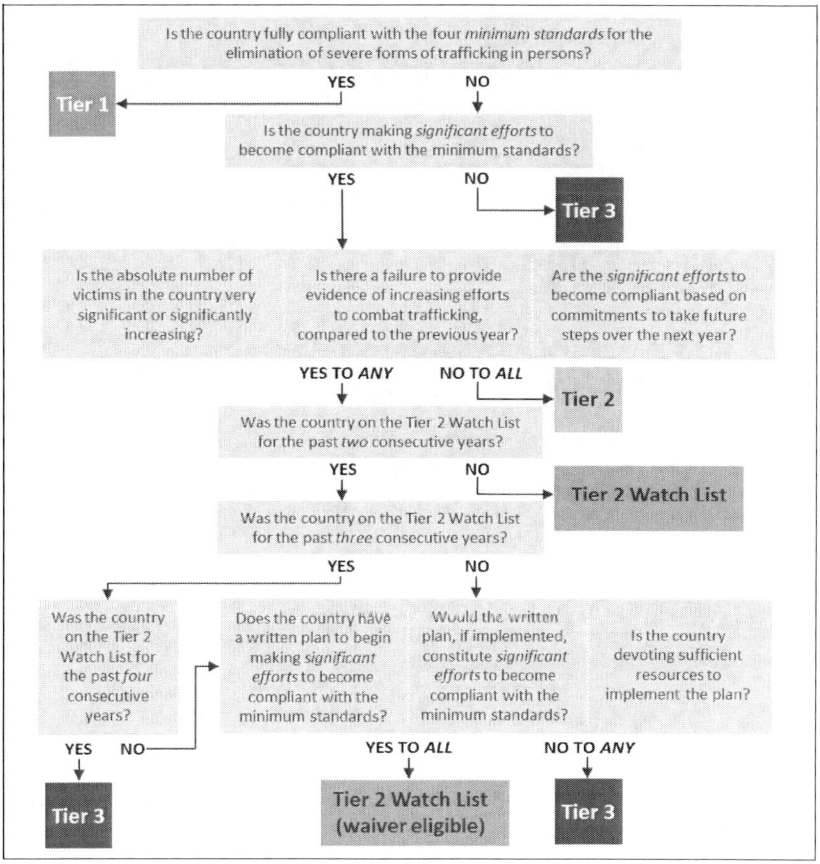

Source: CRS, based on the TVPA, as amended.

Figure 3. Country Ranking Decisions: Which Tier in the TIP Report?

[38] §110 of the TVPA; 22 U.S.C. 7107.

FAQ: What constitutes *significant efforts*?

In determining whether a government is making significant efforts to become compliant with the four minimum standards for the elimination of trafficking, the TVPA requires the Secretary of State to consider three factors:

- the extent to which a country is a source, transit, or destination for severe forms of trafficking in persons;
- the extent of noncompliance with the minimum standards by the countries, including in particular whether public officials are involved in severe forms of trafficking in persons; and
- what measures are reasonable, due to resource and capability constraints, to bring the government into compliance with the minimum standards.[39]

Aid Restrictions in the TVPA

The TVPA's provisions to restrict certain types of U.S. aid and certain other categories of U.S. and multilateral funding to Tier 3 countries began with the 2003 TIP Report. Funding subject to potential restriction includes *nonhumanitarian, non-trade-related foreign assistance* authorized pursuant to the Foreign Assistance Act of 1961, sales and financing authorized by the Arms Export Control Act (AECA), and educational and cultural exchange funding, as well as loans and other funding provided by multilateral development banks and the International Monetary Fund.

Aid Authorized by the Foreign Assistance Act of 1961

Nonhumanitarian, non-trade-related foreign assistance is defined in the TVPA[40] as assistance authorized pursuant to the Foreign Assistance Act of 1961 (FAA) except for the following:

[39] Ibid.
[40] §103 of the TVPA; 22 U.S.C. 7102.

- Assistance authorized under Chapter 4 of part II of the FAA in support of programs, projects, or activities conducted by nongovernmental organizations and eligible for Development Assistance under Chapter 1 of part I of the FAA;
- International Narcotics Control assistance authorized under chapter 8 of part I of the FAA;
- Any other counternarcotics assistance authorized under Chapters 4 or 5 of part II of the FAA (Economic Support Fund and International Military Education and Training), subject to certain congressional notification procedures;[41]
- Disaster relief assistance, including any assistance under Chapter 9 of part I of the FAA (International Disaster Assistance);
- Antiterrorism assistance authorized under Chapter 8 of part II of the FAA;
- Refugee assistance;
- Humanitarian and other development assistance in support of programs conducted by nongovernmental organizations under Chapters 1 and 10 of the FAA;[42]
- Overseas Private Investment Corporation programs authorized under Title IV of Chapter 2 of part I of the FAA; and
- Other trade-related or humanitarian assistance programs.

Sales and Financing Authorized by the Arms Export Control Act

Pursuant to the TVPA, *nonhumanitarian, non-trade-related foreign assistance* subject to aid restriction also includes

- Sales or financing on any terms authorized by the AECA—with the exception of sales or financing provided for narcotics-related purposes if congressionally notified.[43]

---

[41] For the notification procedures, see Section 634 of the FAA, as amended (22 U.S.C. 2394-1).

[42] Pursuant to notes in the U.S. Code, the TVPA's reference to Chapters 1 and 10 of the FAA probably refers to Chapters 1 and 10 of part I of the FAA, which authorize development assistance and the Development Fund for Africa.

[43] For the notification procedures, see Section 634 of the FAA, as amended (22 U.S.C. 2394-1).

Funding for Educational and Cultural Exchanges

In the case of countries that do not receive such *nonhumanitarian, non-trade-related foreign assistance*, the TVPA authorizes the President to withhold funding for participation by officials or employees of Tier 3 in educational and cultural exchange programs.[44]

Loans and Other Funds Provided by Multilateral Development Banks and the International Monetary Fund

The TVPA authorizes the President to instruct the U.S. Executive Directors of each multilateral development bank and of the International Monetary Fund to vote against and otherwise attempt to deny loans or other uses of funds to Tier 3 countries.[45]

Presidential Determinations, Waivers, and Certifications

Between 45 and 90 days after submission of the annual TIP Report (due June 1), the TVPA[46] requires the President to make a determination regarding whether and to what extent antitrafficking aid restrictions are to be imposed on Tier 3 countries during the following fiscal year. (See Table 6 below.) Typically issued near the beginning of the fiscal year and published in the *Federal Register*, the presidential determinations address the following:

- *Applicability of aid restrictions*—whether to withhold *nonhumanitarian, nontrade-related assistance* authorized by the FAA and the AECA, including whether to withhold funding for education and cultural exchanges and loans and other funds

[44] §110 of the TVPA; 22 U.S.C. 7107.

[45] Pursuant to §110 of the TVPA (22 U.S.C. 7107), the U.S. Executive Directors of each multilateral development bank and the International Monetary Fund may support loans and other uses of funds to Tier 3 countries for humanitarian assistance; trade-related assistance; or development assistance that directly addresses basic human needs, is not administered by the government of the Tier 3 country, and confers no benefit to that government.

[46] The TVPA specifies that Presidential determinations are to be made between 45 and 90 days after submission of the annual TIP Report or an "Interim Report" pursuant to §110(b)(2) of the TVPA. The Interim Report may be in reference to provision that was struck by §1205(2) of the 2013 VAWRA.

provided by multilateral development banks and the International Monetary Fund;

- *Duplication of aid restrictions*—whether ongoing, multiple, broad-based restrictions, comparable to those specified by the TVPA, on assistance in response to human rights violations are already in place;
- *Subsequent compliance*—whether the Secretary of State has found that the government of a Tier 3 country is now compliant with the minimum standards or is making significant efforts to become compliant; and
- *National interest concerns*—whether to continue assistance, in part or in whole, because it would promote the purposes of the TVPA or is otherwise in the national interest of the United States—including when the continuation of assistance is necessary to avoid significant adverse effects on vulnerable populations, such as women and children.

Pursuant to the TVPA, the President may selectively waive aid restrictions for national interest concerns, including exercise of the waiver for one or more specific programs, projects, or activities. Following the initial presidential determination required by the TVPA, as amended, the President may make additional determinations to waive, in part or in whole, aid restrictions on Tier 3 countries.[47]

As part of the President's determinations, the TVPA also requires the President to include a certification by the Secretary of State that no counternarcotics or counterterrorism assistance authorized by the FAA or arms sales and financing authorized by the AECA is intended to be received or used by any agency or official who has participated in, facilitated, or condoned a severe form of trafficking in persons.[48]

[47] §110 of the TVPA, as added by §6 of the 2003 TVPRA; 22 U.S.C. 7107.
[48] §110 of the TVPA, as amended with technical edits by §1212 of the 2013 VAWRA; 22 U.S.C. 7107.

Table 6. Aid Restrictions and Waivers for Tier 3 Countries, Pursuant to the TVPA, FY2004-FY2017

Fiscal Year	Aid Restricted	Full National Interest Waivers	Partial National Interest Waivers	Waivers due to Subsequent Compliance
FY2004	Burma, Cuba, North Korea	none	Liberia, Sudan	Belize, Bosnia and Herzegovina, Dominican Republic, Georgia, Greece, Haiti, Kazakhstan, Suriname, Turkey, Uzbekistan
FY2005	Burma, Cuba, North Korea	none	Equatorial Guinea, Sudan, Venezuela	Bangladesh, Ecuador, Guyana, Sierra Leone
FY2006	Burma, Cuba, North Korea	Ecuador, Kuwait, Saudi Arabia	Cambodia, Venezuela	Bolivia, Jamaica, Qatar, Sudan, Togo, United Arab Emirates
FY2007	Burma, Cuba, North Korea	Saudi Arabia, Sudan, Uzbekistan	Iran, Syria, Venezuela, Zimbabwe	Belize, Laos
FY2008	Burma, Cuba	Algeria, Bahrain, Malaysia, Oman, Qatar, Saudi Arabia, Sudan, Uzbekistan	Iran, North Korea, Syria, Venezuela	Equatorial Guinea, Kuwait
FY2009	Burma, Cuba, Syria	Algeria, Fiji, Kuwait, Papua New Guinea, Qatar, Saudi Arabia, Sudan	Iran, North Korea	Moldova, Oman
FY2010	Cuba, North Korea	Chad, Kuwait, Malaysia, Mauritania, Niger, Papua New Guinea, Saudi Arabia, Sudan	Burma, Eritrea, Fiji, Iran, Syria, Zimbabwe	Swaziland

Fiscal Year	Aid Restricted	Full National Interest Waivers	Partial National Interest Waivers	Waivers due to Subsequent Compliance
FY2011	Eritrea, North Korea	Democratic Republic of Congo, Dominican Republic, Kuwait, Mauritania, Papua New Guinea, Saudi Arabia, Sudan	Burma, Cuba, Iran, Zimbabwe	none
FY2012	Eritrea, Madagascar, North Korea	Algeria, Central African Republic, Guinea-Bissau, Kuwait, Lebanon, Libya, Mauritania, Micronesia, Papua New Guinea, Saudi Arabia, Sudan, Turkmenistan, Yemen	Burma*, Cuba, Democratic Republic of Congo, Equatorial Guinea, Iran, Venezuela, Zimbabwe	none
FY2013	Cuba, Eritrea, Madagascar, North Korea	Algeria, Central African Republic, Kuwait, Libya, Papua New Guinea, Saudi Arabia, Yemen	Democratic Republic of Congo, Equatorial Guinea, Iran, Sudan, Syria, Zimbabwe	none
FY2014	Cuba, Iran, North Korea	Algeria, Central African Republic, China, Guinea-Bissau, Kuwait, Libya, Mauritania, Papua New Guinea, Russia, Saudi Arabia, Uzbekistan, Yemen	Democratic Republic of Congo, Sudan, Equatorial Guinea, Eritrea, Syria, Zimbabwe	none
FY2015	Iran, North Korea, Russia	Algeria, Central African Republic, The Gambia, Guinea-Bissau, Kuwait, Libya, Malaysia, Mauritania, Papua New Guinea, Saudi Arabia, Thailand, Uzbekistan, Yemen	Cuba, Democratic Republic of Congo, Equatorial Guinea, Eritrea, Syria, Venezuela, Zimbabwe	none

Table 6. (Continued)

Fiscal Year	Aid Restricted	Full National Interest Waivers	Partial National Interest Waivers	Waivers due to Subsequent Compliance
FY2016	Iran, North Korea	Algeria, Belarus, Belize, Burundi, Central African Republic, Comoros, The Gambia, Guinea-Bissau, Kuwait, Libya, Marshall Islands, Mauritania, Thailand	Equatorial Guinea, Eritrea, Russia, South Sudan, Syria, Venezuela, Yemen, Zimbabwe	none
FY2017	Iran, North Korea	Algeria, Belarus, Belize, Burma, Burundi, Central African Republic, Comoros, Djibouti, The Gambia, Guinea-Bissau, Haiti, Marshall Islands, Mauritania, Papua New Guinea, Suriname, Turkmenistan, Uzbekistan	Equatorial Guinea, Eritrea, Russia, South Sudan, Sudan, Syria, Venezuela, Zimbabwe	none

Sources: Determination of the President of the United States, Nos. 2003-35 (68 FR 53871), 2004-46 (69 FR 56155), 2005-37 (70 FR 57481), 2006-25 (71 FR 64431), 2008-4 (72 FR 61037), 2009-5 (73 FR 63839), 2009-29 (74 FR 48365), 2010-15 (75 FR 67017, 68411), 2011-18 (76 FR 62599), 2012-16 (77 FR 58921, as amended by 77 FR 61046), 2013-16 (78 FR 58861), 2014-16 (79 FR 57699), 2016-01 (80 FR 62435), 2016-12 (81 FR 7031 1).

Notes: Following the President's delegation of authority on February 3, 2012 (see 77 FR 11375), the Secretary of State revised Presidential Determination No. 2011-18 on February 6, 2012, to waive prohibitions on U.S. support for assistance to Burma through international financial institutions. See U.S. Department of State Public Notice No. 7799 (77 FR 9295). Other presidential delegations of authority were issued on July 29, 2013, for Syria (78 FR 48027) and on October 5, 2015, for Yemen (78 FR 6505).

Security Assistance Restrictions in the CSPA

Countries listed in the current TIP Report as having recruited and used child soldiers are prohibited from receiving certain types of security assistance, including

- excess defense articles;[49]
- international military education and training;[50]
- peacekeeping operations and other programs;[51]
- foreign military financing for the procurement of defense articles and services, as well as design and construction services;[52] and
- issuance of licenses for direct commercial sales of military equipment to countries listed in the current TIP Report for child soldiers recruitment and use.

(For further discussion about the CSPA's relationship to security cooperation programs and activities, see text box "FAQs on Child Soldiers Prohibitions")

Exceptions and Presidential Determinations, Certifications, and Waivers

CSPA security assistance restrictions may not apply if one of four circumstances is invoked. (See Table 7 below.)

Peacekeeping Exception

Assistance may continue to child soldier countries for peacekeeping operations that support military professionalization, security sector reform,

---

[49] As authorized by §516 of the FAA, as amended; 22 U.S.C. 2321j.
[50] As authorized by §541 of the FAA, as amended; 22 U.S.C. 2347.
[51] As authorized by §551 of the FAA, as amended; 22 U.S.C. 2348.
[52] As authorized by §23 of the Arms Export Control Act, as amended; 22 U.S.C. 2763.

heightened respect for human rights, peacekeeping preparation, or the demobilization and reintegration of child soldiers.

International Military Education and Training and Nonlethal Supplies Exception

Assistance for international military education, training, and nonlethal supplies to child solider countries may continue for up to five years, if the President certifies to appropriate congressional committees that such assistance will directly support professionalization of the military. The President must also certify that the country is taking "reasonable steps to implement effective measures to demobilize child soldiers ... and is taking reasonable steps in the context of its national resources to provide demobilization, rehabilitation, and reintegration assistance to those former child soldiers."

National Interest Waiver

The President may waive the CSPA security assistance restrictions if it is determined that such a waiver is in the national interest of the United States and the President submits a notification and justification to appropriate congressional committees within 45 days of granting a waiver. The presidential determination is also typically published in the *Federal Register*, though the President's memorandum of justification is not. (See Table 7 below.)

Reinstatement Certification

Security assistance otherwise prohibited by the CSPA may be reinstated if the President certifies to appropriate congressional committees that the government of the listed country has (1) implemented measures, including an action plan and actual steps to stop recruiting and using child soldiers, and (2) implemented policies and mechanisms to prohibit and prevent future use of child soldiers.

Table 7. Aid Restrictions and Waivers to Child Soldier Countries, Pursuant to the CSPA, FY2011-FY2017

Fiscal Year	Aid Restricted	Full National Interest Waivers	Partial National Interest Waivers	Waivers Due to Subsequent Compliance
FY2011	Burma, Somalia	Chad, Democratic Republic of Congo, Sudan, Yemen	none	none
FY2012	Burma, Somalia, Sudan	Yemen	Democratic Republic of Congo	Chad
FY2013	Burma, Sudan	Libya, South Sudan, Yemen	Democratic Republic of Congo, Somalia[a]	none
FY2014	Burma, Central African Republic, Rwanda, Sudan, Syria	Chad, South Sudan, Yemen	Democratic Republic of Congo, Somalia	none
FY2015	Burma, Sudan, Syria	Rwanda, Somalia, Yemen	Central African Republic, Democratic Republic of Congo, South Sudan	none
FY2016	Burma, Sudan, Syria, Yemen	Democratic Republic of Congo, Nigeria, Somalia	South Sudan	none
FY2017	Syria, Yemen, Sudan	Burma, Iraq, Nigeria	Democratic Republic of Congo, Rwanda, Somalia, South Sudan	none

Sources: Determination of the President of the United States, Nos. 2011-4 (75 FR 75855), 2012-01 (76 FR 65927), 2012-18 (77 FR 61509), 2013-17 (78 FR 63367), 2014-18 (79 FR 69755), 2015-13 (80 FR 62431), 2016- 14 (81 FR 72683).

[a] Following the President's delegation of authority on August 2, 2013 (see 78 FR 72789), the Secretary of State revised Presidential Determination No. 2012-18 on August 14, 2013, to partially waive restrictions on Somalia to allow for assistance under the Peacekeeping Operations authority for logistical support and troop stipends in FY2013. This State Department decision was not published in the *Federal Register*. In at least two other years, the President also delegated authority to the Secretary of State to make additional CSPA determinations with respect to Yemen: on September 29, 2015 (80 FR 62429), and on September 28, 2016 (81 FR 72681).

SECURITY ASSISTANCE RESTRICTIONS IN FY2017 APPROPRIATIONS

The Consolidated Appropriations Act, 2017 (P.L. 115-31), contains two provisions that additionally prohibit certain types of security assistance from being used to support military training or operations that involve child soldiers. Similar provisions have also been included in prior appropriations measures in recent years.

- Section 8088 of the Department of Defense Appropriations Act, 2017 (Division C of P.L. 115-31), states that CSPA-listed countries may not receive certain funds appropriated by this act "to support any military training or operation that includes child soldiers" unless the President issues a determination pursuant to the CPSA that permits such assistance.[53]
- Section 7034(b)(1) of the Department of State, Foreign Operations, and Related Programs Appropriations Act, 2017 (Division J of P.L. 115-31), states that funds appropriated by this act "should not be used to support any military training or operations that include child soldiers."[54]

---

[53] Specified funds, subject to restriction in Section 8088 of the FY2017 Defense Department Appropriations Act, include those made available for excess defense articles, assistance under Section 1206 of the National Defense Authorization Act for Fiscal Year 2006, and peacekeeping operations. Similar provisions have been included in recent past Defense Department Appropriations Acts. For FY2016, see Section 8088 of P.L. 114-113; for FY2015, see Section 8092 of P.L. 113-235; for FY2014, see Section 8116 of P.L. 113-76; for FY2013, see Section 8115 of P.L. 113 6; and for FY2012, see Section 8128 of P.L. 112-74.

[54] Similar provisions have been included in recent past Department of State, Foreign Operations, and Related Programs Appropriations Acts. For FY2016, see Section 7034(b)(1) of P.L. 114-113; for FY2015 see "peacekeeping operations" heading under Title IV of P.L. 113-235; for FY2014, see "peacekeeping operations" heading under Title IV of P.L. 113-76; for FY2013, see Section 1101 (extending Department of State, Foreign Operations, and Related Programs Appropriations Act, 2012) of Title I, Division F of P.L. 113-6; for FY2012, see "peacekeeping operations" heading under Title IV of P.L. 112-74; and for FY2011, see Section 2111 (adding a child soldiers provision to the extension of FY2010 appropriations provisions for "peacekeeping operations") of Title XI of P.L. 112-10.

FAQs on Child Soldiers Prohibitions

Are countries that recruit and use child soldiers eligible to receive DOD security assistance?

Despite the CSPA and recent provisions in annual appropriations acts, it may be possible for CSPA-listed countries to receive U.S. security assistance. One category of such assistance may include security cooperation programs and activities authorized in Title 10 of the U.S. Code (Armed Forces), funded in annual Defense Appropriations, and executed by the U.S. Department of Defense (DOD). Although the FY20 17 Defense Department Appropriations Act prohibits a few types of security assistance, most Title 10 security cooperation authorities are not addressed.

Has the President waived or partially waived DOD security assistance in annual CSPA determinations?

Presidential determinations to waive or partially waive CSPA security assistance restrictions have made reference in the past to some DOD security cooperation authorities that have been used to provide assistance to countries identified as recruiting and using child soldiers. In the most recent presidential determination with respect to the CSPA, issued by then-President Barack Obama on September 28, 2016, Somalia received a partial waiver to receive assistance in FY2017 authorized pursuant to 10 U.S.C. 2282.[55] South Sudan received a partial waiver to receive assistance in FY2017 authorized pursuant to Section 1208 of the FY2014 NDAA.[56]

Are security forces units that recruit and use children banned from assistance under the Leahy Laws?

The U.S. Leahy Laws—codified at 22 U.S.C. 2378d and 10 U.S.C. 362—prohibit U.S. security assistance otherwise provided by the U.S. Departments of State and Defense to foreign security forces when there is credible information that a recipient unit has committed a gross violation of human rights (GVHR). Although the recruitment and use of child soldiers is often described as a human rights concern, it is not specifically addressed by the Leahy Laws, which do not define GVHR. As a matter of policy, the U.S. government vets for credible information that indicates (1) torture, (2) extrajudicial killing, (3) enforced disappearance, or (4) rape under color of law.

---

55 See Determination of the President of the United States No. 2016-14 (81 FR 72683). 10 U.S.C. 2282, used by DOD to train, equip, and build the capacity of foreign security forces for counterterrorism and military or stability operations, may not be used to provide assistance "that is otherwise prohibited by any provision of law." Moreover, it may not be used to provide assistance "to any foreign country that is otherwise prohibited from receiving such type of assistance under any other provision of law."

56 Section 1208 of the FY2014 NDAA, used by DOD to support operations to counter the Lord's Resistance Army, may not be used to provide assistance "that is otherwise prohibited by any provision of law."

Trade Restrictions in the TPA

Pursuant to the Bipartisan Congressional Trade Priorities and Accountability Act of 2015 (TPA), as amended, trade authorities procedures may not apply to any implementing bill submitted with respect to an international trade agreement involving the government of a country listed as Tier 3 in the most recent annual TIP Report.[57] The trade authorities procedures described in the TPA are critical for the fast-tracking of international trade agreements, such as a free trade agreement.

The Trade Facilitation and Trade Enforcement Act of 2015 created an exception to the TPA's initial prohibitions.[58] This exception authorizes trade agreement negotiations to proceed with Tier 3 countries, but only if the President specifies in a letter to appropriate congressional committees that the country in question has taken "concrete actions to implement the principal recommendations with respect to that country in the past recent annual report on trafficking in persons."[59] The letter must include a description of the *concrete actions* and supporting documentation of *credible evidence* of each concrete action (e.g., copies of relevant laws, regulations, and enforcement actions take, as appropriate). Moreover, the letter must be made available to the public.

TIP Report Methodology

The TVPA created the Office to Monitor and Combat Trafficking in Persons (J/TIP) within the State Department, whose director holds the rank of Ambassador-at-Large.[60] The J/TIP director is charged with overseeing

---

[57] §106 of the TPA added this statutory restriction; it was subsequently amended by §914 of the Trade Facilitation and Trade Enforcement Act of 2015; See 19 U.S.C. 4205.

[58] §914 of the Trade Facilitation and Trade Enforcement Act of 2015.

[59] *Appropriate congressional committees* in §106 of the TPA, as amended, refer to the Senate Finance Committee, SFRC, House Ways and Means Committee, and HFAC (the TVPA, in contrast, uses the term to refer to the SFRC, SJUD, HFAC, and HJUD). The definition was added by §914 of the Trade Facilitation and Trade Enforcement Act of 2015; 19 U.S.C. 4205. The President delegated this authority to the Secretary of State. See 81 FR 35579.

[60] §105 of the TVPA; 22 U.S.C. 7103.

the annual publication of the TIP Report, among other responsibilities laid out in the TVPA. In parallel to the drafting of the introductory material and the country narratives, the department's Bureau of Democracy, Human Rights, and Labor (DRL) initiates the process for identifying countries to be included in the list of governments that recruit and use child soldiers. Although not specified in law, each TIP Report typically covers country developments beginning in April of each year and ending in March of the following year.

Information Sources

According to the State Department, information used to prepare the report is based on a variety of sources, including U.S. embassies, government officials, nongovernmental and international organizations, published reports, news articles, academic studies, and research trips. U.S. diplomatic posts and domestic agencies report on human trafficking issues throughout the year and the TIP Report incorporates information based on meetings with government officials, local and international non-governmental representatives, officials of international organizations, journalists, academics, and survivors.

Global Law Enforcement Data

Pursuant to the TVPA reauthorization of 2003, Congress added a new criterion for governments to achieve full compliance with the minimum standards for the elimination of severe forms of trafficking in persons: providing the State Department with data on trafficking investigations, prosecutions, convictions, and sentences.[61] (See Figure 4.) Beginning with the 2004 TIP Report, the State Department has included this information in its TIP Reports—on a country-by-country basis, as well as in aggregate on a global and regional basis.

[61] §108 of the TPVA, as amended by §6 of the 2003 TVPRA.

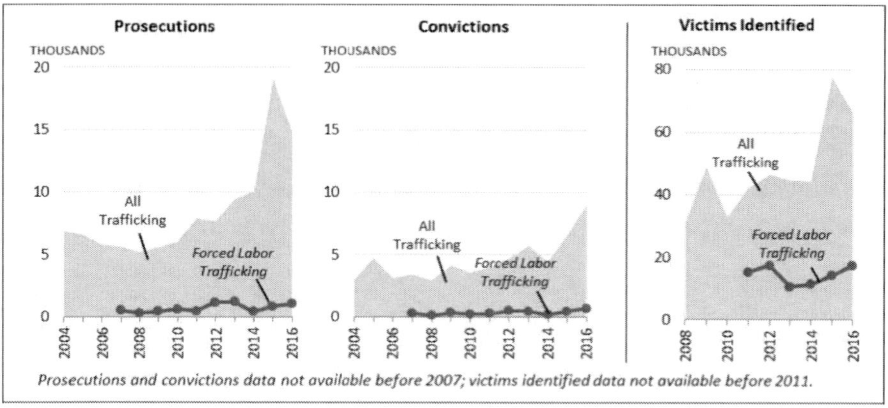

Source: CRS based on U.S. Department of State, TIP Reports, June 14, 2010, p. 45, and June 28, 2017, p. 34.

Notes: According to the most recent TIP Report (2017), with data covering the years 2009-20 1 6:"The above statistics are estimates derived from data provided by foreign governments and other sources and reviewed by the Department of State. Aggregate data fluctuates from one year to the next due to the hidden nature of trafficking crimes, dynamic global events, shifts in government efforts, and a lack of uniformity in national reporting structures. The numbers in parentheses are those of labor trafficking prosecutions, convictions, and victims identified."

Figure 4. Global Law Enforcement Data from TIP Reports, 2004-2016.

Information on Forced Labor

Pursuant to Title XII of the Violence Against Women Reauthorization Act of 2013, Congress requires the Departments of State and Labor to share information on forced labor, with the objective of informing both the State Department's TIP Report and the Labor Department's report on goods produced by forced or child labor in violation of international standards.[62]

Illustrative Draft Cycle

The annual process for drafting and releasing the TIP Report involves a period of worldwide information gathering, followed by an intense

[62] §105 of the 2005 TVPRA, as amended by §1232 of the 2013 VAWRA; 22 U.S.C. 7112.

process of report drafting, led by J/TIP, but involving significant input from U.S. diplomatic missions and consular posts overseas as well as regional and functional bureaus. (See Figure 5.) According to the State Department's Office of Inspector General (OIG), the annual rush to meet the report's statutory release deadline has often led to tensions and disagreements between bureaus and J/TIP regarding the draft country narratives and proposed tier rankings.[63]

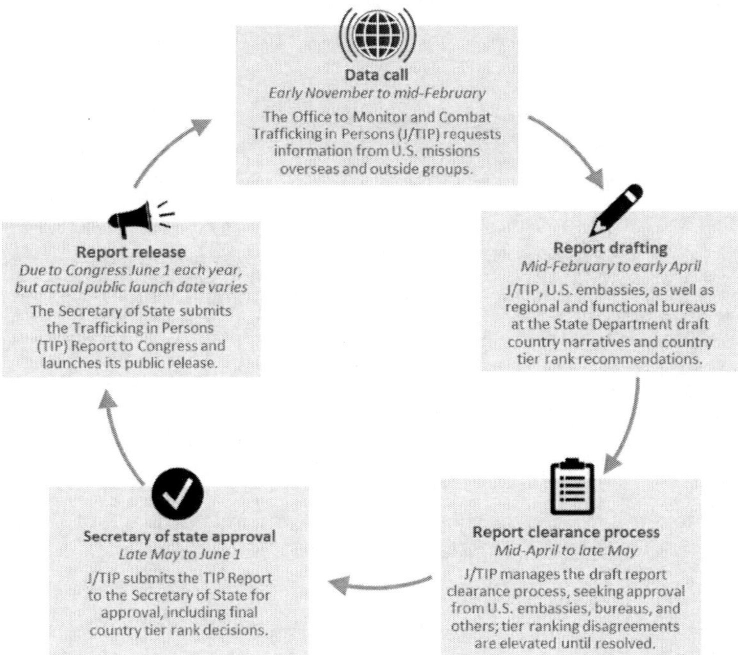

Source: U.S. Government Accountability Office (GAO), Human Trafficking: State Has Made Improvements in Its Annual Report but Does Not Explicitly Explain Certain Tier Rankings or Changes, GAO-17-56, December 2016 and U.S. Department of State and the Broadcasting Board of Governors, Office of Inspector General, Inspection of the Office to Monitor and Combat Trafficking in Persons, ISP-I-12-37, June 2012.

Figure 5. TIP Report: Typical Draft and Review Process.

---

[63] U.S. Department of State and the Broadcasting Board of Governors, Office of Inspector General, *Inspection of the Office to Monitor and Combat Trafficking in Persons*, ISP-I-12-37, June 2012.

FAQ: What other required reports address international human trafficking matters?

Congress requires the executive branch to prepare and submit several other reports that address, at least in part, human trafficking matters. These include reports prepared by the Departments of State, Justice, and Labor.

- State Department. The TVPA and the CSPA require the State Department's annual Country Reports on Human Rights Practices to include information on human trafficking and child soldiers. In practice, the State Department satisfies this requirement by including a heading on *Trafficking in Persons* for each country in the report and a subheading on *Child Soldiers* for the CSPA-listed countries, referring and hyperlinking to the TIP Report. The most recent version of this report was released in 2017, covering human rights practices in 2016.
- Justice Department. The TVPA's reauthorization in 2003 added a provision to require the Attorney General to annually report, beginning in 2004, on U.S. government efforts to combat trafficking in persons.[64] The most recent publicly available edition of this report covers FY2015.
- Labor Department. The TVPA's reauthorization in 2005 added a provision to require the Bureau of International Labor Affairs to develop and make available a public list of goods from countries it has reason to believe are produced by forced labor or child labor in violation of international standards.[65] The list was most recently updated in September 2016. The Labor Department is also responsible for preparing an annual report on the Worst Forms of Child Labor.[66]

Over time, the report draft cycle has evolved. Beginning with preparations for the 2010 TIP Report, for example, the State Department

[64] §6 of the 2003 TVPRA amended §105 of the TPVA; it was also amended by §205 of the 2005 TVPRA, §§231 and 304 of the 2008 TVPRA, and §1231 of the 2013 VAWRA. See 22 U.S.C. 7103.

[65] §105 of the 2005 TVPRA, as amended by §§1232 and 1233 of the 2013 VAWRA; 22 U.S.C. 7112.

[66] §412 of the Trade and Development Act of 200 (P.L. 106-200) amended the Trade Act of 1974 (P.L. 93-618) to create this reporting requirement on the worst forms of child labor; 19 U.S.C. 2464.

began to issue annual notices in the *Federal Register*, requesting information from nongovernmental groups on whether governments meet the TVPA's minimum standards for the elimination of trafficking.[67] A 2012 OIG inspection report of the J/TIP Office identified several other internal process changes that resulted in a significant reduction of tier ranking disputes.[68]

FAQ: How has Congress reacted to Malaysia's ranking in recent TIP reports?

Many observers alleged that Malaysia's rankings in the 2015 and 2016 TIP Reports were influenced by factors unrelated to the Malaysian government's efforts to eradicate human trafficking. After four consecutive years on the Tier 2 Watch List from 2010 through 2013, Malaysia was downgraded in 2014, as required by law, to Tier 3 for lack of significant progress to combat human trafficking. In 2015 and 2016, however, the State Department ranked Malaysia as a Tier 2 Watch List country (see Figure 6 below).

The timing of the State Department's upgrade in 2015 was criticized by outside advocacy groups and many Members of Congress as politically motivated by the Trans-Pacific Partnership (TPP) trade deal negotiations with Malaysia, which were ongoing at the time. Just before release of the 2015 TIP Report, the 114th Congress enacted the TPA, which specified that authorities for fast-tracking trade deals like the TPP would not be applicable to Tier 3 countries.

Following the June 30, 2016, release of the 2016 TIP Report, in which Malaysia remained on the Tier 2 Watch List for a second consecutive year, several Members of Congress continued to express concerns over Malaysia's ranking. In the 2017 TIP Report, the department upgraded Malaysia to Tier 2. While Malaysian officials point to this year's TIP Report ranking as proof of the country's improved commitment to combating human trafficking, advocacy groups have expressed skepticism.

---

67 For the 2017 TIP Report, see 81 FR 90039.

68 Ibid, p. 8. Among the changes identified by the OIG report were the inclusion of footnotes in internal drafts and the use of SharePoint software to make country-specific information accessible across different parts of the State Department.

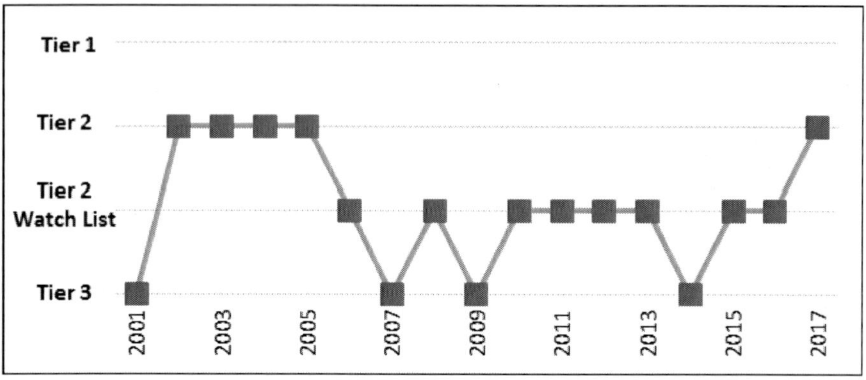

Source: U.S. Department of State, *TIP Reports*, 2001-2017.

Notes: Malaysia received full waivers from aid restrictions when it was rated Tier 3 in 2007, 2009, and 2014.

Figure 6. Malaysia: Historical TIP Rankings, 2001-2017.

Ranking Dispute Resolution

Although Congress has prescribed a range of expectations for the elimination of trafficking, ranking designations are not based on a concrete formula. Rather, country-specific considerations often leave State Department officials considerable discretion in categorizing countries. Consequently, some country rankings, initially proposed by J/TIP in early drafts of the TIP Report, have reportedly been disputed by other parts of the State Department, including regional bureaus and senior leadership. According to the 2012 OIG report, "the number of tier-ranking disputes between regional bureaus and J/TIP declined from 46 percent of all countries ranked in 2006 to 22 percent of those ranked in 2011."[69]

On August 3, 2015, a *Reuters* news article reported that tier-ranking disputes for 2015 TIP Report involved 17 countries and that the J/TIP Office "won only three of those disputes, the worst ratio in the 15-year history of the unit."[70] The article indicated that countries whose rankings were disputed included China, Cuba, India, Malaysia, Mexico, and

[69] Ibid.

[70] Jason Szep and Matt Spetalnick, "Special Report: State Department Watered Down Human Trafficking Report," *Reuters*, August 3, 2015.

Uzbekistan—all of which reportedly received better rankings than the J/TIP Office had recommended. The article further reported that, typically, J/TIP "wins more than half" of the tier-ranking disputes.

In testimony before the Senate Foreign Relations Committee, J/TIP Director and Ambassador-at-Large Susan Coppedge declined to identify the specific number of tier-ranking disputes that preceded the release of the 2016 TIP Report. She noted, however, that the "vast majority" of the State Department's staff recommendations to the Secretary of State—encompassing those of J/TIP and the regional bureaus—were consensus recommendations.[71] In testimony before the Senate Foreign Relations Committee on the 2017 TIP Report, Coppedge noted that department staff could not agree on five countries' tier rankings.[72]

On June 24, 2017, a *Reuters* news article reported that Secretary of State Tillerson removed Burma and Iraq from the child soldiers list, overruling his own staff's assessments that children remain in the ranks of the Burmese Army and Iraqi government-affiliated militias.[73] Advocacy groups have also long suggested that Afghanistan be included on the child soldiers list—a proposal that was reportedly floated within the State Department this year as well.[74] According to the same *Reuters* article, an anonymous official stated that Tillerson's decision to leave Iraq and Afghanistan off the list was "made following pressure from the Pentagon to avoid complicating assistance to the Iraqi and Afghan militaries."

Allegations of Political Influence in Country Rankings

Although many observers view the TIP Report as a credible reflection of global efforts to address human trafficking, some have been critical of the methodology used to evaluate foreign country efforts and assign tier

---

[71] CQ transcript of SFRC hearing on "Review of the 2016 Trafficking in Persons Report," July 12, 2016.

[72] CQ transcript of SFRC hearing on "Review of the 2017 Trafficking in Persons Report," July 13, 2017.

[73] Szep and Spetalnick, "Exclusive: Overruling Diplomats, U.S. to Drop Iraq, Myanmar from Child Soldiers' List," *Reuters*, June 24, 2017.

[74] See for example "U.S.: Return Burma, Iraq to Child Soldier List," *Human Rights Watch*, June 26, 2017.

rankings. In a 2012 OIG report, the TIP Report was praised as having "gained wide credibility for its thoroughness" and "recognized as the definitive work by the anti-trafficking community on the status of anti-trafficking efforts."[75] The OIG report, however, also noted that some view the TIP Report as subjective and influenced by political pressures.

In December 2016, the U.S. Government Accountability Office (GAO) issued a report assessing the State Department's TIP Report and country ranking procedures.[76] In general, the State Department describes its tier ranking designations as not based on a concrete formula, but rather country-specific considerations that leave department officials considerable discretion. In analyzing its TIP Report methodology, the December 2016 GAO report assessed that the State Department lacked consistent and explicit explanations to justify upgrades and downgrades, which the report found problematic. It stated: "The lack of an explicit explanation for most of State's decisions to upgrade or downgrade countries to a different tier could limit the ability of internal and external stakeholders to understand the justification for tier changes and, in turn, use the report as a diplomatic tool to advance efforts to combat trafficking."[77]

Report Release

Although not required by law, the State Department has always publicly released the report and the Secretary of State has personally presided over the launch of the annual TIP Report. The report, however, has never been published by its statutory June 1 deadline.[78] In addition to the statutory deadline for the annual release of the report, current law includes two other provisions related to the TIP Report's release, one that

---

[75] ISP-I-12-37 (June 2012).
[76] GAO-17-56 (December 2016).
[77] Ibid.
[78] Publications dates of the TIP Report were as follows: July 12, 2001; June 19, 2002; June 11, 2003; June 14, 2004; June 3, 2005; June 5, 2006; June 12, 2007; June 4, 2008; June 16, 2009; June 14, 2010; June 27, 2011; June 19, 2012; July 11, 2013; June 20, 2014; July 27, 2015; June 30, 2016; and June 28, 2017.

requires its translation and a second that connects the report's release with the presentation of the *Presidential Award for Extraordinary Efforts to Combat Trafficking in Persons.*

Translation Requirement

Pursuant to the Advance Democratic Values, Address Nondemocratic Countries, and Enhance Democracy Act of 2007, the Secretary of State is required to "expand the timely translation of applicable parts" of the TIP Report, among other reports prepared by the State Department.[79] Current law further specifies that the applicable parts of the TIP Report are to be translated "into the principal languages of as many countries as possible, with particular emphasis on nondemocratic countries, democratic transition countries, and countries in which extrajudicial killings, torture, or other serious violations of human rights have occurred."[80]

Award Ceremony

Pursuant to the TVPA reauthorization of 2008, the timing of the TIP Report's release corresponds to a requirement for the Secretary of State to host an annual ceremony for recipients of the Presidential Award for Extraordinary Efforts to Combat Trafficking in Persons.[81] Current law provides that the Secretary-hosted ceremony occur "as soon as practicable after the date on which the Secretary submits to Congress the [TIP R]eport...."[82]

---

[79] See §2122 of Title XXI of the Advance Democratic Values, Address Nondemocratic Countries, and Enhance Democracy Act of 2007 (P.L. 110-53); 22 U.S.C. 8222. See also §107 of the 2008 TVPRA; 22 U.S.C. 7107 note.

[80] The provision, codified at 22 U.S.C. 8222, additionally required the Secretary of State to submit annual reports to appropriate congressional committees in 2008 through 2010 on the status of the law's implementation.

[81] §112B of the TVPA, as added by §109 of the 2008 TVPRA; 22 U.S.C. 7109b.

[82] The provision, codified at 22 U.S.C. 7109b, additionally authorizes the Secretary of State to pay the travel costs for each award recipient and for a guest of each recipient who attends the ceremony. For the fiscal years 2008 through 2011, Congress had authorized to be appropriated such sums as may be necessary to carry out the provision. This authority has since lapsed.

HUMAN TRAFFICKING TRENDS

An implicit objective of the TVPA was to leverage the country ranking process of the TIP Report as a foreign policy tool to motivate foreign governments to prioritize and address human trafficking.

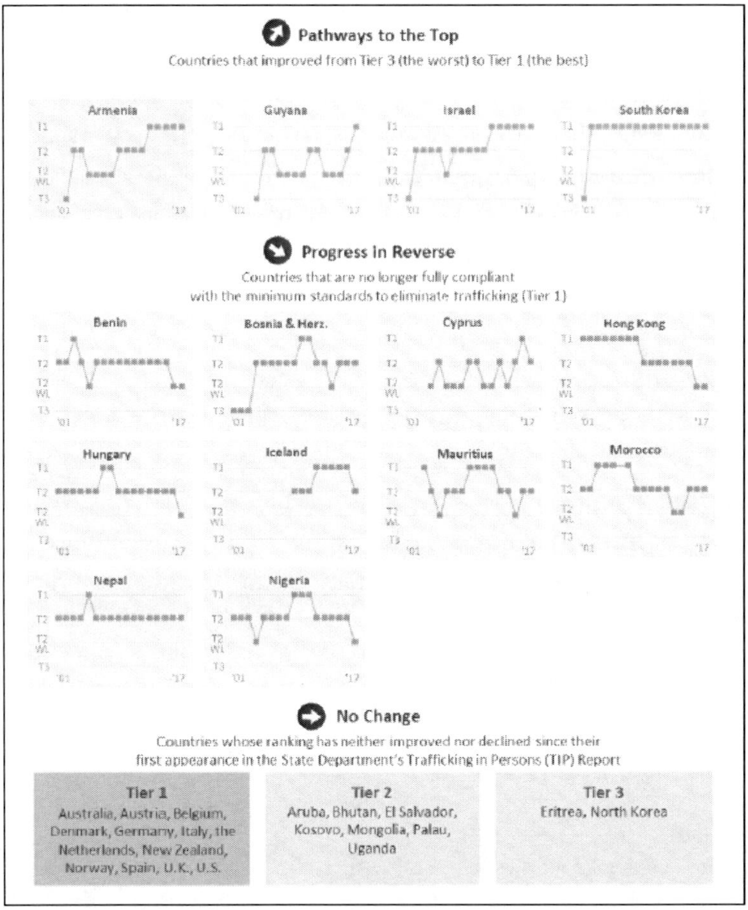

Source: U.S. Department of State, *TIP Reports*, 2001-2017.

Figure 7. Selected TIP Report Country Ranking Trends: Pathways, Progress, and Change, 2001-2017.

Some suggest the TIP Report can be used as a potent form of soft power as both a "name-and-shame" or "blacklist" process and a mechanism for country-by-country monitoring of antitrafficking progress. In theory, publications like the TIP Report can mobilize domestic and international pressure for policy change.[83] In practice, while some countries appear to be responsive to the TIP Report, others remain intractable. Out of 187 countries ranked in the 2017 TIP Report, 36 countries were ranked Tier 1 and more than 80% of the ranked countries in this year's TIP Report remained noncompliant with the minimum standards laid out by the TVPA for eliminating trafficking in persons.

Pathways to the Top

Several countries' rankings have improved from noncompliant to Tier 1, including

- *Armenia,* which was rated Tier 3 in 2002 and eventually improved to Tier 1 by 2013.
- *Guyana,* which was rated Tier 3 in the 2004 and experienced multiple years on the Tier 2 Watch List before attaining a Tier 1 rating for the first time in 2017.
- *Israel,* which was rated Tier 3 in 2001 and eventually improved to Tier 1 by 2012.
- *South Korea,* which was rated Tier 3 in 2001 and immediately improved to Tier 1 the following year.

Progress in Reverse

Other countries, which used to be fully compliant with the minimum standards to eliminate trafficking (Tier 1), have since become noncompliant, including

---

[83] Judith G. Kelley and Beth A. Simmons, "Politics by Numbers: Indicators of Social Pressure in International Relations," *American Journal of Political Science*, Vol. 59, No. 1 (January 2015), pp. 55-70.

- *Benin,* which attained Tier 1 status in 2003, but after many years on Tier 2, further declined to the Tier 2 Watch List in 2016 and 2017.
- *Bosnia and Herzegovina,* which began as a Tier 3 country in 2001, attained Tier 1 status in 2010, but later declined to Tier 2 Watch List in 2014. It has been a Tier 2 country since 2015.
- *Cyprus*, which attained Tier 1 status in 2016 after many years vacillating between Tier 2 and Tier 2 Watch List, dropped back down to Tier 2 in 2017.
- *Hong Kong,* which began as a Tier 1 country in 2001 and remained so until 2008. In 2009, it dropped to Tier 2 and dropped again in 2016 to Tier 2 Watch List, where it remained in 2017.
- *Hungary,* which attained Tier 1 status in 2007, but dropped to Tier 2 Watch List in 2017.
- *Iceland,* which attained Tier 1 status in 2012, but dropped to Tier 2 in 2017.
- *Mauritius,* which began as a Tier 1 country in 2003 and has since vacillated between compliant and noncompliant. After dropping to Tier 2 Watch List in 2015, it rose to Tier 2 in 2016, where it remained in 2017.
- *Morocco,* which attained Tier 1 status in 2003, but has been rated Tier 2 since 2015.
- *Nepal,* which attained Tier 1 status in 2005, but has since been rated Tier 2.
- *Nigeria,* which attained Tier 1 status in 2009, but dropped to Tier 2 Watch List in 2017.

No Change

The rankings of several other countries have been unchanged.

- *Unchanged Tier 1:* Australia, Austria, Belgium, Denmark, Germany, Italy, the Netherlands, New Zealand, Norway, Spain, United Kingdom, and United States.[84]
- *Unchanged Tier 2:* Aruba, Bhutan, El Salvador, Kosovo, Mongolia, Palau, and Uganda.[85]
- *Unchanged Tier 3:* Eritrea and North Korea.[86]

Of the 45 countries on the Tier 2 Watch List in the 2017 TIP Report, 22 had been Tier 2 Watch List in 2016 and 9 required waivers to remain on the Tier 2 Watch List for their third or fourth consecutive year. (See Table 4 for the list of Tier 2 Watch List countries in the 2017 TIP Report and discussion in section on "Watch List Downgrades" above.)

LEGISLATIVE OVERSIGHT AND OUTLOOK

The State Department's TIP Report is highly anticipated each year in Congress, with congressional oversight and evaluation taking the form of hearings, requests for GAO reports, and legislation.

- *Hearings.* In recent years, the Senate Foreign Relations Committee has held closed briefings with State Department officials in anticipation of the TIP Report's release as well as public hearings after its publication.[87] The House Foreign Affairs Committee,

[84] Denmark and Norway were first ranked in 2003, Australia and New Zealand were first ranked in 2005, and the United States was first ranked in 2010.

[85] Mongolia was first ranked in 2005, Kosovo and Palau were first ranked in 2009, Aruba was first ranked in 2011, and Bhutan was first ranked in 2013.

[86] North Korea was first ranked in 2003 and Eritrea was first ranked in 2009.

[87] See SFRC hearings in the 115th and 114th Congresses: "Review of the 2017 Trafficking in Persons Report," July 13, 2017; "Closed: Preparing for the 2017 Trafficking in Persons Report," June 21, 2017; "Ending Modern Slavery: Building on Success," February 15, 2017; "Closed/Secret: Trafficking in Persons: Preparing the 2016 Annual Report," May 25, 2016; "Review of the 2016 Trafficking in Persons Report," July 12, 2016; "Closed Briefing: State Department Processes in Establishing Tier Rankings for the 2015 Trafficking in Persons Report," September 17, 2015; "Review of the 2015 Trafficking in Persons Report," August 6, 2015.

particularly its Subcommittee on Africa, Global Health, Global Human Rights, and International Organizations, has also long held hearings on the TIP Report.[88]

- *Comptroller reports.* To date, GAO has prepared two reports that directly address the State Department's TIP Report, one in 2006 and a second in 2016.[89] Both contain GAO recommendations that remain pending or unimplemented.
- *Legislation in the 115th Congress.* Several bills in the 115th Congress have been introduced to further modify requirements associated with the TIP Report, including H.R. 2200, the Frederick Douglass Trafficking Victims Prevention and Protection Reauthorization Act of 2017, which passed the House on July 12, 2017, and contains several changes to the TIP Report's country ranking process. Other bills introduced in the 115th Congress that, if passed, would modify requirements associated with the TIP Report include H.R. 436, the Human Trafficking Prioritization Act; S. 377, the Trafficking in Persons Report Integrity Act; H.R. 1191, the Child Soldier Prevention Act of 2017; and H.R. 2219 and S. 952, the End Banking for Human Traffickers Act of 2017.

Common themes in the legislative proposals to modify the TIP Report's methodology focus on reducing the prospects for political interference, while also increasing public transparency and congressional oversight into the State Department's country ranking process.

A key focus of the proposals involves changes to the special watch list or Tier 2 Watch List. Various bills seek to modify:

---

[88] See HFAC Subcommittee on Africa, Global Health, Global Human Rights, and International Organizations hearings in the 115th and 114th Congresses: "Winning the Fight Against Human Trafficking: The Frederick Douglass Reauthorization Act," May 2, 2017; "Accountability Over Politics: Scrutinizing the Trafficking in Persons Report," July 12, 2016; and "Demanding Accountability: Evaluating the 2015 Trafficking in Persons Report," November 4, 2015.

[89] GAO-17-56 (December 2016); GAO, *Human Trafficking: Better Data, Strategy, and Reporting Needed to Enhance U.S. Antitrafficking Efforts Abroad*, GAO-06-825, July 18, 2006.

- the number of years a country may remain on the Tier 2 Watch List, from a maximum of four years (two consecutive years on Tier 2 Watch List, plus a maximum of two waivers to remain on the list for two more years) to three (two consecutive years on Tier 2 Watch List, plus one waiver);
- the conditions under which a country may remain on the Tier 2 Watch List (excluding those that have committed to take future antitrafficking steps, but have not already taken concrete steps to implement policies that would constitute significant efforts toward becoming compliant with the TVPA's minimum standards for eliminating trafficking);
- expectations for upgrading a Tier 2 Watch List country that exhausted its permitted time on that list and was subsequently downgraded to Tier 3 for lack of progress, including whether or how long it would be permitted to return to the Tier 2 Watch List in the future;
- public documentation requirements to justify the continued listing of a country on the Tier 2 Watch List; and
- country narratives in the TIP Report to explicitly rationalize a country's upgrade or downgrade compared to its previous-year ranking.

Some bills also seek to further define key terms in the TVPA used by the State Department to determine country rankings, including proposed

- changes to the scope of foreign assistance subject to restriction;
- changes to the TVPA's four minimum standards for the elimination of trafficking;
- additions to the currently 12 criteria used to evaluate whether a country is making serious and sustained efforts to eliminate trafficking (the fourth minimum standard);

- revisions to what constitutes *significant efforts* to become compliant with the four minimum standards for the elimination of trafficking; and
- new definitions for the terms *concrete actions* and *credible evidence*.

If these proposals are enacted, they would constitute significant changes to the current TIP Report's methodology. A critical issue is whether changes to the TIP Report's methodology would motivate countries to do more to combat human trafficking or, in contrast, could undermine its value as a tool of soft power diplomacy. Some countries, which criticize the current ranking process as opaque, may prefer more detailed statutory instructions for how to assign tier rankings. Additional transparency in the TIP Report's rankings and country narratives could clarify expectations for future upgrades. Other countries, particularly those with limited resources and capabilities to address human trafficking, may have more difficulty proving progress in the report. If changes to the TIP Report's ranking process result in more countries falling to Tier 3, additional policy question may arise, including whether the President would subject more Tier 3 countries to foreign aid restrictions or whether the Administration would use waivers to minimize the consequences of poor rankings in the TIP Report.

In: Criminal Justice
Editor: Quincy Franks
ISBN: 978-1-53614-196-2

Chapter 6

CHARLOTTESVILLE CAR CRASH ATTACK: POSSIBILITY OF FEDERAL CRIMINAL PROSECUTION*

CRS Reports and Analysis

LEGAL SIDEBAR

Attorney General Jeff Sessions has announced a federal civil rights investigation into the incident in Charlottesville, Virginia, in which a woman was killed and several others were injured when a car plowed into a group of counter-protesters on a day when protesters had clashed with participants in a white supremacist rally. Virginia authorities have arrested the Ohio driver of the car and charged him with second degree murder, a crime punishable under Virginia law by imprisonment for not less than five or more than forty years.

---

* This is an edited, reformatted, and augmented version of a CRS Reports and Analysis Legal Sidebar, dated August 15, 2017.

For both constitutional and practical reasons, law enforcement is first and foremost a state responsibility. Nevertheless, the protection of civil rights has been thought to be an important federal concern. It's too early to tell what, if any, prosecutable federal offenses the Justice Department's investigation might discover. However, various civil rights and terrorist offenses may be implicated.

CIVIL RIGHTS OFFENSES

Media reports have cited two potential civil rights violations – the federal hate crime offense and the offense of interfering with federally protected activities. The federal hate crime statute applies to anyone who "willfully causes bodily injury to any person ... because of the actual or perceived race ... of any person." The woman who was killed was white, and several of those injured with her were African-American. Conviction under the hate crime statute would require, among other things, evidence that the driver targeted his victims because of their race rather than because of their political beliefs, such as their perceived anti-white supremacist views. In cases where a death results, the hate crime statute carries a sentence of imprisonment for any term of years or for life.

The "protected activities" statute creates a number of civil rights crimes including those involving interference with the access to public benefits, services, facilities, and accommodations. The statute also applies to anyone who "by force ... willfully injures ... any citizen because he ... has been ... participating lawfully in speech or peaceful assembly" relating to opposition to any denial of public benefits, services, facilities, or accommodations on the basis of race, religion, or national origin. The Charlottesville attack reportedly followed sometimes violent clashes between white supremacist demonstrators and counter-demonstrators. Conviction would require, among other things, evidence that the driver targeted his victims because they had participated in lawful speech or peaceful assembly in opposition to the denial of access to federal or state benefits, services, facilities, or accommodations on the basis of race, religion, or national origin. In cases of a resulting second degree murder, the protected activities offense carries a sentence of imprisonment for any term of years or for life.

DOMESTIC TERRORISM

The federal criminal code defines the term "domestic terrorism" to encompass those federal or state crimes, "dangerous to human life ... [that] appear to be intended – (i) to intimidate or coerce a civilian population; [or] to influence the policy of a government by intimidation or coercion ... [and that] occur primarily within the ... United States." Domestic terrorism as such, however, is not a separate federal crime, but an element or aggravating factor in the case of other crimes, such as port security bribery in furtherance of domestic terrorism or false statements for purposes of domestic terrorism. Federal law does feature a number of individual terrorism offenses. One of these bans the use of weapons of mass destruction. The commercial airlines that terrorists flew into the Pentagon and the World Trade Center were treated as "weapons of mass destruction" for purposes of the statute. Whether a court would consider a car driven into a crowd constitutes comparable use of a weapon of mass destruction remains to be seen. If so, conviction would require, among other things, proof of one of the statute's jurisdictional elements, such as interstate travel in furtherance of the offense or an effect of the offense on interstate or foreign commerce. Here too, the offense is punishable by imprisonment for any term of years or for life. The facts to date do not appear to implicate any of the other individual federal terrorism statutes.

CONSPIRACY AND ACCOMPLICES

Initial reports have said nothing of the culpability of others in the crash. No one other than the driver has been charged. Evidence of the involvement of others would suggest the possibility of criminal liability under several other provisions of federal criminal law. More specifically, it is a federal crime to conspire to commit a federal offense; to solicit the commission of a federal violent felony of violence; or to conspire to intimidate others from enjoying "the rights and privileges" secured by federal law. Moreover, those who counsel, command, aid, or abet the commission of a federal offense by another are treated as though they had committed the underlying offense themselves.

DUAL OR SEQUENTIAL STATE-FEDERAL PROSECUTION

There is no constitutional impediment to both state and federal prosecution for the same misconduct, although prosecution in both forums occurs only infrequently.

In: Criminal Justice
Editor: Quincy Franks

ISBN: 978-1-53614-196-2

Chapter 7

SPECIAL COUNSELS, INDEPENDENT COUNSELS, AND SPECIAL PROSECUTORS: OPTIONS FOR INDEPENDENT EXECUTIVE INVESTIGATIONS*

Cynthia Brown

ABSTRACT

Under the Constitution, Congress has no direct role in federal law enforcement and its ability to initiate appointments of any prosecutors to address alleged wrongdoings by executive officials is limited. While Congress retains broad oversight and investigatory powers under Article I of the Constitution, criminal investigations and prosecutions have generally been viewed as a core executive function and a responsibility of the executive branch. Historically, however, because of the potential conflicts of interest that may arise when the executive branch investigates itself (e.g., the Watergate investigation), there have been calls for an independently led inquiry to determine whether officials have violated

---

* This is an edited, reformatted and augmented version of a Congressional Research Service report, R44857, dated June 1, 2017.

criminal law. In response, Congress and the U.S. Department of Justice (DOJ) have used both statutory and regulatory mechanisms to establish a process for such inquiries. These responses have attempted, in different ways, to balance the competing goals of independence and accountability with respect to inquiries of executive branch officials.

Under the Ethics in Government Act of 1978, Congress authorized the appointment of "special prosecutors," who later were known as "independent counsels." Under this statutory scheme, the Attorney General could request that a specially appointed three-judge panel appoint an outside individual to investigate and prosecute alleged violations of criminal law. These individuals were vested with "full power and independent authority to exercise all investigative and prosecutorial functions and powers of the Department of Justice" with respect to matters within their jurisdiction. The independent counsel provisions included sunset provisions, but were reauthorized regularly until 1992, when Congress allowed the law to expire. Although it was again reauthorized in 1994, debate over the scope, cost, and effect of the investigations (perhaps most notably the Iran-Contra investigation and the Whitewater investigation) resulted in the law's expiration and nonrenewal in 1999.

Following the lapse of the statutory independent counsel provisions, DOJ promulgated regulations authorizing the Attorney General (or, if the Attorney General is recused from a matter, the Acting Attorney General) to appoint a "special counsel" to conduct specific investigations or prosecutions that may be deemed to present a conflict of interest if pursued under the normal procedures of the agency. Under these regulations, the Attorney General may appoint an individual from outside the federal government to investigate and prosecute criminal matters within his or her assigned jurisdiction. Two instances in which the Attorney General has invoked this authority include the investigation of the Branch Davidian incident in Waco, Texas, and the current investigation of alleged Russian interference in the 2016 election. Special counsels appointed under this authority are vested "within the scope of his or her jurisdiction, the full power and independent authority to exercise all investigative and prosecutorial functions of any United States Attorney." Special counsels are not subject to "day-to-day supervision" by any official, but may be asked to report to the Attorney General during the course of their work. The Attorney General must "give great weight to the views of the Special Counsel" but may conclude that particular actions should not be pursued and must notify Congress accordingly if the Attorney General rejects a particular course of action. Additionally, the Attorney General maintains the authority to discipline or remove the special counsel for cause.

Ultimately, under the previous statutory authorization for independent counsel appointments or under the existing regulatory authority to appoint special counsels, the Attorney General holds the sole authority to initiate the appointment for such investigations and prosecutions. However, other alternatives of investigation and oversight of actions by federal officials—whose methods are beyond the scope of this chapter—are available, such as inspector general investigations and congressional oversight investigations.

Under the Constitution, Congress has no direct role in federal law enforcement and its ability to initiate a prosecution to address alleged wrongdoings by executive officials is limited.[1] While Congress retains broad oversight and investigatory powers under Article I of the Constitution,[2] criminal investigations and prosecutions have generally been viewed as a core executive function and a responsibility of the executive branch under Article II.[3] Historically, however, because of the potential conflicts of interest that may arise when the executive branch investigates itself, there have been calls for independent inquiries to determine whether officials have violated criminal law.[4] In response, Congress and the U.S. Department of Justice (DOJ) have used both statutory[5] and regulatory[6] mechanisms to establish a process for such inquiries. These responses have attempted, in different ways, to balance the competing goals of independence and accountability with respect to inquiries of executive branch officials.

---

[1] The U.S. Constitution is structured to establish a principle known as "separation of powers," which assigns particular functions to each of the three branches of government. For a historical background on separation of powers, see CRS Report R44334, *Separation of Powers: An Overview*, by Matthew E. Glassman.

[2] *See* McGrain v. Daugherty, 273 U.S. 135 (1927) (describing congressional oversight authority as "an essential and appropriate auxiliary to the legislative function"); Watkins v. United States, 354 U.S. 178, 187 (1957) ("The power of the Congress to conduct investigations is inherent in the legislative process. That power is broad.").

[3] *See* Morrison v. Olson, 487 U.S. 654, 706 (1988) ("Governmental investigation and prosecution of crimes is a quintessentially executive function.").

[4] *See generally* Kimberly Robinson, *Comey Firing Could Wake a Constitutional Wolf*, BLOOMBERG LAW (May 11, 2017), *available at* https://bol.bna.com/comey-firing-could-wake-a-constitutional-wolf/; George D. Brown, *The Ethics Backlash and the Independent Counsel Statute*, 51 RUTGERS L. REV. 433 (1999); Niles L. Godes and Ty E. Howard, *Independent Counsel Investigations*, 35 AM. CRIM. L. REV. 875 (1998).

[5] *See* Ethics in Government Act of 1978, P.L. 95-521, title VI, 92 Stat. 1867, as amended by P.L. 97-409, 96 Stat. 2039 (1983); P.L. 100-191, 101 Stat. 1293 (1987); P.L. 103-270, 108 Stat. 732 (1994).

[6] *See* 28 C.F.R. Part 600.

This chapter analyzes the use of *special prosecutors* and *independent counsels* that were authorized under now-expired provisions of the Ethics in Government Act of 1978,[7] as well as the use of *special counsels* that are currently authorized by DOJ regulations.[8] A glossary of terms at the beginning of the chapter briefly defines these italicized terms (see Table 1). The chapter also addresses constitutional considerations in establishing independent inquiries to address perceived conflicts of interest between investigating officials and the officials being investigated. Other methods of oversight, including investigations by congressional committees or under the authority of agency inspectors general, may also be available with respect to executive branch investigations, but are beyond the scope of this chapter.

Table 1. Glossary of Terms

Independent Counsel	Now-expired provisions of the Ethics in Government Act of 1978 (P.L. 95-521, as amended) authorized the Attorney General to request that a three-judge panel within the federal judiciary appoint an independent counsel. Independent counsels had more independence than regular DOJ officials and employees, though the breadth of their investigations led to debate and ultimately to the expiration of the statutory authorization.
Special Counsel	The DOJ's general administrative hiring authority (28 C.F.R. Part 600) authorizes the Attorney General to appoint special counsels. Special counsels exercise more independence than regular DOJ officials and employees, but because the Attorney General generally appoints, supervises, and may remove special counsels, they are considered to be less independent than independent counsels were. (The term "special counsel," when used in the context of independent criminal investigations of executive officials, is entirely distinct from the Office of Special Counsel, an independent federal agency, which investigates certain federal personnel practices.)
Special Prosecutor	The Attorney General historically has appointed special prosecutors to investigate scandals involving public officials. The term "special prosecutor" was also initially used to describe independent investigations authorized by the Ethics in Government Act, though the term was later changed under that statute to "independent counsel." Historically, these appointments were used to provide for the investigation of any related allegations without political interference.

[7] *See supra* note 5.
[8] *See* 28 C.F.R. Part 600.

BACKGROUND ON THE USE OF INDEPENDENT INVESTIGATIONS OF ALLEGED WRONGDOING

To counter perceptions that executive officials suspected of criminal wrongdoing may be subject to different standards than individuals outside the government, independent investigations have historically been used, in some circumstances, to determine whether officials have violated the law.[9] The government has used a range of options to conduct these types of inquiries: special prosecutors, independent counsels, and special counsels. It has been noted, however, that "there is no perfect solution" to achieving the goal of avoiding potential conflicts or the appearance thereof that may arise as a result of the executive branch investigating its own officials.[10]

While special prosecutors had been used historically in investigations of executive officials, the events commonly known as Watergate led to perhaps the most famous use of an independent investigation in U.S. history.[11] Specifically, the break-in and burglary of the Democratic National Committee Headquarters at the Watergate Hotel in 1972 led to widespread allegations of wrongdoing by senior officials in the executive branch and calls for the appointment of a prosecutor who could conduct an investigation independent of political interference.[12] In the midst of the Watergate controversy, Elliot Richardson, whose nomination to be Attorney General was being considered by the Senate Committee on the Judiciary, agreed to name an independent special prosecutor to pursue the Watergate allegations.[13] Once confirmed by the Senate, the Attorney

---

[9] *See* Elliot L. Richardson, *Special Counsels, Petty Cases*, N.Y. TIMES (June 5, 1995), *available at* http://www.nytimes.com/1995/06/05/opinion/special-counsels-petty-cases.html; Jim Mokhiber, *A Brief History of the Independent Counsel Law*, FRONTLINE (May 1998), *available at* pbs.org (noting the use of "special prosecutors" to investigate the Teapot Dome scandal of the 1920s and tax scandals of the 1950s).

[10] *See* Office of Special Counsel, 64 Fed. Reg. 37,038 (July 9, 1999) (codified at 28 C.F.R. Part 600) (introducing regulations to replace the expired implementing regulations of the independent counsel statute).

[11] *See generally* Joseph S. Hall, Nicholas Pullen, and Kandace Rayos, *Independent Counsel Investigations*, 36 AM. CRIM. L. REV. 809 (1999).

[12] *See* Mokhiber, *supra* note 9.

[13] *Nomination of Elliot L. Richardson, of Massachusetts, to be Attorney General: Hearing Before the S. Comm. on the Judiciary*, 93d Cong. 4-7, 18-20 (1973).

General, under his own authority, appointed Archibald Cox as special prosecutor for the Watergate investigation in 1973.[14] The President subsequently ordered DOJ officials to fire the special prosecutor later that year,[15] leading to public outcry, the appointment of another special prosecutor, and, ultimately, the initiation of impeachment proceedings by Congress.[16] Following these events, Congress enacted a new mechanism—discussed in the following section—for the use of special prosecutors who would be appointed by a three-judge panel upon the request of the Attorney General.[17]

SPECIAL PROSECUTORS AND INDEPENDENT COUNSELS, AS AUTHORIZED UNDER THE ETHICS IN GOVERNMENT ACT

Congress enacted the Ethics in Government Act of 1978 out of a broad intent "to preserve and promote the integrity of public officials and institutions."[18] The statute addressed a number of concerns about the ethical behavior of some public officials in the wake of the Watergate scandal.[19] Most relevantly, Title VI of the statute (hereinafter "the independent counsel statute") established a mechanism for the appointment of individuals to lead independent investigations and prosecutions in certain circumstances.[20] The statute originally designated these individuals

---

[14] 38 Fed. Reg. 14,688 (June 4, 1973).

[15] DOJ regulations "gave the Watergate Special Prosecutor very broad power to investigate and prosecute offenses arising out of [the events comprising Watergate]," and provided that the special prosecutor could only be removed "for extraordinary improprieties on his part." *See* Nader v. Bork, 366 F. Supp. 104 (D.D.C. 1973), *vacated by* Nader v. Levi, No. 1954-73, 1975 U.S. Dist. LEXIS 16791 (D.D.C. 1975) (concluding that the discharge of the special counsel was unlawful under the regulations).

[16] *See* Mokhiber, *supra* note 9.

[17] *See* Ethics in Government Act of 1978, P.L. 95-521, title VI, 92 Stat. 1867.

[18] *Id.* at 1824 (1978).

[19] In part, the statute required disclosure of certain financial interests by specified government employees; established the Office of Government Ethics within the executive branch; and provided criminal regulation of certain outside employment and lobbying activities by former government officials. *Id.* at 1824-67.

[20] *Id.*

as "special prosecutors"[21] and later renamed them as "independent counsels."[22]

Two of the most commonly known examples of appointments of independent counsels under the statute involved incidents known as Iran-Contra and Whitewater.[23] In 1986, Lawrence E. Walsh[24] was appointed as independent counsel[25] to investigate potential criminal misconduct of government officials related to the sale of arms to Iran and alleged diversion of profits from the sale to support the "the military activities of the Nicaraguan contra rebels" in violation of federal law.[26] That investigation resulted in criminal charges for 14 individuals, most of whom were convicted, though some convictions were overturned on various grounds.[27] In 1994, Kenneth Starr[28] was appointed as independent counsel[29] to investigate potential violations of federal criminal or civil law related to President Clinton or First Lady Hillary Rodham Clinton's relationship with Madison Guaranty Savings & Loan Association, Whitewater Development Corporation, or Capital Management Services, as well as any allegations arising out of that investigation.[30] That

---

[21] *See id.* § 601, 92 Stat. 1867.

[22] *See* P.L. 97-409, § 2(a)(1)(A).

[23] *See generally* NAT'L ARCHIVES AND RECORDS ADMIN., *Records of Independent Counsels*, *available at* https://www.archives.gov/research/guide-fed-records/groups/449.html.

[24] Walsh formerly had served as a federal judge, private litigator, deputy attorney general, and negotiator in peace talks for the Vietnam War. *See* Neil A. Lewis, *Lawrence E. Walsh, Prosecutor in Iran-Contra Scandal, Dies at 102*, N.Y. TIMES (Mar. 20, 2014), *available at* https://www.nytimes.com/2014/03/21/us/politics/lawrence-e-walsh-iran-contraprosecutor-dies-at-102.html?_r=0.

[25] *See* 28 C.F.R. § 601.1.

[26] Lawrence E. Walsh, *Final Report of the Independent Counsel for Iran/Contra Matters, Vol. I: Investigations and Prosecutions* (Aug. 4, 1993), *available at* https://archive.org/stream/WalshReport/Walsh%20Report%20volume%201%20Investigations%20and%20Prosecutions#page/n0/mode/2up.

[27] *Id.* at xiv-xv.

[28] Starr formerly had served as a law professor, private litigator, and as Solicitor General. *Biography*, Baylor University, *available at* http://www.baylor.edu/inauguration/index.php?id=75013. He was later succeeded by Robert W. Ray and Julie F. Thomas as independent counsels related to that investigation.

[29] 28 C.F.R. § 603.1.

[30] *Id.*

investigation led to a myriad of charges for a number of individuals, but did not include indictments of the President or First Lady.[31]

Appointment Process

Appointment of independent counsels under the statute occurred in two steps, requiring the involvement of both the Attorney General and a panel of federal judges.

Role of the Attorney General

The independent counsel statute generally directed the Attorney General to conduct a preliminary investigation upon receiving information about potential wrongdoing by certain officials in the executive branch or from presidential campaign committees.[32] If, within 30 days of receiving such information, the Attorney General determined that the information was specific and from a credible source,[33] the Attorney General was required to conduct a preliminary investigation for a period of up to 90 days.[34] The statute did not require the Attorney General to acknowledge or notify any other parties that such information had come to his attention, but did require that the Attorney General inform the court that he had commenced a preliminary investigation.[35]

---

[31] Robert Ray, *Final Report of the Independent Counsel in Re Madison Guaranty Savings & Loan Association* (Jan. 5, 2001), *available at* https://www.gpo.gov/fdsys/pkg/GPO-ICREPORT-MADISON/content-detail.html; Neil A. Lewis, *Final Report By Prosecutor on Clintons is Released*, N.Y. TIMES (Mar. 21, 2002), *available at* http://www.nytimes.com/2002/03/21/us/final-report-by-prosecutor-on-clintons-is-released.html.

[32] 28 U.S.C. § 591. The individuals subject to investigation generally included the President; Vice President; designated heads of federal agencies; certain high-level officials in the Executive Office of the President; certain senior executive officials in DOJ, the Central Intelligence Agency, or the Internal Revenue Service; and officers of campaign committees for the President. *See id.* § 591(b). Other individuals, including Members of Congress, could be investigated under certain circumstances as well. *See id.* § 591(c). The statute allowed for investigations of potential violations of "any Federal criminal law other than a violation classified as a Class B or C misdemeanor or an infraction." *See id.* § 591(a).

[33] *Id.* § 592(d).

[34] *Id.* § 592(a).

[35] *Id.* § 592(a)(1).

The conclusions reached based upon that initial investigation determined whether an independent counsel would be appointed to investigate the underlying allegations further.[36] The statute required that the Attorney General request appointment of a special prosecutor by the special division of a federal court (discussed below) under three sets of circumstances. First, if the 90-day window for the preliminary investigation passed without a determination that further investigation or prosecution was not warranted, the Attorney General was required to request the appointment by the court.[37] Second, if the Attorney General's initial investigation determined that further investigation or prosecution was warranted, the Attorney General was also required to request the appointment by the court.[38] Finally, if the preliminary investigation indicated that further action was not warranted, but additional information was subsequently revealed which led the Attorney General to determine that further investigation or prosecution was indeed warranted, the Attorney General was mandated to conduct a preliminary investigation based on that information.[39] Following that investigation, the statute required the Attorney General to seek appointment of an independent counsel under the same circumstances—i.e., if no determination had been made within 90 days or if the Attorney General determined further investigation was warranted.[40] The Attorney General's decision to request an appointment under the statute was not subject to judicial review.[41]

While the Attorney General was not authorized under the statute to appoint the independent counsel, he was required to provide the court with

---

[36] If the Attorney General determined from the initial investigation that "there were no reasonable grounds to believe that further investigation [was] warranted," he or she was required to notify the three-judge panel, which would then have no authority to appoint a special prosecutor for the allegations. *Id.* § 592(b)(1). The Attorney General was required to provide a summary of the information received and the results of the preliminary investigation. *Id.* § 592(b)(2).

[37] *Id.* § 592(c)(1)(B).

[38] *Id.* § 592(c)(1)(A).

[39] *Id.* § 592(c)(2).

[40] *Id.*

[41] *Id.* § 592(f).

"sufficient information to assist" the court in the selection of the appointed individual and to define the jurisdiction of the inquiry.[42]

Role of the Court

While the Attorney General conducted the initial investigation to determine whether an independent investigation was warranted, the independent counsel statute required that a special division of the U.S. Court of Appeals for the D.C. Circuit (D.C. Circuit), composed of three federal judges or Justices, appoint the independent counsel.[43]

The Chief Justice of the U.S. Supreme Court assigned three federal judges or Justices to that division for two-year assignments.[44] The statutory rules regarding assignment of the three-judge panel required that the panel include a judge from the D.C. Circuit and that not more than one judge or Justice be from any single court.[45] Any judge or Justice serving in the special division of the court that appointed the independent counsel was barred from participating in any judicial proceeding involving the independent counsel while he or she was still serving in that position or any proceeding involving the exercise of the independent counsel's official duties.[46]

Based on recommendations from the Attorney General regarding the selection and jurisdiction of the independent counsel, the three-judge panel had the final authority to make the appointment and define the prosecutorial jurisdiction.[47] The court was expressly barred from appointing "any person who holds or recently held any office of profit or trust under the United States."[48]

---

[42] *Id.* § 592(d).
[43] *Id.* § 593(a) (cross-referencing 28 U.S.C. § 49).
[44] *Id.* § 49.
[45] *Id.* § 49(d).
[46] *Id.* § 49(f).
[47] *Id.* § 593(b).
[48] *Id.* § 593(b)(2).

Scope of Authority

"[W]ith respect to all matters in [the] independent counsel's prosecutorial jurisdiction," Congress granted the independent counsel "full power and independent authority to exercise all investigative and prosecutorial functions and powers of the Department of Justice, the Attorney General, and any other officer or employee of the Department of Justice...."[49] Examples of the independent counsel's enumerated authorities included

- conducting investigations and grand jury proceedings;
- engaging in judicial proceedings, including litigation and appeals of court decisions;
- reviewing documentary evidence;
- determining whether to challenge the use of testimonial privileges;
- receiving national security clearances, if appropriate;
- seeking immunity for witnesses, warrants, subpoenas, and other court orders;
- obtaining and reviewing any tax return; and
- carrying out prosecutions in court, including filing indictments.[50]

Furthermore, the independent counsel could request DOJ assistance in the course of his or her investigation, including access to materials relevant to the jurisdiction of the inquiry and the necessary resources and personnel to perform his or her assigned duties.[51]

Removal

Other than impeachment, the independent counsel could be subject to removal "only by the personal action of the Attorney General and only for

[49] *Id.* § 594(a).
[50] *Id.*
[51] *Id.* § 594(d).

good cause, physical or mental disability ..., or any other condition that substantially impairs the performance of such independent counsel's duties."[52] In other words, the independent counsel was generally not subject to the control and oversight of any other official within the executive branch.[53] If the Attorney General exercised his removal authority, he or she was required to notify the special division of the court responsible for the initial appointment and the Committees on the Judiciary of both the House of Representatives and the Senate, identifying his reasons for removal.[54]

Termination of Independent Counsel Inquiries

The inquiry led by the independent counsel under the statute could be terminated under two methods. First, the statute directed that the office of the independent counsel would terminate upon notification by the independent counsel to the Attorney General that the investigation and any subsequent prosecutions had been completed.[55] Second, the statute permitted the special division of the court—by its own choice or by the recommendation of the Attorney General—to terminate the office at any time if the investigation had been completed or sufficiently completed, allowing the DOJ to formally complete the inquiry under its own processes.[56] In either case, the independent counsel was required to submit

---

[52] *Id.* § 596(a)(1).

[53] The standard of removal "for good cause" indicates that the independent counsel could not be removed at will, but rather for reasons related to the specific performance of his or her assigned duties. *See* Free Enter. Fund v. Pub. Co. Accounting Oversight Bd., 561 U.S. 477, 502-03 (2010) (describing the "good cause" standard as an "unusually high standard" which included willful violations of law, willful abuse of authority, or failure to comply with rules without reasonable justification). *But see* Morrison v. Olson, 487 U.S. 654, 692 (1988) (explaining that the independent counsel statute's "good cause" requirement for removal nonetheless allows the Attorney General "ample authority to assure that the counsel is competently performing his or her statutory responsibilities in a manner that comports with the provisions of the Act").

[54] 28 U.S.C. § 596(a)(2).

[55] *Id.* § 596(b)(1). If the investigation or prosecutions were not fully completed, but were sufficiently completed to allow DOJ to complete them under normal processes, the independent counsel could also terminate the inquiry. *Id.*

[56] *Id.* § 596(b)(2).

a report to the special division of the court detailing the work completed.[57] The report was required to include "a description of the work of the independent counsel, including the disposition of all cases brought."[58]

Statutory Reauthorizations and Eventual Lapse of the Independent Counsel Statute

When the independent counsel statute was originally enacted in 1978, Congress provided that its authority would lapse five years after enactment.[59] Investigations that had already started pursuant to the provisions were permitted to continue, but no new investigations could be initiated at that time.[60] Rather than allow the statute to lapse, Congress reauthorized the law, with some amendments, several times. It was reauthorized in 1983[61] and 1987,[62] and remained in effect until 1992, when Congress allowed the law to expire. The statute was again reauthorized in 1994, following concerns related to the investigation of the Whitewater controversy during the interim years.[63] However, concerns over whether the independent counsel possessed too much power, which arose after the extensive independent counsel investigations of the Iran-Contra affair and the Whitewater controversy, resulted in the law's ultimate expiration and nonrenewal in 1999.[64]

Special Counsels, as Authorized under Current DOJ Regulations

Following the expiration of the independent counsel statute, DOJ promulgated regulations in 1999, which are currently still in effect, to

[57] *See id.* § 596(b).
[58] *Id.* § 594(h)(1)(B).
[59] P.L. 95-521, § 601 (then codified at 28 U.S.C. § 598).
[60] *Id.*
[61] Ethics in Government Act Amendments of 1982, P.L. 97-409, 96 Stat. 2039 (1983).
[62] Independent Counsel Reauthorization Act of 1987, P.L. 100-191, 101 Stat. 1293 (1987).
[63] Independent Counsel Reauthorization Act of 1994, P.L. 103-270, 108 Stat. 732 (1994).
[64] *See generally Brown, supra* note 4.

establish procedures for the appointment of special counsels pursuant to the Attorney General's general administrative hiring authority.[65] DOJ described these regulations as "strik[ing] a balance between independence and accountability in certain sensitive investigations."[66] DOJ acknowledged at the time the regulations were promulgated, however, that "there is no perfect solution" to achieving that goal.[67]

Thus far, it appears the special counsel regulations have been used infrequently.[68] In 1999, shortly after the regulations were promulgated, the Attorney General appointed former U.S. Senator John Danforth as special counsel to investigate events related to the government actions that occurred six years earlier at the Branch Davidian compound in Waco, Texas.[69] The special counsel's investigation found no wrongdoing on the part of federal law enforcement officials.[70] In May 2017, Deputy Attorney General Rod Rosenstein (acting in place of Attorney General Jeff Sessions, who had recused himself from the investigation) appointed former Federal Bureau of Investigation Director Robert S. Mueller III as special counsel to investigate efforts of the Russian government "to influence the 2016 election and related matters."[71]

It may be noted that the Attorney General has general statutory authority to appoint DOJ staff to conduct or coordinate particular investigations.[72] DOJ has used this authority previously to appoint "special counsel" to investigate particular matters. This authority differs from the special counsel regulations because it involves assignment of an internal

---

65 28 C.F.R. Part 600.

66 *See* Office of Special Counsel, 64 Fed. Reg. 37,038.

67 *See id.*

68 Matt Zapotosky, *Explaining the Precedent for and Role of a Special Counsel*, ORLANDO SENTINEL (May 19, 2017).

69 Lorraine Adams, *Reno Asks Danforth to Run Waco Probe*, THE WASHINGTON POST (Sept. 8, 1999).

70 Jim Yardley, *A Special Counsel Finds Government Faultless at Waco*, N.Y. TIMES (July 22, 2000).

71 Office of the Deputy Att'y Gen., *Appointment of Special Counsel to Investigate Russian Interference with the 2016 Presidential Election and Related Matters*, Order No. 3915-2017 (May 17, 2017), *available at* https://www.justice.gov/opa/press-release/file/967231/download.

72 28 U.S.C. §§ 509, 510, 515.

agency official rather than an individual from outside the government.[73] For example, in 2003, then-Deputy Attorney General James Comey (acting in place of then-Attorney General John Ashcroft, who had recused himself from the investigation) used this statutory authority to appoint Patrick Fitzgerald to lead an investigation of whether White House or other federal officials unlawfully leaked the identity of a Central Intelligence Agency officer to a reporter.[74] Fitzgerald was serving as a U.S. Attorney when named as "special counsel," which would have precluded his appointment under the special counsel regulations.[75] While "special counsel" thus may be appointed under either the general statutory authority or under the specific special counsel regulations, those named under the regulations are considered to be more independent, given that they are not appointed from within the agency.

Appointment and Selection by the Attorney General or the Acting Attorney General

Under the DOJ regulations that supplanted the independent counsel provisions, the authority to appoint and select a special counsel resides solely with the Attorney General (or his surrogate, if the Attorney General has recused himself from the matter), rather than being shared with the judicial branch.[76] The regulations generally state that the Attorney General "will appoint a Special Counsel" to conduct certain investigations or prosecutions.[77] To make such an appointment, the Attorney General must determine that (1) a criminal investigation is warranted; (2) the normal processes of investigation or prosecution would present a conflict of interest for DOJ, or other extraordinary circumstances exist; and (3) public

---

[73] 28 C.F.R. § 600.3(a).

[74] Letters from James B. Comey, Acting Attorney General, to Patrick J. Fitzgerald, U.S. Attorney (Dec. 30, 2003 and Feb. 6, 2004), *available at* https://www.justice.gov/archive/osc/documents/2006_03_17_exhibits_a_d.pdf.

[75] *Id.*; *see also* 28 C.F.R. § 600.3.

[76] *See* 28 C.F.R. 600.1.

[77] *Id.* § 600.1.

interest requires a special counsel to assume those responsibilities.[78] When DOJ promulgated the special counsel regulations, it explained the type of conflicts that might lead to the appointment of a special counsel: "[t]here are occasions when the facts create a conflict so substantial or the exigencies of the situation are such that any initial investigation might taint the subsequent investigation, so that it is appropriate for the Attorney General to immediately appoint a Special Counsel."[79]

After receiving information that could warrant consideration of an independent investigation, the Attorney General generally has discretion under the regulations to determine whether and when the appointment of a special counsel would be appropriate.[80] The Attorney General may appoint a special counsel immediately; may require an initial investigation to inform his decision about whether to appoint a special counsel; or "may direct that appropriate steps be taken to mitigate any conflicts of interest, such as recusal of particular officials," to permit the investigation to be concluded within "the normal processes."[81]

In the event that the Attorney General has recused himself from a particular matter upon which a special counsel appointment might be appropriate, the regulations contemplate that the Acting Attorney General will take responsibility for the appointment process.[82] Federal law provides that the Deputy Attorney General would serve as the Acting Attorney General.[83]

Individuals who may be appointed as special counsels under these regulations must be chosen from outside the federal government.[84] Such individuals must be "a lawyer with a reputation for integrity and impartial decisionmaking, and with appropriate experience to ensure both that the investigation will be conducted ably, expeditiously and thoroughly, and

---

[78] *Id.* § 600.1.

[79] *See* Office of Special Counsel, 64 Fed. Reg. 37,038, 37038.

[80] 28 C.F.R. § 600.2.

[81] *Id.* § 600.2.

[82] *Id.* § 600.1.

[83] 28 U.S.C. § 508(a). If the Deputy Attorney General is likewise recused, the appointment authority would pass to the Associate Attorney General. *Id.* § 508(b). *See also* Exec. Order 13,787, 3 C.F.R. 16,723 (Mar. 31, 2017) (identifying the order of succession within DOJ if the Attorney General or other senior officials are unable to serve).

[84] 28 C.F.R. § 600.3(a).

that investigative and prosecutorial decisions will be supported by an informed understanding of the criminal law and Department of Justice policies."[85] Furthermore, the special counsel may hold other professional roles during his or her service, but is required to agree that the duties of the appointment will take "first precedence."[86]

Scope of Jurisdiction and Authority

Like the appointment and selection process, the sole authority to determine the scope of the special counsel's inquiry rests with the Attorney General.[87] The jurisdiction of the inquiry is determined by "a specific factual statement" about the matter to be investigated, which is provided by the Attorney General to the special counsel at the outset of the appointment.[88] Beyond that general jurisdiction, the special counsel is also authorized "to investigate and prosecute federal crimes committed in the course of, and with intent to interfere with, the Special Counsel's investigation, such as perjury, obstruction of justice, destruction of evidence, and intimidation of witnesses."[89] While these are the original parameters of a special counsel's jurisdiction, additional matters may be assigned to the special counsel as the inquiry proceeds.[90] To expand the jurisdiction, the special counsel must find such an expansion is necessary to complete the original assignment or necessary "to investigate new matters that come to light in the course of his or her investigation."[91] Upon such finding, the special counsel's jurisdiction may be expanded only after consultation with the Attorney General, who then has the authority to

---

[85] *Id.* § 600.3(a).

[86] *Id.* § 600.3(a). The regulations state "that it may be necessary to devote their full time to the investigation, depending on its complexity and the stage of the investigation." *Id.*

[87] *Id.* § 600.4.

[88] *Id.* § 600.4(a).

[89] *Id.* § 600.4(a). The special counsel also has authority to appeal any decisions arising in the course of the inquiry. *Id.* The regulations explicitly state that special counsels "shall not have civil or administrative authority unless specifically granted such jurisdiction by the Attorney General." *Id.* § 600.4(c).

[90] *Id.* § 600.4(b).

[91] *Id.*

determine whether to assign the additional matters to the special counsel or "elsewhere."[92]

Within the jurisdiction identified by the Attorney General, the special counsel has relatively broad authority to carry out his or her inquiry. According to the regulations, "the Special Counsel shall exercise, within the scope of his or her jurisdiction, the full power and independent authority to exercise all investigative and prosecutorial functions of any United States Attorney."[93]

Oversight and Removal

The DOJ special counsel regulations limit the special counsel's relatively broad authority to conduct an inquiry by first subjecting his or her conduct to DOJ rules, regulations, procedures, practices, and policies.[94] Special counsels are directed to consult with the appropriate offices within DOJ or the Attorney General directly if necessary.[95] Additionally, special counsels are subject to discipline for misconduct and breach of ethical duties that are generally applicable to DOJ employees.[96]

Second, the DOJ regulations contemplate some oversight of the special counsel by the Attorney General.[97] Specifically, they direct the special counsel to "determine whether and to what extent to inform or consult with the Attorney General or others within the Department about the conduct of his or her duties and responsibilities."[98] While the regulations indicate that special counsels "shall not be subject to the day-to-day supervision of any official,"[99] the rules authorize the Attorney General to "request that the

---

[92] *Id.*

[93] *Id.* § 600.6.

[94] *Id.* § 600.7(a).

[95] *Id.*

[96] *Id.* § 600.7(c).

[97] *See id.* § 600.7. Special counsels are required to comply with DOJ rules, regulations, procedures, practices, and policies and are directed to consult with the appropriate offices within DOJ or the Attorney General directly if necessary. *Id.* § 600.7(a). Additionally, special counsels are subject to discipline for misconduct and breach of ethical duties that are generally applicable to DOJ employees. *Id.* § 600.7(c).

[98] *Id.* § 600.6.

[99] *Id.* § 600.7(b).

Special Counsel provide an explanation for any investigative or prosecutorial step."[100] If, after giving the views of the special counsel "great weight," the Attorney General's review of such actions leads him to "conclude that the action is so inappropriate or unwarranted under established Departmental practices that it should not be pursued," the Attorney General must notify the Chairman and Ranking Members of the Judiciary Committees in Congress of that decision with an explanation.[101]

Aside from review of particular actions, the regulations also grant the Attorney General authority to discipline or remove the special counsel. This authority may be exercised "only by the personal action of the Attorney General."[102] In other words, to comply with the regulations,[103] the Attorney General himself must remove the special counsel, not the President or a surrogate (unless, as noted previously4 in this chapter, the Attorney General has recused himself in the matter under investigation).[104] A decision to remove the special counsel must be made with "good cause," such as misconduct, a dereliction of duty, incapacity, or the existence of conflicts of interest.[105] The Attorney General must report his decision to remove the special counsel, with an explanation of that decision, to both the Chairman and Ranking Members of the Judiciary Committees of Congress.[106]

Review and Conclusion of Special Counsel Inquiries

Although the special counsel regulations do not provide an explicit timeline for inquiries or a special counsel appointment, they do require the

[100] *Id.* § 600.7(b).
[101] *Id.* § 600.7(b).
[102] *Id.* § 600.7(d).
[103] Commentators have noted the possibility that, regardless of the regulations, the President arguably may still be able to remove special counsels. *See* Neal Katyal, *Trump or Congress Can Still Block Robert Mueller. I Know. I Wrote the Rules*, THE WASHINGTON POST (May 19, 2017); Josh Blackman, *Could Trump Remove Special Counsel Robert Mueller? Lessons from Watergate*, Josh Blackman's Blog (May 23, 2017), http://joshblackman.com/blog/2017/05/23/could-trump-remove-special-counsel-robert-mueller-lessons-from-watergate/.
[104] *Id.* § 600.7(d).
[105] *Id.* § 600.7(d). *See supra* note 53 for an explanation of the "good cause" standard.
[106] *Id.* § 600.9(a)(2).

special counsel to report to DOJ periodically about the budget of operations for the inquiry as well as with status updates in some circumstances. Specifically, the special counsel must provide a proposed budget within 60 days of the appointment.[107] The special counsel must also provide annual reports regarding the status of the investigation and budget requests 90 days prior to the beginning of the fiscal year.[108] The Attorney General is required to review the special counsel's annual report and determine whether the investigation should continue and with what budget.[109]

When the special counsel's inquiry concludes, the special counsel must provide a confidential report to the Attorney General with explanations of the decisions made in the course of the inquiry in favor of or declining to prosecute any charges.[110] The regulations do not expressly provide for disclosure of this chapter to any other parties.

CONSTITUTIONAL ISSUES RELATING TO THE INVESTIGATION OF ALLEGATIONS OF WRONGDOING BY EXECUTIVE OFFICIALS

Under separation-of-powers principles provided structurally within the U.S. Constitution, each branch of government is assigned particular functions that may not be delegated to, nor usurped by, another branch.[111] Congress may initiate and conduct congressional investigations and hearings to conduct oversight of executive agencies or consider the need

---

[107] *Id.* § 600.8(a)(1).
[108] *Id.* § 600.8(a)(2).
[109] *Id.* § 600.8(a)(2).
[110] *Id.* § 600.8(c).
[111] Under what is commonly known as the nondelegation doctrine, Congress cannot delegate its authority to another branch of government. *See* Touby v. United States, 500 U.S. 160, 164-65 (1991) (quoting Mistretta v. United States, 488 U.S. 361, 371 (1989)) ("The nondelegation doctrine is rooted in the principle of separation of powers that underlies our tripartite system of Government.").

for possible remedial legislation,[112] but it may not engage in criminal prosecutions on behalf of the United States—a function generally provided to the executive branch.[113]

Accordingly, designing a mechanism to provide for criminal inquiries of executive officials by officers independent from the executive branch has raised questions about whether such a goal can be accomplished in accordance with constitutional mandates. This issue was addressed directly in response to the now-expired independent counsel statute in *Morrison v. Olson*, a 1988 U.S. Supreme Court decision involving a constitutional challenge to the authority of Congress to vest the appointment of an independent counsel outside the executive branch and limit the removal authority of the President.[114] *Morrison* ultimately upheld the independent counsel statute as constitutional,[115] although, perhaps notably, the Court's analysis has been criticized in the decades since the decision.[116]

In *Morrison*, noting that the constitutional text of the Appointments Clause permitted Congress to "vest the Appointment of such inferior Officers, as they think proper, in the President alone, *in the Courts of Law*, or in the Heads of Departments,"[117] Chief Justice Rehnquist, writing on behalf of the majority, concluded that independent counsels are "clearly" inferior officers.[118] Such officers, according to the Court, could constitutionally be appointed by the court under the statute because they (1) could be removed by a higher-ranking official; (2) had a limited scope of authorized duties; and (3) held an office with limited jurisdiction.[119] The

[112] *See* McGrain v. Daugherty, 273 U.S. 135 (1927) (describing congressional oversight authority as "an essential and appropriate auxiliary to the legislative function"); Watkins v. United States, 354 U.S. 178, 187 (1957) ("The power of the Congress to conduct investigations is inherent in the legislative process. That power is broad.").

[113] *See* Morrison v. Olson, 487 U.S. 654, 706 (1988) ("Governmental investigation and prosecution of crimes is a quintessentially executive function.").

[114] 487 U.S. 654 (1988).

[115] *Id.* at 659-60.

[116] While the Court's holding in *Morrison* remains the controlling opinion, at least one lower court, in an opinion that has been vacated pending en banc review, has more recently afforded significant weight to the dissent's analysis. *See* PHH Corp. v. Consumer Fin. Prot. Bureau, 839 F.3d 1, 20 (D.C. Cir. 2016) (vacated).

[117] U.S. CONST. art. II, § 2, cl. 2 (emphasis added).

[118] *Morrison*, 487 U.S. at 671.

[119] *Id.* at 671-72. Perhaps notably, the Court expressly indicated its decision did not mean "that Congress' power to provide for interbranch appointments of 'inferior officers' is unlimited."

Court likewise concluded that Congress had not interfered with executive authority by providing for the independent counsel's removal only for good cause for similar reasons.[120]

Morrison was decided 7-1, with Justice Scalia dissenting from the Court's opinion and Justice Kennedy not participating in the case. In dissent, Justice Scalia argued that the independent counsel statute should be read as a violation of the separation of powers because, under his reading, the Constitution vested authority for criminal investigations and prosecutions exclusively in the executive branch.[121] Under this rationale, Justice Scalia warned that the Court must be very careful to guard against the "'gradual concentration of the several powers in the same department'" that can be likely to occur as one branch seeks to infringe upon another's distinct constitutional authorities.[122]

In the years since *Morrison*, especially in the wake of the Whitewater investigation, a number of legal scholars have also criticized the independent counsel statute on both policy and constitutional grounds.[123] While *Morrison* remains good law, it is unclear whether the Court would necessarily view a reauthorization of the independent counsel statute or a similar statute in the same vein as it did in *Morrison.*[124]

Morrison, 487 U.S. at 675 ("In this case, however, we do not think it impermissible for Congress to vest the power to appoint independent counsel in a specially created federal court.").

[120] *Id.* at 686.

[121] *Id.* at 703-05 (Scalia, J., dissenting).

[122] *Id.* at 699 (quoting Federalist No. 51, p. 321 (J. Madison)) ("Frequently an issue of this sort will come before the Court clad, so to speak, in sheep's clothing: the potential of the asserted principle to effect important change in the equilibrium of power is not immediately evident, and must be discerned by a careful and perceptive analysis. But this wolf comes as a wolf.").

[123] *See Starr Opposes Independent Counsel Act*, CNN.com (Apr. 14, 1999), *available at* http://www.cnn.com/ ALLPOLITICS/stories/1999/04/14/test.top/; Julie O'Sullivan, *The Independent Counsel Statute: Bad Law, Bad Policy*, 33 Am. Crim. L. Rev. 463 (1996); Julian A. Cook III, *Mend It or End It? What To Do With the Independent Counsel Statute*, 22 Harv. J. L. & Pub. Pol'y 279 (1998); Ken Gormley, *Monica Lewinsky, Impeachment, and the Death of the Independent Counsel Law: What Congress Can Salvage from the Wreckage – A Minimalist View*, 60 MD. L. REV. 97 (2001).

[124] *See PHH Corp.*, 839 F.3d at 20 (noting that Justice Kagan, who joined the Court after the *Morrison* decision, regards Justice Scalia's dissent in *Morrison* as "one of the greatest dissents ever written and every year it gets better").

INDEX

A

B

C

D

E

F

G

H

I

J

K

L

M

N

O

P

T

U

V

W

Y

Z